Early Intervention For Children With ASD

Considrations

S. K. Lund & Alan Schnee

INFINITY PUBLISHING

ISBN 978-1-4958-2126-4
Library of Congress Control Number: 2018902816

Published April 2018

INFINITY PUBLISHING
1094 New DeHaven Street, Suite 100
West Conshohocken, PA 19428-2713
Toll-free (877) BUY BOOK
Local Phone (610) 941-9999
Fax (610) 941-9959
Info@buybooksontheweb.com
www.buybooksontheweb.com

Children with Autism Spectrum Disorders have characteristic impairments in social, language and communication abilities. Many have severe impairment qualifying them for early intensive intervention. The nature of interventions for children with autism is predicated on how the disorder is understood, and understandings abound. A survey of clinical approaches would reveal a myriad of perspectives ranging from the reasonable and well-founded to the naïve and absurd. Such a survey will not be done here. Nor are we concerned with advancing a particular clinical approach or articulate some rigorous system of implementation. Our purpose is to offer some considerations concerning certain practice or more precisely, certain curricular practice in early behavioral intervention for children with autism. The considerations we offer are not necessarily reflective of our own clinical practice and we claim no ownership of the various 'programs' we discuss.

S. K. Lund
Rhode Island, September 2017

"Teaching is the arrangement of contingencies of reinforcement under which the students learn. They learn without teaching in their natural environment, but teachers arrange special contingencies which expedite learning, hastening the appearance of behavior which would otherwise be acquired slowly or making sure of the appearance of behavior which might otherwise never occur"

(B.F. Skinner, 1968)

INTRODUCTION

In 1977 Ole Ivar Lovaas published *"The Autistic Child: Language Development through Behavior Modification"* where he laid out many discoveries of his pioneering behavioral research on language intervention for young children with autism. *"The Autistic Child"* discusses many features and components of language intervention with an agreeable blend of technical and empathetic prose. Many of the issues outlined were integral to the treatment protocols of the influential outcome study published in 1987 as well as subsequent research projects [1].

When viewed in a historical perspective, the scope of *"The Autistic Child"* is impressive and Lovaas' patient elucidation and passion for detail is exemplary. For instance, he describes in great detail novel procedures such as 'expanded trials' and 'interspersed trials.' He provides explanations for selecting individual teaching objectives, as well as sketched progression lines for these objectives or domains. The book includes commentary of core epistemic targets such as object naming, functions of objects, and facets of superordinate categorization (taxonomy of classes), and it offers accounts for more complex and subtle components of language such as plural-singular, nominal and genitive pronouns, locative prepositions, time-related concepts, and verb tenses. Moreover, Lovaas describes a variety of exercises aimed at advancing faculties such as memory and attention and embarks upon intricate linguistic problems such as deixis. His discussion of personal pronouns is particularly inspiring. This deictic category is notoriously challenging for the majority of children with ASD, and their confusion is sometimes so severe that amelioration seems forlorn. Lovaas dedicates several pages to expounding genitive and nominal case pronouns and describes ways to get these concepts 'off the ground.' His insights are well worthy of consideration.

Although we have had only tangential professional relations to Lovaas and his colleagues, the groundbreaking work captured in *"The Autistic Child"* has influenced our

---

1   The first author participated in a UCLA replication research project at Bancroft NeuroHealth Haddonfield, New Jersey in 1993/94. Many programs and implementation techniques used in this project corresponded with those used in the 1987 study (Lovaas, 1987)

clinical practice in substantial ways for more than 20 years. It has served as a basis for intervention and a subject of analysis, elaboration, conceptual reconstruction, and outline of programmatic trajectories. While we have moved in many new directions well beyond "*The Autistic Child,*" some elements are still present in our clinical practice and many of the new roads we have taken can be traced back to Lovaas' pioneering work[2]. We are not alone. The impact of Lovaas' work is evident in some form or another in large segments of contemporary behavioral intervention for children with ASD. There are replication sites, extensions and elaborations by students and collaborators (e.g., Leaf and McEachin, 1999), direct adaptations of core 'programs' (e.g., Taylor and McDonough 1996), although some without explicit acknowledgement, application of core curriculum items reconstructed within a different conceptual framework (Sundberg & Partington, 1998[3]), and widespread criticism giving way to alternative clinical frameworks (e.g., Koegel & Koegel, 1995; Schreibman & Pierce, 1993).

Our purpose of this book is to offer considerations concerning some programs or curricular items common in early intensive behavioral intervention. Many of which originated with Lovaas. While we consider many core areas, we by no means capture all aspects of early behavioral intervention. Our selective sample is designed to bring to light a few general principles. First, we want to place emphasis on the importance of looking beyond specific content. We must keep in mind that many children with ASD have significant impairment of basic capacities such as attention dexterity, inhibition, tracking, and working memory. Many common programs in early behavioral intervention are vehicles to develop such 'standard equipment.' For example, when teaching imitation, we are not just concerned with the outcome – "do as I do," but also with implicit capacities involved in a range of other domains. If for example, a student is to imitate someone who is placing a block on a red box in a field of four boxes, he must track the person's movements and the object being manipulated (a block), scan the array of boxes, and shift attention to his own set of stimuli. By altering various dimensions of imitation tasks (e.g., complexity, time delay, and distance), we can strengthen capacities such as scanning, tracking, shifting attention between stimulus sets and working memory. Thus, imitation training is not just about imitation proper; it is also a vehicle for developing components involved in virtually all learning and performances (Lund, 2004). "Matching to sample" is another common domain that lends itself to strengthen standard equipment. As with imitation, we are not merely concerned with teaching children to relate stimuli (placing objects together or pointing to

---

2   Notably, as significant technological and conceptual advancements have occurred in neuro-science, the neural mechanisms by which early behavioral intervention works are becoming better understood (e.g., Niemann, 1996; Thompson, 2005), and neurological abnormalities associated with autism are coming into focus. This edifice informs our current practice in a measurable manner. Moreover, our conception of 'language' has more in common with the conception of late Wittgenstein (1953) than the assumptions that underlie Lovaas' work. These and other variables have led us to an intervention paradigm that is discontinuous with that of Lovaas.

3   The assessment offered by Sunberg and Partington (ABLLS) encompasses many elements found in the work of Lovaas and colleges. While the targets described in ABLLS is wrapped in the conceptual garment of Skinner's concept of "Verbal Behavior" and his attendant neologisms, there are many striking similarities once we look beyond the conceptual idiosyncrasies.

corresponding pairs), but also with dimensions such as scanning, tracking, referencing, and working visual memory[4]. Consequently, we may take advantage of matching programs to teach children to track someone's index finger and eye-gaze, scan large arrays of stimuli, and search for objects that are not immediately available (retrieving objects from a distance or turning pages in a book). We provide several examples of how conventional matching can be elaborated and appropriated for different purposes.

Secondly, in constructing comprehensive intervention for a young child with ASD, a clinician must consider how certain abilities or lack thereof impact the child's learning and development. What does it take to learn a particular skill or ability? What are the sub-elements of the skill and how does it influence other skills and abilities? (Lund, 2001) We thus offer a range of considerations concerning the relation between individual programs. However, this book is *not a curriculum*. The word 'curriculum' is commonly associated with standardized sequences of skills to be taught or a list of objectives or intended learning outcomes. The present work does not fit such descriptions. Clearly, there can be no universal sequence of skills to be taught for children with ASD. The neurological complications and behavioral patterns exhibited by individuals within this group are vastly different. While there are many overlapping behavioral features and sets of resemblances across members of this category, we find considerable differences at fine-grained levels of clinical observation. Thus, each child requires an individualized plan. This book aims to help aspiring clinicians to consider critical issues, enhance his or her understanding of these issues by considering reasons for teaching certain skills and the relationship between 'programs' (i.e., 'internal structure') that has become part and parcel of early intensive behavioral intervention. We hope we have provided enough examples to illustrate the analysis and synthesis we believe is critical in all stages and domains of early intensive intervention.

---

4   We are here adopting the common vocabulary of 'working memory' (Miller, Galanter, & Pribram, 1986) although this term is potentially misleading; for 'transient holding, processing, and manipulation of information' is the domain of attention. Memory is 'knowledge retained" and the way working memory is ordinarily used concerns 'holding of information' during tasks. It is altogether unclear whether the "information processing" and "storing" metaphor is intelligible thus whether the term 'working memory" is an appropriate term concerning human capacities. Here we give it a pass.

CONTENTS

LIST OF CORE EXERCISES

Core Exercises (1)

Matching
1. Basic Identity Matching
2. Matching Objects to Pictures
3. Bring Same
4. Bring Same: Two Steps
5. Sorting (1)
6. Sorting (2)
7. Touch Same
8. Find Same

Selection-Based Imitation
9. Selection-Based Imitation (SBI) (1)
10. Selection-Based Imitation (2)
11. Selection-Based Imitation: Two Steps

Task Completion
12. Task Completion
13. Sequential Matching (TPSM)
14. Following Lists ("shopping")
15. Search (1)
16. Search (match1)
17. Search (match 2)

Imitation
18. Gross Motor Imitation
19. Fine Motor Imitation
20. Multi-Step Imitation
21. Object Imitation (1)
22. Object Imitation (2)
23. Block Imitation (1)
24. Block Imitation (2)
25. Block Imitation (3)
26. Follow the Leader
27. Verbal Imitation
28. Third Person Imitation
29. Observational Learning

Basic Receptive Language
30. One Step Instructions
31. Two Step Instructions
32. Receptive Object Identification
33. 2-D Object Identification
34. Receptive Person Identification
35. Receptive Body Parts Identification
36. Bring Me
37. Receptive Block Building
38. Two-Step Receptive Objects

Tracking/Joint Attention
39. Tracking 1
40. Tracking 2 (Direct Point)
41. Tracking 3 (Object Location)
42. Tracking 4 (Two Objects)
43. Tracking 5 (Go to Location)
44. Tracking 6 (Combined Tracking and Receptive)
45. Tracking 7 (Alternated Tracking and Receptive)
46. Shifting Between Instruction Modalities

Core exercises (2)

Naming and requesting
47. Expressive Naming (Objects)
48. Expressive Naming 2 (Body Parts)
49. Expressive Naming 3 (Persons)
50. Expressive Naming: Multiple Presentation Forms
51. Tracking and Orienting
52. Sequential Naming
53. Self-Paced Naming
54. Naming through Observational Learning
55. Requesting Desired Objects and Activities
56. Sequential Matching: Interrupted chain
57. Blocked Response (Instruction)
58. Requesting from second person
59. Managing Listener's Responses

Integrating basic learning skills
60. Naming to Requesting (contrived)
61. Requesting to Naming
62. Receptive-Expressive Correspondence
63. Receptive to Requesting

Personal pronouns

*All figures referenced in the text appear in the appendix

CORE EXERCISES (1)

MATCHING

| # 1 | **Basic Identity Matching** |

Purpose	• To establish a basic routine of *receive, look, scan, and decide (making a comparison)*. • This routine targets fundamental perceptual and cognitive abilities including scanning, shifting attention between objects, and basic-level categorization. • Learn to compare and contrast.
Set up	• Place three distinct objects on the child's worktable. The objects should be separated by a few inches.
Procedure	1. Hand the child an object corresponding to one of the objects on the table and say: "Put with same" (or "match"). 2. When the child makes the match, remove the object and introduce another trial. 3. Use conventional discrete trial instruction.
Considerations	• If the child has difficulty with this exercise, it is usually because the child is not looking at the items the child holds or the objects on the table, or both. In other words, the child does not *compare* by shifting attention between the object in their possession and the array of objects on the table. • Strengthening attention to the object often requires ample practice (repetition), and use of a highly discrete routine (DTI). Instruction should be modified over time as children begin to shift attention flexibly to compare objects. • Increase the field size gradually (the number of objects on the table). This strengthens the child's scanning or searching ability and persistence. Eventually, the objects on the table should be presented in varied arrangements (linear, horizontally, random/disorganized). • Once the child can match identical objects, make the objects increasingly more dissimilar (non-identical). This kind of basic-level categorization or 'stimulus generalization' requires considerable multiple exemplary teaching where the objects vary across many different kinds of details. • Once the child is able to match objects that are quite dissimilar, introduce identical *picture* matching. Follow the same procedure as object matching. Introduce non-identical pictures as he makes progress. Once the child can match dissimilar pictures, start "Matching Object to Pictures" (#2). • Some children have difficulty with picture matching, and special stimulus shaping procedures may be necessary. For instance, the pictures

may be initially cut out to remove the background so they retain their idiosyncratic contours.

2   Matching Objects to Pictures

Purpose	• To further establish visual recognition of kinds and "unite" three-dimensional objects and their representations (two-dimensional objects).
Set up	• Place three distinct pictures on the worktable. The pictures should be separated by a few inches. • Use conventional discrete trial instruction
Procedure	• Hand the child a picture corresponding to one of the pictures on the table and say: "Put with same." • When the child matches, remove the object and introduce another trial. • Increase the field size gradually (the number of pictures on the table). This strengthens the child's scanning ability and persistence. Eventually, present pictures in varied arrangements (linear, horizontally, random/disorganized).
Considerations	• Once the child is proficient, make the objects and pictures increasingly more dissimilar. • Once the child is proficient with the previous step, reverse the arrangement; Present a picture and require the child to identify the corresponding object (see "Bring Same" #3).

#3   Bring Same

Purpose	• To promote working memory (remember what you saw and go find it), sustained focus, persistent searching/problem solving, and basic social awareness. • To develop the routine of *look, search, return, and deliver.* • To combine Basic Identity Matching, simple problem solving and basic social awareness.
Set up	• Place items around the room
Procedure	1. Hold up a picture and say: "Find same." The child should search for and retrieve the corresponding object. 2. After presenting the picture, guide the child to the corresponding object, assist the child to pick it up and to deliver it to you (use open hand cue). 3. If the child deviates from the task or loses track of what the child is looking for (i.e., forgets), interrupt gently, bring the child back to the point of origin and re-present the picture.

4. As progress is made, increase the distance and radius (spread) of the objects. The objects should be placed in different kinds of positions (on the floor, eye-level, and above eye-level such as on shelves).

5. With increased progress, make sure that the objects are more difficult to locate. At this level, the child may forget what the child is looking for and may look back at you for information. If so, present the picture immediately. This "re-check" (information seeking) is a crucial skill.

Considerations	• All the elements of the *look, search, return and deliver* routine should be addressed systematically and individually: • *Look:* Alter presenting the picture; hold it up in different positions so the child must strive to see it. • *Search:* Place objects in different kinds of positions (on the floor, eye-level, and above eye-level) and eventually partially (or fully hidden) so the child must manipulate the environment to find it (e.g., behind or in other objects). • *Return:* Initially, wait at the point of origin until the child returns with the object. When this routine is established, move yourself around (including out of sight) so that the child must strive to locate you. • *Deliver:* Initially, use an explicit open hand cue (prompt). As the child reliably delivers the object, discontinue the hand cue and require the child to 'capture your attention' (such as moving into your visual field, tapping your arm in, holding the object up in front of you). Such 'initiations' may be shaped in a systematic manner with the assistance of a second instructor who provides manual guidance from behind the child. • "Bring same" combines Basic Identity Matching with simple problem solving and basic social awareness.

#4   Bring Same: Two Steps

Purpose	• To increase visual working memory, introduce multiple-step. instructions, motor planning/problem solving. • To expand "Bring Same" (#3).
Set up	• Place items around the room.
Procedure	1. Present a picture and say: "Get this" and wait for the child to find the corresponding object. When the child picks it up, present another picture and guide the child to pick up the second corresponding object. Use an open hand cue to prompt the child to hand you the objects. Initially, the objects should be in close proximity and easy to locate. 2. As the child demonstrates success, decrease the time between the picture presentations until they are presented in immediate succession and eventually, simultaneously.
Considerations	• The transition from single-step to two-step may be challenging for some

children and may require extensive practice. Be prepared that children often put down the first object when the second picture is presented. Prolonged practice involving only one object ("Bring Same" #3) may amplify this problem. Therefore, transition to multiple steps should be made as soon as possible.

- As progress is made, make sure that the objects are more difficult to locate (encourages searching).
- The child may forget what the child is looking for and look back at you for a reminder. Continue to display both pictures until the child has completed the two-step task).

#5 Sorting (1)

Purpose	• To strengthen sustained attention to task (task completion). • Disentangle visual matching from instructor cues (building proficiency). • To establish sequences of *select, scan, match, select.* • *Decide which things go together.*
Set up	• Place three plates on the table with a sample object on each. Have the child stand a few feet away from the table with a bin of objects next to the plates. The objects in the bin should correspond to the objects on the plates (a minimum of two of each kind).
Procedure	1. Instruct the child to "sort" or provide another relevant cue. The child should then match the objects one by one until the bin is empty. Provide manual guidance from behind and fade assistance over successive trials. 2. Gradually increase (a) the kinds of items on the table (up to a field of at least five), and (b) the number of items of each kind (up to at least four). (There is no magic number; the idea is simply to build toward greater proficiency). 3. Initially, the objects should be similar (identical).
Considerations	• Sorting may be implemented when the child is proficient with "Basic Identity Matching" (see #1). • Sorting may have to be built from smaller steps; starting with two objects in each of two bins and only two corresponding objects on the table. • Avoid verbal prompting. If the child deviates from the task, guide the child back manually. • Ideally, sorting should be addressed at the same time as "Bring Same" (#3). Thus, the child will be expanding matching abilities across different contexts.

#6	Sorting (2)

Purpose	<ul><li>To teach the child to organize items by kind without any environmental cues (pre-arranged sample).</li><li>To address basic inference and decision making.</li><li>To decide which things go together by organizing conditions for sorting.</li></ul>
Set up	<ul><li>Place three plates on the table <u>without</u> a sample object on each. The child should stand a few feet from the table containing a bin of objects (a minimum of two of each kind; a total of six items).</li></ul>
Procedure	1. Instruct the child to "sort" or provide another relevant cue. The child should pick one item from the bin and place it on an empty plate and then return to the bin and pick another item. If that second object corresponds to the object already on the plate, the child should place it on that plate. If the object does not match, the child should place it on an empty plate. This process continues until all the objects are sorted correctly. 2. Provide manual guidance from behind. 3. Increase the number of kinds of objects (plates) as the child becomes more proficient.
Considerations	<ul><li>This is a challenging task for many children and success may not follow directly from "Sorting (1)" (#5).</li><li>This exercise deviates from conventional matching exercises as it does not offer explicit antecedent cues (presentation of an object as in "Basic Identity Matching," #1) or pre-arranged comparison fields (as in "Sorting 1," #5). Instead, the child must *choose* an item from the bin in the absence of any environmental guidance, *decide* where to place items based on likeness, *select* other items from the bin, place items with similar kinds or place it on an empty plate if similar kinds are not available (decision by comparison).</li><li>If the child does not demonstrate progress within three to four sessions (i.e., manual guidance cannot be faded), the program should be postponed and re-introduced when progress is made in other matching programs such as "Find Same" (#8) and "Selection-Based Imitation" (#9).</li></ul>

#7	Touch Same

Purpose	<ul><li>To further develop scanning, shifting attention, and working visual memory.</li><li>To shift modality of matching from handling objects/pictures (placing objects/pictures together, retrieving objects) to pointing.</li></ul>
Set up	<ul><li>Place an array of pictures on a table.</li></ul>
Procedure	1. Display a picture and instruct the child to "point to same." He should look at the picture, scan the pictures on the table, and point to the corresponding one.

2. With progress, you may (a) gradually reduce the time the picture is available (eventually just "flash" it), and (b) gradually increase the number of pictures on the table (extend scanning requirement).
3. Use conventional discrete trial instruction.
4. If the child makes consecutive errors, decrease the field size or prime the child with conventional picture matching (see "Basic Identity Matching" (#1), "Matching Objects to Pictures" (#2).

| Considerations | • Discontinue conventional matching exercises (#1, #2) when progress is made with this exercise. |
| | • Consider using pictures that are *slightly* dissimilar to enhance visual acuity (e.g., one car with white roof and one with black roof, two different kinds of dogs). |

#8   Find Same

Purpose	• To further develop the executive function skills of working visual memory and searching.
	• To teach the child to seek information when they forget.
	• To establish appropriate eye contact.
	• To establish the sequence of *look, search, point and check back.*

| Set up | • Place a picture on each page in small binder or photo album. |

Procedure	1. Present a picture and tell the child to "find same." The child turns pages in the binder and points to the corresponding picture when it appears. Initially, use manual guidance.
	2. As the child makes progress, you should withhold praise/reinforcement until he looks at you after pointing to the target picture.
	3. Initially, the target picture should be on the first or second page. As he makes progress, more pages should be added to the binder, and the target picture should be placed further into the back. When extending the task this way, the child may forget which picture they are looking for and may therefore look back at you for information (communicating non-verbally that he seeks information). When looking back is habitual, wait to present the picture until eye contact occurs (see also "Bring Same," #3).
	4. Use conventional discrete trial instruction.

| Considerations | • As children look consistently to you for information, change the format: Rather than presenting a single picture, place an array of pictures on the table and point to one of them when giving the instruction "find same." When the child looks up to find out what you want them to 'find,' wait for eye contact before pointing to the target picture. |

| Troubleshooting | • Some children have difficulty turning the pages. Use thicker pages or tabs to make it easier. |

SELECTION BASED IMITATION

#9   Selection-Based Imitation (SBI) (1)

Purpose	• To facilitate the development of pointing, flexible shift of attention, joint attention, and tracking. • Strengthen executive function.
Set up	• Sit directly across the child at the table. Both of you have a line of corresponding pictures. The two lines are arranged so the pictures correspond in terms of position. The lines may be arranged so both are oriented toward the child (Fig. 1.1). • Begin with a field of three pictures and increase with success.
Procedure	• Say: "Do this" and point to a picture in front of you. The child should then point to the corresponding picture in front of the child. • Use "Touch Same" (#7) as a bridge to establish SBI: Instead of pointing to a picture, pick up a picture and say; "Touch same." As the child catches on, change from holding a picture up to pointing to one (on the table).
Considerations	• SBI is a 'tool skill' rather than a goal in itself. • SBI is a hybrid of matching and imitation. While both selection-based and conventional imitation (topography-based imitation) involve imitation, they are quite different. In selection-based imitation, the response is the same every time (pointing), while in topography-based imitation, the response is different from instance to instance. SBI also differs from topography-based imitation in that it requires elements of joint attention, shifting attention, increased memory load, and tracking. This is a complex social event. • SBI may serve as a tool for establishing "receptive object naming" (Lund, 2001) and may aid in development of imitation for children who struggle with conventional imitation training (see "Gross Motor Imitation" #18).

#10   Selection-Based Imitation (2)

Purpose	• To further develop pointing, flexible shift of attention, joint attention, and tracking. • A direct extension of "Selection-Based Imitation (1)" (#9). • This version of SBI controls for the problem of positional prompts.
Set up	• Sit directly across the child at the table. Have a row of pictures in front of

you and a row of corresponding pictures in front of the child. Arrange the field so the pictures <u>no longer correspond</u> by position within the rows. The rows may be arranged so both are oriented toward the child (see Figure 1.2).

Procedure	• Say "do this" and point to a picture displayed in the array in front of you. The child then points to the matching picture in front of the child.

Considerations	• The child may copy the position of your finger as opposed finding the target picture (e.g., if you point to the far left picture. He may do the same whether the pictures match or not, or he may first point to the picture corresponding to the position of your finger and then switch to the correct picture. To address these problems you could, (a) scale back to two pictures and increase the field size when the child performs proficiently, (b) block the child's response to permit sufficient scanning time. (For instance, the child's effort may be blocked until he observes your response and shifts attention to his own array) and (c) interrupt "position pointing" and introduce a new trial after a brief delay (two, three seconds).

#11   Selection-Based Imitation: Two Steps

Purpose	• To extend observational abilities, curb impulsive responding, and enhance working memory. • To teach sequential ordering.

Set up	• Same arrangement as "Selection-based imitation (2)."

Procedure	• Say: "do this" while pointing to a picture. Then say "and this" and point to another picture. The child should point to the corresponding pictures in his row. Use a shaping/time delay procedure, i.e., point to the first picture and wait for the child to initiate his response. When the child responds, point to the second picture. Keep your finger on the second picture until the child responds correctly. Increase the speed gradually as he is able to follow along.

Considerations	• Multi-step instruction is very difficult for many children. Common problems include attention drift, impulsivity, and order conflation (i.e., reversing the order of stimulus input/pointing to the picture in the opposite order). This exercise is designed to improve these issues. • Establishing this skill often requires meticulous and creative shaping. The time delay procedure described above is one example. • If the child does not demonstrate progress after three to four sessions, the exercise may be postponed and reintroduced when the child demonstrates success with other multiple step exercises such as "Multi-Step Imitation" (#20) and "Bring Same: Two Steps" (#4).

TASK COMPLETION

#12	**Task Completion**

Purpose	• To complete tabletop tasks such as pegboards, puzzles, bead stringing, shape sorter etc. • To promote sustained attention to task with minimal assistance.
Set up	• The child sits at a table and you stand behind the child.
Procedure	• Use Manual guidance and systematic prompt fading.
Considerations	• Start with very simple activities such as stacking rings and pegboards and then move to more complex activities such as shape sorter, island puzzles, and stringing beads. • Eye-hand coordination is often challenging, and it is often necessary to break tasks down into incremental steps.

#13	**Sequential Matching (TPSM)**

Purpose	• To teach a multi-component sequence of *turn, point, select, match* (TPSM). • To strengthen executive functions including working memory, scanning, searching, and shifting attention between components of tasks.
Set up	• Place four to six pictures on a table, face down, in a row. Place a bin containing a set of corresponding items to the child's left (on a separate table or chair). (Fig. 2.1)
Procedure	• The child should turn the first picture (T), (Fig. 2.2) point to it (P), select the corresponding item from the bin (S), and place it on the picture (M) (Fig. 2.3). Continue until the child has completed all the matches (up to six pictures). • Assist (manual guidance) from behind until independent.
Considerations	• Sequential matching or "Turn-Point-Select-Match" (TPSM) may be introduced when the child has mastered "Sorting" (#5, #6) and "Matching Objects to Pictures" (#2). • TPSM is a 'tool' that may later be used to enable development of basic communication skills. • When the child performs fluently, omit the first part of the sequence. Thus,

the pictures are placed face up. The child should then point (P), select the corresponding object (S), and match it (M).

- As the child progresses, include items that are similar so that finer discriminations are required to make accurate matches.

#14   Following Lists ("Shopping")

Purpose	• To strengthen executive function skills of working memory, scanning, searching, and shifting attention.
	• To generalize matching skills and searching (this program is a version of the *turn, point, select, match*, see "Sequential Matching," #13).
	• To strengthen task completion (independent problem solving).
Set up	• Place familiar pictures in a binder (one on each page) and arrange corresponding objects around the room.
Procedure	• Give the binder to the child along with a relevant instruction (e.g., "Do your schedule"). The child should open the binder, point to the picture (can be omitted), retrieve the corresponding object, place it in a bin, turn to the next page, etc.
Considerations	• If the child has mastered "Sequential Matching" (#13), this skill is often easily acquired "Following Lists" is a tool used for later language goals such as requesting objects and information, teaching yes/no, and other pragmatic language exercises.

#15   Search (1)

Purpose	• To develop persistent searching and exploration.
	• Teach the child to reposition himself and manipulate the environment to obtain objects.
Set up	• Place three or more cups/containers on the table spaced far enough apart so it is not possible for the child to view their contents.
	• Place a highly preferred item in one of the cups.
Procedure	• Guide the child to each of the containers so the child may see what is inside. When the child encounters the cup with the preferred item allow the child to take it. Fade guidance so the child eventually searches for the item independently.
Considerations	• When the child demonstrates proficiency, introduce more challenging tasks so that the child must use a variety of actions to gain access to the objects. For instance, change the containers so that (a) the child needs to 'pour' out

the contents to see what is inside (e.g., opaque bottles), (b) pulling things apart to see what is inside, (c) nested items (e.g., a small paper bag inside closed containers), (d) place a highly preferred item in an opaque container (bag, box) that allows an item's removal only if child reaches in and pulls it out. (Fig. 26)

- Keep in mind the importance of teaching children to problem solve as opposed to requesting assistance. While requesting help and assistance is a critical target, it should not overshadow development of practical problem-solving. Be alert to the 'passivity fallacy' in which the child routinely defers attempts to problem solve and explore.

#16   Search (Match 1)

Purpose	• To develop search routines, memory.
Set up	• Present an opaque container which contains several items.
Procedure	• Visually, present a matched item which corresponds to one of those in the box and ask the child to find same. • Manually guide. • Fade guidance.
Considerations	• Limit the number of items in box b to two until the child is independent and then increase the number. • Use easily 'recognizable' items, e.g., a ball, a block, a book.

#17   Search (Match 2)

Purpose	• To develop search routines, memory.
Set up	• Present two opaque containers. • In one is only one item (box a). • In the other are several items, one of which matches the item in the other container (box b).
Procedure	• Instruct the child to 'find out what is in the box' (box a). Guide the child to reach in, feel for the item but not to remove it. • Direct child to 'find same' in the other box. • Guide the child to reach into the other.
Considerations	• Use easily recognizable items, e.g., a ball, a block, a book. • Limit the number of items in box b to two until the child is independent and then increase the number. • This exercise is an extension of "Touch Same" (#7) and "Find Same" (#8). • This exercise may be seen as a pre-condition for "Naming by Touch" (#103)

Imitation

#18   Gross Motor Imitation

Purpose	• To teach the child to observe and copy other person's simple gross motor movements.
Set up	• Sit face to face.
Procedure	• Say: "Do this," and simultaneously model a simple movement. Prompt the corresponding movement immediately (manual guidance). Fade prompts over successive trials. • Use conventional discrete trial instruction. • Start with simple gross motor movements such as waving, clapping, touching the head, raising the arms, and eventually introduce 'out of the chair' movements such as walking around the chair and running. • When the child masters a particular movement, introduce another and randomize it with mastered ones (expanded trials). Continue to introduce novel movements until the child imitates new ones without specific training (generative behavior).
Considerations	• Establishing imitation may require considerable repetition with extensive manual guidance. • See "Teaching Developmentally Disabled Children: The Me Book" (Lovaas, 1981) for an extended discussion of imitation training. • For some children, it is easier to learn gross motor imitation when using objects (see "Object Imitation (1)" #21).
Troubleshooting	• If the child is not making progress, it may be necessary to strengthen subservient skills such as shifting attention, sustained attention, and working memory. These skills are addressed systematically in various matching programs ("Basic Identity Matching" #1, "Sequential Matching" #13, "Selection-Based Imitation" #9).

#19   Fine Motor Imitation

Purpose	• To teach the child to attend to and imitate fine motor movements, facial expressions (including mouth movements). • Strengthen observational acuity, fine-tune child's attention to small differences in movements.

Set up	• Sit face to face.
Procedure	• Say: "Do this," and simultaneously model a simple movement. Prompt the corresponding action immediately (manual guidance). Fade prompts over successive trials. • Use conventional discrete trial instruction. • Start with simple fine motor movements such as shaking and nodding head, pointing, thumbs up, folding hands, and putting index fingers together. Eventually introduce facial expressions and mouth movements such as smacking lips, sticking tongue out, puff up cheeks with air, pout, bite lip, and smile. • Once the child masters a particular movement, introduce another and randomize it with mastered ones ("expanded trials"). Continue to introduce novel movements until the child imitate new ones without specific training (generative behavior).
Considerations	• If the child struggles, use more salient targets and then, over time, increase subtlety. • Be mindful of developmental norms. • As fluencies develop, link some of these items into normative uses, e.g., shaking or nodding head paired with saying "yes" and "no," pointing for pointing *to* things.

#20   Multi-Step Imitation

Purpose	• To expand imitation skills. • To reproduce a sequence of movements in the order they were observed. • To exercise executive function skills such as order of motor skills (motor planning; praxis), working memory and the suppression of incorrect pre-potent responding.
Set up	• Sit face to face.
Procedure	• Say "Do this," and model two movements. The movements should be distinctly different (e.g., clap and wave) and presented consecutively with minimal time delay. Upon completion of the sequenced model, the child should perform them in the order they were presented.
Considerations	• Multi-step imitation requires the child to, (a) observe compound movements (sustained attention to transient events), (b) remember the sequence (movements and their order), and (c) refrain from copying the last movement until the child performs the first (impulse suppression). • The step from single step to two-step imitation is dramatic and extensive practice is often necessary.

Troubleshooting	•	*The child* imitates only the first movement and/or responds to the first movement before observing the second. To address this problem, have a second person provide prompts from behind. The second person should prevent (physical blocking) the child from responding until both movements are presented. Also, consider postponing the exercise and establish or strengthen "Selection-Based Imitation: Two Steps" (#11) then re-introduce.
	•	*The child* imitates only the second movement. To address this problem, slow things down, i.e., present the first movement and when the child imitates it, introduce the second. Increase the speed gradually. If the problem persists, it may be helpful to establish multi-step imitation with objects (see "Object Imitation 2", (#22) before returning to this exercise. Also, consider postponing the exercise and establish or strengthen "Selection-Based Imitation: Two Steps" (#11), then re-introduce.
	•	*The child* reverses the order. To address this problem, practice segments in which you present the first movement, wait for the child to imitate and then present the second. Also, consider postponing the exercise and establish or strengthen "Selection-Based Imitation: Two Steps" (#11), then re-introduce. Fluency with "Sequential Matching" (#13) may also aid the child with this difficulty.

#21   Object Imitation (1)

Purpose	•	To see that the child learns to observe and copy another person's simple, actions with objects.
Set up	•	Face each other; two sets of identical objects are separated on the child's table.
Procedure	•	Say "do this" while picking up an item and manipulating it in a particular way (e.g., placing it in a particular location, banging it, turning it). The child should select the corresponding object and imitate the movement.
	•	Arrange 'distractor objects' (extra objects which won't be used) to ensure discrimination. For instance, if you put a block in a bucket, there should be a block and one additional object for the child to choose from. Increase the number of objects as the child demonstrates success.
Considerations	•	Start with simple actions such as putting a block in a bucket, peg in pegboard, banging the table with a hammer, etc.
	•	Upon success with simple actions, introduce more complex ones. For instance, turning a cup upside down and putting a block inside, taking apart two pop-beads and placing them in a bucket, taking a peg out of the pegboard and banging it on the table.
	•	It is important that objects are not always used in the same manner. For instance, a hammer should not always be used to bang on the table, but sometimes placed in the bucket, on the floor, etc. Likewise, a block can be

used to bang on the table rather than placing it in a bucket. This will prevent memorization of object-action sequences and compels the child to observe the entire action every time.
- Some children have an easier time learning imitation with objects before imitation without objects.

#22   Object Imitation (2)

Purpose	• To expand the child's ability to observe and copy another person's actions with objects.
Set up	• *Multiple steps:* Place two sets of identical objects on the child's table. • *Distance and delay:* Place two sets of identical objects are spread out on the floor.
Procedure	• *Multiple-steps*: Both of you have a set of corresponding objects. Say: "do this" and manipulate an object, then say "and this" while manipulating another. After the last movement, the child should imitate both in the order presented. Start with simple combinations such as *place block in a bucket + bang the table with a hammer*; *put a peg in a peg-board + turn a cup upside down*; *unsnap two pop-beads + roll a car across the table.* • *Distance and delay*: Both of you should each have a set of corresponding objects. The child's objects are placed on the floor, out of reach and out of the immediate visual field (peripherally). Say "do this" while picking up an item and manipulating it in a particular way (e.g., placing it in a particular location, banging it, turning it). The child should then *search for* the corresponding object and imitate the movement.
Considerations	• *Multiple-steps:* • Common problems: Similar to "Multi-Step Imitation" (#20). • If the child continues to struggle, consider postponing the exercise and establish or strengthen "Selection-Based Imitation: Two Steps" (#11), then re-introduce. Fluency with "Sequential Matching" (#13) may also help the child with this exercise. • As the child makes progress with this program, omit the second verbal cue ("and this"). Thus, say; "do this" and then model two consecutive movements • This exercise may serve as a bridge to "Follow the Leader" (# 26) and "Observational Learning" (#29). • *Distance and delay:* • This task is quite challenging for many children and must be built up gradually (i.e., incremental changes in the object's position relative to the child). • When the child masters this exercise, combine it with "multiple-steps."

#23

Block Imitation (1)

Purpose	• To teach block building and strengthen imitation skills.
	• To refine visual-motor coordination and establish "triadic attention shift:" shifting attention systematically from model to set of blocks to own structure. This sequence of *look, select, construct, check back* is essential to advanced skill learning.
	• To foster development of spatial awareness, and visual perspective taking.
	• To increase searching and scanning, and develop early understanding of part-whole relations.
	• To establish block building as a platform for teaching language and problem-solving abilities.

Set up	• Sit next to each other at a table. You each have a set of colored wood blocks which includes distractors.

Procedure	• Place one of the blocks, from your pile on the table in front of the child, and say: "do this." The child needs to select the corresponding block from their own pile and place it in front of your block (Fig. 3). When done, you should select another block and place it on top of the first (Fig. 4). The child does the same. Use manual guidance if necessary.
	• Once the two-block sequence is mastered, gradually increase the number of blocks to seven or eight.
	• Start with simple vertical structures and make the structures increasingly more complex over time. (Fig. 5)

Considerations	• Initially, the child should build his structure just below the model. When the child does well, start building side-by-side. (Fig. 6)
	• If the child struggles, focus on "Selection-Based Imitation" (#9, #10) in order to promote flexible shift of attention between sets of objects.
	• Block imitation and block building are crucial to the development of core cognitive skills and will be used extensively in later language building exercises.

Troubleshooting	• If the child selects the wrong block from his own pile: Strengthen "Object Imitation" (#21, #22) and return to the exercise. Alternatively, line the blocks up in a corresponding fashion so it is easier for the child to discern the correct one.
	• If the child places the block in the wrong position: Slow down the pace and simplify the structure. In the initial phases of this exercise, do not challenge the child with subtle positions or orientation (e.g., placing a block in the middle of a base block versus at the edge) and the aspect of blocks (standing up versus laying flat).
	• If the child continues to build his structure using 'distractor' blocks: Provide mass trials and abruptly interrupt upon completion of the model (and reinforce of course).

#24	**Block Imitation (2)**

Purpose	• To move from step-by-step imitation to copy a pre-built structure.
	• To establish the ability to 'keep track' of progression within a complex task,' and to further establish "triadic attention shift" (*look, select, construct, check back*).

Set up	• Sit next to each other at a table. Build a block structure (out of colored wood blocks) behind a barrier and then reveal it. The child has a set of blocks, including distractors.

Procedure	• Instruct the child to build the model revealed. Provide manual guidance if necessary.
	• Start with a two-block structure (a base block and one other). For some children, it may be helpful to begin with a stationary base block (a block placed in front of the child before revealing the model. The base block marks the starting point.
	• Start with only one "distractor." It is critical for the child to learn to omit the extra block. This can be challenging, and it may be useful for the child to place the extra block on a designated area (i.e., a plate). As he becomes successful, more distracters can be introduced.
	• Gradually increase the number of blocks and the complexity in the structures (i.e., from straight towers to more complex three-dimensional arrangements). (Fig. 8)

Considerations	• The change from step-by-step imitation to copying pre-built structures may require gradual transitions. For instance, you may need to extend step-by-step building by incrementally speeding up the modeling process from discrete building (one block at a time and wait for the child to complete the effort) to continuous building (introducing the next block right before the child completes the first block).
	• The cognitive challenges involved in copying pre-built structures are many and include flexible and systematic shift of attention between three domains (the model, an array of blocks, and own construction), comparison between two structures and discerning discrepancies, tracking progress/continuous tracking (knowing which step is current and which step has been completed), motor planning, and eye-hand coordination. As the block structures become more complex, so do the challenges: depth perception, judging and probing distance between blocks (how close do two pillars have to be to support a "roof?"), judging which block to build first (foundation versus subsequent blocks, understanding the concept of "support"), correcting detected errors, fine-grained adjustments to make things fit, discerning aspect (e.g., is the block laying flat or standing up, is it aligned or across), and position (e.g., is the block in the middle of another or at the edge? Is it set back or in the foreground of its base?).
	• This exercise challenges motor-planning abilities. Some children pick

up a block with each hand and have subsequent difficulties coordinating/ sequencing their actions. It may be necessary to prompt the child to pick up one block at the time (i.e., gently block the less dominant hand).

#25   Block Imitation (3)

Purpose	• To advance imitation of pre-built block structures. • To relate three-dimensional to two-dimensional structures. • To ensure that the child is able to relate complex stimuli of different dimensions and scale.
Set up	• Sit next to each other at a table with pictures of different kinds of block structures and a corresponding set of blocks.
Procedure	• Present a picture of a block structure and say: "Do this" (or "build this"). The child should build a corresponding structure with his own set of blocks. • Gradually increase the number of blocks and complexity of the structure (i.e., from "vertical" to more complex three-dimensional arrangements).
Considerations	• Before starting this exercise, children should be fluent with building from pre-built structures (#24)

#26   Follow the Leader

Purpose	• To advance imitation skills and continuous tracking of other person's movements.
Set up	• Practice this exercise in the child's natural environment.
Procedure	• Say: "Do this" (or "follow me" or "do what I do") and perform a simple movement that may or may not involve an object (e.g. clapping versus knocking on the door). The child should imitate the movement and you move about the room and model additional movements. • Place a strong emphasis on imitation that involves objects (kicking a ball, walking around a table, throwing a bean bag, etc.). • Initially, the instruction "do this" may be presented before each movement (a more discrete format), but as the child becomes fluent, the verbal instruction should be presented only at the beginning of the sequence. • Gradually increase the length of the imitation segments. Start with two movements.
Considerations	• This exercise represents a break from a discrete trial format and requires sustained and flexible shift of attention.

- A reasonable goal is a four to five step sequence.
- "Object Imitation (2)" (#22) may serve as a bridge to this exercise.

#27   Verbal Imitation

Purpose	• To establish vocal imitation.
Set up	• Sit face to face.
Procedure	• Present the instruction _"Say"_ followed by a target sound, word or sentence. The target sound should (a) be presented slightly louder that than _"Say"_ and (b) there should be a short delay (one second) between _"Say"_ and the target sound. • Initially, any approximation to the target sound should be reinforced. • Increase complexity/length of vocalizations with increasing success.
Considerations	• Verbal imitation should be considered when the child is compliant and competent with basic imitation (#18, #19). • We also like to wait until the child begins to imitate sounds or words spontaneously (without effort or direct intervention). We often see this occur following the commencement of receptive label exercises or receptive instruction exercises. However, such repetitive imitation can result in echolalia, and it is therefore important that verbal imitation comes under conditional antecedent control as soon as possible (see next bullet point). • Initially, the child may imitate "say," and it may be tempting to omit this instruction. However, verbal imitation training that omits "say" could induce or perpetuate echolalia. It is imperative that imitation is brought under conditional stimulus control (in this case "say" is the controlling stimulus). While the instructor may omit "say" in the very beginning, this conditional cue should be introduced as soon as the child begins to imitate sounds. • When children reliably imitate words or approximations to words, "Expressive Naming (1)" should be considered (#47).

#28   Third Person Imitation

Purpose	• To address aspects of imitation, tracking and flexible shift of attention. • To break away from a one-to-one teaching format. • To address an emergent understanding of pointing and the deixis "this" and "that."
Set up	• Two instructors are required for this exercise.
Procedure	• Point to another person and say; "do that" or "do like [name]." The child should imitate the movement of the second person. Deliver the cue ("do

that" + point) and guide the child manually to attend to the other person. Initially, the second person may be in the child's immediate visual field (i.e., next to you).

- Randomize "do that" (imitating the second person) and "do this" (imitating you).
- With progress, alternate your role and second person's role.

Considerations	• This is a later imitation program. The child must be able to track (#39-45) and demonstrate ability to "Follow the Leader" (#26).
	• Many children have difficulty shifting from one model to another. Extensive practice is often necessary. If the child shows persistent difficulty, postpone this exercise and strengthen tracking and Observational Learning (#29). With progress in these areas, reinstatement should be considered.
	• Third person imitation is a crucial ability and is essential to further social and language development. It involves (1) the basic deixis of "this" and "that", (2) the ability to track and to sustain attention to events at a distance, (3) conditions which promote understanding of speaker roles (i.e., a person's role shifts, speakers provide information and gives directives).

#29   Observational Learning

Purpose	• To teach the child to observe others and imitate the actions of others at a later time. For instance, the child observes an action in one location, and imitates it in a different location or when a similar situation requires a similar action.
	• To strengthen working memory and problem solving (i.e., using information obtained at one point in time at a later time).
Set up	• Practice this exercise in the child's natural environment, with familiar objects.
Procedure	• Model an action with an object, then guide the child to a different location where the child has access to the same kind of problem. The child should imitate the action at the second location in order to solve the problem (e.g., use some object as a tool).
	• Start with very short distances. For instance, model an action at a table, then turn the child around to face another table that contains the relevant objects. Increase the distance to the second table gradually.
Considerations	• The child should be able to "Follow the Leader" (#26) and perform multi-step imitation with objects (#22).
	• "True" observational learning, in which the child imitates actions after a considerable time delay, (e.g., sees something at school and imitates at home) is not likely to follow automatically from this exercise. Rather, this exercise is designed to begin the process of developing observational learning.

- Once the child develops basic observational learning, numerous opportunities should be provided throughout the day. In other words, observational learning must become a regular feature of the child's everyday environment.

Basic Receptive Language

#30 — One Step Instructions

Purpose	• To teach the child to follow simple directions.
Set up	• Sit or stand facing each other.
Procedure	• Present an instruction (e.g., "clap") and manually guide the child's response. Repeat the instruction and fade the prompt over successive trials. • When the child responds independently, introduce a second instruction and follow the same procedure. Randomize the first and the second instruction. • Introduce new instructions when the child discriminates between the two initial instructions (expanded trials).
Considerations	• Some children are more successful when two or more instructions are randomized from the outset. • Mastered instructions should eventually be introduced in less contrived settings. Alter dimensions such as location, setting, and proximity to the instructor. • Proficiency with programs like "Tracking" (#39-45) and "Selection Based Imitation" (#9-11) may facilitate development of receptive instructions. • A small subset of children struggle to learn simple receptive language. In some cases, it may be wise to postpone receptive language training and strengthen "tool" skills such as scanning, tracking, and working visual memory (see "Selection Based Imitation"). • Some children learn to name objects expressively before receptively.

#31 — Two-Step Instructions

Purpose	• To teach the child to follow two-part instructions • To develop executive function skills such as ordering of motor responses (**praxis**), suppressing pre-potent but incorrect responding (impulsivity) and working memory.
Set up	• Sit face to face. Practice this exercise in the child's natural environments.
Procedure	• Instruct the child to do two distinct things using the conjunction *"and"* (e.g., "clap" and "wave"). After the last instruction is presented, the child should do them in the order they were presented.

- Initially, you may need to present the first instruction (e.g., "clap") and wait for the child to respond before introducing the next ("...<u>and</u> wave"). As the child develops fluency with this sequence, instructions may be presented without time delay.

Considerations	<ul><li>The objective is to teach the child to respond to novel combinations, not fixed sequences.</li><li>Multi-step instructions place considerable demands on executive functions including working memory, inhibition of prepotent (impulsive) but incorrect responding and motor planning (praxis).</li><li>In order to increase the likelihood of success, the child needs to be (a) fluent with several single receptive instructions (#30) and acquire new ones with relative ease, (b) show steady acquisition of receptive labels, (c) and proficiency with "Multiple-step Imitation" (#20).</li></ul>

#32   Receptive Object Identification

Purpose	• To teach the child the names of common objects.
Set up	• Present three objects on a table separated by a few inches.
Procedure	<ul><li>Use instructions such as "Where is [object]?" "Give me [object]," or "Find [object]."</li><li>Prompt by guiding the child's hand to the object and fade prompts over successive trials (conventional discrete trial instruction).</li></ul>
Considerations	<ul><li>Object identification concerns assigning words to objects; it is the basic element of symbolic or referential understanding.</li><li>In contrast to receptive *instructions*, object identification requires that the child scan an array of objects rather than perform a specific motor program. In this sense, receptive object labeling is "selection-based" rather than topography-based (based on form).</li><li>Many children struggle with identifying objects and may demonstrate inconsistency even after considerable teaching. It may be helpful to omit extra words in early instructions (i.e., simply "cup" as opposed to "find cup," etc.). If problems persist, the exercise should be discontinued, and an emphasis should be placed on strengthening "tool skills" such as scanning, shifting attention, tracking, and working memory within 'matching' exercise formats.</li><li>Some children learn expressive object naming before receptive language, and the former may serve as a tool to teaching the latter.</li><li>Use **multiple exemplars** (many different cars, many different balls, etc.).</li><li>As the child demonstrates proficiency with the basic arrangements, alter different aspects of the instructional setting by (a) increasing the field size to expand scanning and searching, (b) broaden the radius; displaying</li></ul>

objects on a wider radius around the child (see "Bring Same" #3), and (c) requested objects are hidden behind barriers, in drawers, under containers, etc. in order to strengthen searching routines.

#33   2-D Object Identification

Purpose	• To expand receptive object identification.

Set up	• Present three pictures on a table separated by a few inches.

Procedure	• Use instructions such as "Where is [object]?" "Show me [object]," or "Find [object]."
	• Prompt by guiding the child's hand to the appropriate picture and fade prompts over successive trials (conventional discrete trial instruction).

Considerations	• The child should have mastered "Matching Objects to Pictures" (#2) and be able to identify several 3D objects (see #32).
	• Use multiple exemplars (many different cars, many different balls, etc.).
	• Object identification is a foundation for development of other language skills.

Additional step and permutation	• With success, introduce different formats: (a) Place a picture on each page in small binder or photo album. Ask the child to "find the [picture]." The child should turn the pages and point to the target picture when it appears (see "Find Same" #8 for description); (b) use a typical picture book and ask the child to identify objects he knows, (c) place pictures upside down and ask the child for one of them. He should then turn the pictures over until he finds the correct one, point to it and make eye contact.
	• Receptive object identification is the most basic form of word-world relation and is a foundation for expanding to words that denote relations between concrete things or events. Such terms are often referred to as "abstract" and include concepts such as prepositions and temporal relations (e.g., before/after) (e.g., Lovaas, 1977). While it is often necessary to elaborate and expand receptive object identification meticulously, abstract terms may be introduced once the child demonstrates reliable acquisition. Basic prepositions (#183, #184) such as *on*, *in* and *under* are practical starting points for entry into abstract relations (cf. Lovaas, 1977).

#34   Receptive Person Identification

Purpose	• To identify familiar persons.

Set up	• This exercise requires a minimum of two familiar persons in addition to the instructor.

Procedure	• Instruct the child to "go to" [person]?" and then guide the child to the corresponding person. The target person provides feedback (reinforcement). You then guide the child back to the point of origin. Fade prompts over successive trials as discrimination between two persons emerges.
Considerations	• Identifying persons concerns assigning names to persons. This differs from identifying objects (see #32) in several important ways: (a) as opposed to objects, persons do not have a generic nature; persons are individuals and not an example or an instance of a concept, (b) face recognition and object recognition involve different neurological systems. Some children have significant difficulty learning names of persons although they are able to identify many objects, (c) while objects like cups, books, and balls have distinct and unique "interaction properties" persons do not, (d) teaching person names based on pictures is not a good substitute. • Once the child learns the names of a few persons, pictures may be introduced. Pictures should vary considerably in size, angle, background, and focus.

#35   Receptive Body Part Identification

Purpose	• To teach the child to identify their own and others' body-parts. • To teach the child rudimentary apprehension of part-whole concepts.
Set up	• Sit face to face.
Procedure	• Instruct the child to "point to" or "touch" a body part and prompt the correct response. Fade prompts over successive trials. • When the child can identify two body parts, introduce new ones systematically.
Considerations	• Start with the most salient body parts such as head, tummy, foot, knee, nose, etc.
Additional Steps and Permutations	• This exercise should eventually be extended to (a) identification of body parts of persons in pictures, (b) identifying body parts on other persons (see "pronouns"), and (c) identifying animal body parts.

#36   Bring Me

Purpose	• To solidify object identification and concomitant skills of persistence, searching, and executive function skills including working memory. • To enhance the child's ability to search for things and attain the instructor's attention when the mission is accomplished.

- The sequence *listen-search-attain attention* is a basic social routine and essential component of further learning.

Set up	• Place an object on a table a few feet away from you and the child.

Procedure	• Instruct the child to bring you/find [object]."
	• Guide the child to the object, to pick it up and deliver it to you. Fade prompts over successive trials. To ensure that the child returns to you with the item, it may be useful to employ a second person to provide the initial prompting.
	• Once the child can travel to the table independently, begin to increase the distance from the point of instruction and the table with the objects. Eventually, place objects on the floor around the table and finally around the room including their proper locations (shelf, toy bins, etc.).
	• As the child becomes proficient, you should move yourself around (including out of sight) so that the child has to also locate you after obtaining the object.

Consideration	• This exercise should be easy if the child can readily identify several objects (see #32) and search for things "Find Same" (#8).

#37   Receptive Block Building

Purpose	• To advance basic receptive language.
	• To teach the child to build things 'from memory.'

Set up	• Sit with the child at a table with colored wood blocks.

Procedure	• Instruct the child to build a simple structure (e.g., "Make a house"). You should then guide the child to build the structure. Fade assistance over successive trials. Initially, provide only the blocks needed for the target structure.
	• When the child has learned to build a particular structure, introduce another one. Teach the new structure in isolation and then randomize the first and the second structures.
	• Relevant prompting strategies include manual guidance, modeling, and **reversed chaining**.

Considerations	• The treatment team should agree on the exact form of each structure (e.g., Figs. 9, 9a, 9b, 9c, 9d).
	• This program may be introduced when the child can imitate several complex pre-built block structures (#24, #25), and can easily identify several objects (#32).
	• When teaching a new structure, the child should be given the required blocks only. Additional ("distracter blocks") should be introduced once the child can build structures independently.

#38	**Two-Step Receptive Objects**

Purpose	• To teach the child to follow two-part instructions which incorporate additional abilities.
Set up	• See "Receptive Object Identification" (#32), "One step instructions" (#30), Two steps instructions (#31), and "Bring Same" (#3).
Procedure	• _Object ID_: Arrange known objects or pictures on a table and say "point to [object] and [object]." Assist by pointing or using hand over hand guidance. Fade assistance over successive trials. • _Bring me:_ Place objects around the room (those the child has learned to identify). Places should include proper locations (e.g., books on shelves) and random locations. Instruct the child to "bring me/find [object] and [object]." Guide the child to retrieve the objects. Fade prompts over successive trials. • Give to: In the presence of familiar persons and objects tell the child "give the [object] to [person]" and "give a/an [object] to [person]" (see "considerations in Progressive Actions (1) (#81) for extensions).
Considerations	• The child should be fluent with "Bring Same" (#3), "Multiple Step Imitation" (#22) and "Two Step Instruction" (#31). • Some children may be successful with one of these formats (e.g., "Bring Same," #3) but struggle with the other. The order of which to introduce these formats must be based on individual assessment.

Tracking/ Joint Attention

#39   Tracking 1

Purpose	• To teach the child to track/retrieve objects based on pointing. • To develop a *'track-search-attain attention' sequence* as a fundamental social routine that *should be developed along* with *listen-search-attain attention* ("Bring Same," #3). • To teach *a rudimentary understanding* of the deictic word "this."
Set up	• Line up a set of pictures and/or place pictures on a wall. Corresponding items are placed around the room.
Procedure	• Point to one of the pictures and say: "Find this." The child needs to attend (track), locate the object, and give it to you. • Start by touching the picture with your index finger and gradually increase the distance so that your touch becomes a point. Do not increase the distance beyond a reachable level (i.e., you should be able to reach the picture if you stretch your arm). • If the child can identify 2-D objects, the current arrangement should be alternated (i.e., "find this" while pointing to picture versus "find [object]").
Considerations	• This exercise is an extension of "Selection-Based Imitation" (#9) and "Find Same" (#8). • When increasing the distance between index finger and picture, it may be necessary to increase the distance between the pictures.

#40   Tracking 2 (Direct Point)

Purpose	• To teach the child to track/retrieve objects based on pointing. • To teach the child to orient to and track the pointing of others over extended distances. • To teach the child a rudimentary understanding of "this" and "that."
Set up	• Place a few items around the room (on the floor). The objects should be two to three feet apart. You and the child stand in the middle of the room about three feet apart.
Procedure	• Point to one of the objects and say: "get me that" or "give me this." The child should get the object and give it to you. Initially, it may be helpful

if a second person provides manual guidance. When the child hands you the object, provide positive feedback. Wait two to three seconds and then present a new direction. (Fig. 10.1)

- Start with close proximity between your index finger and the target object (10-14 inches) and gradually increase the distance. Eventually, the child should be able to track across the room.
- Start by standing side by side and point to an object within the child's peripheral vision. As the child catches on, begin pointing to objects outside of his visual field. (Fig. 10.2) Thus, the child will have to orient (move his head and body) in order to track.
- Once the child can track across the room, vary the position between you and the child i.e. (a) face to face in close proximity, pointing to objects on each side of the child (Fig. 10.3). face to face in close proximity, pointing to objects behind the child (he has to turn around to locate the object) (Fig. 10.4), (c) face to face in close proximity, but you turn around (back to the child) and point to an object in the direction that the child is facing (Fig. 10.4), (d) as described in a, b, and c, but pointing to objects *at a distance*, (e) face to face, pointing to objects in front of the child (between you and the child), (f) stand behind the child and point as described in a, b, c, d, and e.

Considerations
- Tracking acuity may often require consistent practice over long periods of time. Once the child makes some progress, tracking should be part of most routine interactions. Practice throughout the day as well as during dedicated sessions.
- Practice in all environments and all positions. It is important that the child learns to turn their body so to orient toward the target object.
- Practice across all distances. When pointing to an object in close proximity, the target object can be closer to other objects. When pointing to an object at a far distance (across the room or outside), the target object should be placed further away from other objects.

#41   Tracking 3 (Object/Location)

Purpose
- To teach the child to follow directions involving two-part pointing.
- To teach the child to shift attention; tracking the attention of instructors when they point to an object and then to a location ("put this over there").
- To teach the child a rudimentary understanding of "this," "that," and "there."

Set up
- Place a few items around the room (on the floor). The room should be furnished with objects with large bases such as chairs, tables, and bins. Stand in the middle of the room with the child.

Procedure
- Point and say: "put that" - "over there" (point to a location). The child should track to the object, pick it up, and place it the designated location. Initially, a second person may provide manual guidance.

- When beginning, it may be necessary to separate the two instructions. Thus, delay the second point ("over there") until the child responds to the first ("put that"). With success, gradually decrease the time between the instructions.
- Use "bounded regions" as the designated location (a chair, an empty table, an empty bin).

Considerations	• This exercise should eventually include persons in addition to locations (i.e., "give that to <u>her/him</u>"). For some children, it may be easier to acquire this skill first by using persons rather than locations.
	• Fluency with two-step object imitation (#22) and multi-step instructions (see #31) could lessen the difficulty of this exercise.
	• A common problem is that children act on the first instruction ("put this/that") but not the second ("over there"). If the child does not make notable progress within four to five sessions, this exercise should be postponed and revisited upon success with "Tracking 4 (Two Objects)" (# 42) and/or progress with more advanced receptive language.
	• When the child demonstrates proficiency with bounded regions ("put this/that over there") and persons ("give that to her/him"), introduce open-ended regions (i.e., point to a general area on the floor). Thus, first point to an object ("put this/that"), then point to a general area on the floor ("over there"). The shift from bounded to open-ended regions is often difficult and demands extensive practice. However, an understanding of open-ended regions is a fundamental aspect of pragmatic language and cannot be overlooked.
	• Be mindful that use of "this" and "that" is most often determined by proximity; "this" usually is used to refer to something close-by whereas "that" usually is used to refer to something farther away. However, this is not an absolute; as with many things in language.

#42   Tracking 4 (Two Objects)

Purpose	• To teach the child to retrieve two objects based on 'two-part pointing' ("get me this and that"/that one and that one") as opposed to placing items following a two-part point ("Tracking 3" #41).
Set up	• Place a few items around the room (on the floor). The items should be approximately the same size and easy to pick up and carry. The objects should be two-three feet apart. You should stand in the middle of the room about three feet from the child.
Procedure	• Point to one of the objects and say: "get me that," then point to another and say "and...that." The child should bring you both objects.
	• Initially, it may be necessary to separate the two instructions wherein the second instruction is delayed until the child responds to the first. With

success, the time between the instructions can be reduced.

Considerations	•	Mastery of two-step object imitation (#22) and multi-step instruction (see #31) should assist in success with this exercise.
	•	Mastery of this exercise may facilitate "Tracking 3" (#41).
	•	Eventually, "give me that and that" should be practiced in conjunction with "put that over there" (placing an object in a location based on two-part pointing (see "Tracking 3" #41). If the child demonstrates persistent confusion with this discrimination, these two exercises should be kept separate at this time.

#43   Tracking 5 (Go to Location)

| Purpose | • | To teach the child to go to general/open-ended regions as directed by a point ("go over there |

| Set up | • | Stand next to each other in the middle of the room. |

| Procedure | • | Points to a general area on the floor and say; "go there" or "go over there." A second person providing manual guidance makes this exercise easier to execute and should be continued until the child begins to show increased competence. |

| Considerations | • | Proficiencies in "Tracking 3" (#41) and "Tracking 4" (#42) should lessen difficulties with this exercise. |
| | • | Many children have a great difficulty with such "indeterminate locations" (i.e., location as a open ended 'region' rather than an absolute point). |

#44   Tracking 6 (Combined Tracking and Receptive)

| Purpose | • | To teach the child to attend to instructions involving both gesture (pointing) and description (receptive). |
| | • | To teach the child that the word "that" in conjunction with pointing aids in the specification of an object (e.g., "that cup" in a field of objects involving other cups). |

| Set up | • | Stand next to each other and have several objects spread across the floor. The child must be able to identify all objects. There should be more than one example of each kind (two kinds of cups, two kinds of balls, etc.). Make sure that pairs of objects are placed close to one another (e.g., two cups are placed next to each other). Thus, when you name an object, children cannot determine which is being referenced unless he considers the instructor's gesture. Likewise, non-matching pairs of objects should be placed close to one another (e.g., a cup and a banana) so when you name an object and |

point, the child cannot "over select" on the gesture.

Procedure	• Point to an object and say: "Get me that [object name]" (e.g., "get me that cup"). The child should track and get the designated object.
Considerations	• The objective of this program is to teach the child to respond to two different cues (modalities) with respect to an object. • The child should be able to identify several objects (see #32) and continue to show ease with identifying new ones, and be proficient with basic tracking (see "Tracking (1)" #39, "Tracking (2)" #40, "Tracking (3)" #41).

#45   Tracking 7 (Alternated Tracking/Receptive)

Purpose	• To teach the child to respond to instructions that combine pointing with a description (e.g., "Put the cup over there"). • Place a few items around the room (on the floor). The room should be furnished with larger base objects such as chairs, tables, and bins. Stand together in the middle of the room.
Procedure	• Point to an object and say: "put that one… on the table" (or another familiar location). Do not point to the location. • Name an object and point to a location ("put the cup over there"). Do not point to the object.
Consideration	• Many children struggle when pointing and verbal description are combined into one instruction. Initially, it may be necessary to separate the two instructions wherein the second instruction is delayed until the child responds to the first. With success, the interval between instructions can be reduced.

#46   Shifting Between Instruction Modalities

Purpose	• To strengthen the child's ability to switch flexibly between different kinds of instructions.
Arrangement	• Place pictures on the wall and corresponding pictures on a table in front of the child; place objects around the room (some objects should correspond to the pictures on the wall). The child is sitting at the table and you are standing by the pictures on the wall.
Procedure	• Present random instructions including: *"Touch same"* (while pointing to a picture on the wall; see #39), *"touch this… and this…"* (pointing to two consecutive pictures on the wall: see # 42), *"bring me this…"* (pointing

to picture on the wall and the child retrieves the corresponding object, see #39), *"bring me [object name]"* (the child retrieves the object), *"point to [object name]"* (the child points to the corresponding picture on the desk), *bring me that* (pointing to object on the floor, see #40), *bring me this* [object] (pointing to a pair of the same kind of objects, see #44), *put this over there* (pointing to an object and a destination, see #41).

CORE EXERCISES (2)

NAMING AND REQUESTING

#47	**Expressive Naming 1 (Objects)**

Purpose	• To teach the child to name objects. • To teach word-object correspondence and ensure that the child is able to name familiar objects in a variety of circumstances and extend the name to similar objects ('basic-level categorization').
Set up	• Sit face to face. Have objects selected for teaching readily available.
Procedure	• Present an object along with the question, "What is it?" • Use conventional discrete trial instruction. • Move from mass trials to expanded trials.
Considerations	• Expressive object naming sometimes emerges during receptive object labeling or even at earlier stages of intervention. Some children can already name objects at the onset of intervention. • For some children, it may be better to address receptive identification and expressive naming simultaneously (combined exercises). • For some children, expressive naming is acquired more easily than receptive identification. In such cases, expressive naming may serve as a bridge to teach receptive identification. • Expressive naming is a simple "correspondence skill" (word-object correspondence) and should not be confused with "knowing what an object is." The latter is a much broader issue of which expressive naming is merely an element. • Start with familiar objects that are easy for the child to pronounce (e.g., car, ball, cookie, apple). • Start with items that have been acquired receptively (if applicable).
Additional Steps and permutations	• As the skill emerges begin including pictures • When a few items are acquired, merge "Receptive Object Identification" (#32) and "Expressive Naming (1) (Objects)." • As soon as the child acquires and retains names with ease, move to less contrived teaching (e.g., see "Tracking and Orienting" (#51), "Naming Through Observational Learning" (#54).

#48	**Expressive Naming 2 (Body Parts)**

Purpose	• To teach naming *body-parts*.

Set up	• Sit face to face.

Procedure	• Point to one of the child's body parts and ask: "What is it/that?" • Use conventional discrete trial instruction. • Move from mass trials to expanded trials.

Considerations	• If the child struggles with body parts, consider expanding "Expressive Naming 1(Objects)" (#47) to increase vocabulary, proficiency, and acquisition speed before reintroducing this exercise. • Some children have significant motor coordination impairments and have great difficulty identifying their own body parts. For children with such difficulties consider an increased focus on various eye-hand coordination and gross motor activities.

Steps and permutations	• "Expressive body parts" should eventually involve identifying both the child's and the instructor's body parts. Eventually extend to figurines/dolls, animals and pictures.

#49	**Expressive Naming 3 (Persons)**

Purpose	• To teach naming familiar *persons*.

Set up	• Practice with familiar persons (e.g., family members, instructors). As the child learns to name familiar persons, introduce pictures.

Procedure	• Point to a familiar person/picture and ask: "Who is it?" • Use conventional discrete trial instruction. • Move from mass trials to expanded trials.

Considerations	• Some children find it more difficult to name persons than objects and body parts (see "Receptive Person Identification," #34 for elaboration). • If the child struggles with "Expressive Naming (3)", consider expanding "Expressive Naming 1 (Objects)" (i.e., increase vocabulary and proficiency) before reintroducing the exercises.

#50   Expressive Naming: Multiple Presentation Forms

Purpose	• To teach the child to name things with respect to different kinds of presentations. In conventional naming protocols, the instructor presents objects one at a time in a discrete fashion. In this exercise, items are presented in other kinds of ways. • To teach the child to 'shift his attention' and to track the attention (point) of another person.
Set up	• *Vary modalities*: • Present one item at a time (as "Expressive naming 1"). • Point to an object/picture in an array on the table. • Point to a picture in a book. • Point to an object at a distance ("Tracking and Orienting," #51).
Procedure	• Present the modalities randomly (see "set up"). • If necessary, introduce one modality at a time until child responds flexibly to all modalities.
Considerations	• Some children struggle with the transition from contrived conditions ("Expressive naming 1 (objects)") to less constrained natural and varied situations. Expect transition to take time.
Steps and permutations	• Use only known objects initially. When the child is proficient, new object names should be taught in all of the ways described. • When pointing, start with short distances (2 feet) and unambiguous arrangements (isolate the target from other objects). Distance and ambiguity can be increased as child makes progress with "Tracking and Orienting" (#51).

#51   Tracking and Orienting

Purpose	• To improve the child's ability to track another person's attention (pointing). • To shift visual orientation to align it with another person. • To extend basic naming to less contrived settings. In this exercise, the child names the item to which the instructor points.
Set up	• Place familiar objects and pictures around the room (on a table, wall, floor, shelves, etc.). Instructor and child move around the room.
Procedure	• Point to an object or picture and ask: "What is that?" / "What is this?" and while flexibly shifting your attention (and as the child tracks and orients), also modify the way you ask e.g., "What is this?" "What is that?" "…and what about this? ...and this?"

| **Considerations** | • This is an extension of earlier tracking exercises (# 39, #40). |
| | • Many children struggle when the instructor increases the distance between his finger and the object. When increasing distance, it is often necessary to make the target items more isolated (i.e., increase its distance to surrounding objects). |

| **Additional Steps and permutations** | • When the child develops proficiency, practice across all settings. |

#52   Sequential Naming

| **Purpose** | • To strengthen *see-say* correspondence and keep track of where he is in a sequence.
• To teach the child to name objects as he points to them while *moving* about.
• To 'detach' naming from antecedent verbal instructions. |

| **Arrangement** | • Several familiar objects and/or pictures are placed in a row. The child should stand and face the pictures. |

| **Procedure** | • Point to the table, and say: "What do you see?" or "What are these?"
• Place yourself behind the child, guide his finger (point to the picture farthest to the left) and name each object. When the child imitates your actions, guide the child's finger to the next picture, etc.
• When he begins to name items independently, discontinue manual guidance. |

| **Considerations** | • This skill may take some time to develop as children often lose track of where they are in the sequence. It may be necessary to build sequential naming gradually, starting with only two items, then three, etc. Initially, it may also be wise spread items out across a large surface so the child has to walk from left to right when naming the items.
• Sequential naming may establish a foundation for academic skills such as counting and other cognitive skills that require sustained sequential responding (e.g., describing unfolding events, tracking transactions between persons). |

| **Trouble Shooting** | • If the child continues to struggle after several instructional segments, it may be wise to postpone the exercise and strengthen/build more proficiency with skills such as "Self-Paced Naming" (#53) and "Sequential Matching (TPSM)" (#13). |

#53	**Self-Paced Naming**

Purpose	• Increase naming proficiency (the child names known objects at his own pace). • To detach naming from antecedent verbal instruction.
Set up	• Provide the child with a stack of pictures and/or a bin with objects. Use objects the child can easily name.
Procedure	• Say: "Name these" / "What are these?" (or use similar instructions) and present the materials. The child should select an item, name it, put it away and select the next, etc. • Some children have difficulty maintaining a steady pace with the *see-say* correspondence. It may be necessary to start with only a few items and guide the child to name the item only after the child places it on the table (i.e., the child selects an item, puts it on the table, and when the child releases, the instructor prompts the child to name it).
Considerations	• Self-pace naming may facilitate sequential responding in academic skills such as counting.

#54	**Naming Through Observational Learning**

Purpose	• To teach the child new objects names by observing direct instruction with another person.
Set up	• The child observes another person as the child learns to name an object (the instructor teaches another person). When the trial ends, the instructor tests to determine if the child learned the name through observation. Use multiple exemplars.
Procedure	• Present a novel object to another person and say: "This is a [name]," and follow up with the question: "What is it?" The person answers and receives praise. • Next, turn to the child, present the object and ask; "What is it?" • Repeat the sequence until the child learns the object's name. • Continue until the child learns the names of new objects with ease.
Considerations	• Before implementing this exercise, the child should demonstrate success with "Third Person Imitation" (#28) and "Follow the Leader" (#26). • The time delay from observation to test for acquisition should be increased gradually.

#55	**Requesting Desired Objects and Activities**

Purpose	• To teach the child to approach someone to request a desired item or activity.

Set up	• When the child is engaged in a preferred activity or is eating a preferred food. • See incidental teaching.

Procedure	• Arrange so the child is engaged in a preferred activity or eating a preferred food. • Block further access to the desired item/activity and instruct the child to make a request ("Say, I want X" or "Say, X please"). • The child should follow the direction to receive the item. • After 3 to 5 seconds, block access again and wait for the request. If the child does not request, repeat the earlier sequence. • This procedure corresponds to "incidental teaching" (see glossary) and should take place in all settings.

Considerations	• Requesting should be developed from the outset of language intervention, and many opportunities should be afforded throughout the day. • Practice across all environments. • Requesting is not simply the act of uttering a word corresponding to a needed or desired object. It involves approach, directedness (speaking *to* someone), gestures, answering questions, and repairing communication breakdown (i.e., problem-solving). Consequently "requesting" is a comprehensive skill that requires many incremental levels of instruction. • When teaching the child to request, it is essential to capture or contrive motivation (e.g., capturing desires, arranging tasks where necessary things are missing). • Instruction related to requests and "expressive naming" should be addressed concurrently. • "Requesting" is often used synonymously with "communication" or "functional communication." This conflation could be misleading. In vernacular parlance "communication" denotes a complex social ability in which a person attempts to make something known to another person. This presupposes that the communicator understands that the other person does not know and must be informed. In contrast, requesting can be purely "instrumental" in which another person serves as a tool to fulfill a desire.

#56	**Sequential Matching: Interrupted Chain**

Purpose	• To teach the child to request an item required to complete a familiar task.

Set up	• Place four to six pictures face down, in a row on a table. Place a bin containing a set of corresponding items to the child's left (on a separate table or chair). (see "Sequential Matching" #13). Make sure that one or

more of the pertinent objects are not in the bin.

Procedure	• The child should turn the first picture (T), point to it (P), select the corresponding item from the bin (S), and place it on the picture (M). • When the child discovers a picture that lacks a corresponding object, an assistant prompts the child to approach you and request it. • Reinstitute the procedure and fade assistance over successive trials.
Considerations	• Prompt fading may take some time. • Intersperse interrupted trials (missing item) with uninterrupted trials (all items available). • This procedure was developed as an alternative to the traditional 'Picture Exchange Communication System' (PECS) as PECS often proves ineffective for highly impaired children.[1]
Additional steps and permutations	• Once the child requests a missing item reliably, start to address the quality of requesting (eye-contact, volume) and vary the distance child travels. Eventually place yourself out of view so that the child has to look for you.

#57   Blocked Response (Instruction)

Purpose	• To teach the child to request a needed item in order to carry out an instruction. • To teach the child to ask for information regarding an object's location.
Set up	• Practice this exercise in the child's natural environment with known objects. • This exercise requires two instructors.
Procedure	• Tell the child to get an object ("get the X"). The child should search for the object and bring it to you. Tell the child to get another object. The child should search for the object, but it is hidden. • When the child shows signs of giving up the search (stalling, deviates) an assistant guides the child back to you and models the question: "Where is ___? Or alternatively, "I want___" (see "considerations"). • You point to the object and say; "there it is" or "it's over there". The child should track and retrieve the object.
Considerations	• The child should be fluent with tracking (#39, #40, #,42, #43) and requesting desired objects (#55) and needed objects (# 56).
Troubleshooting	• Many children tend to confuse object requests/demands ("I want ___") with "Where is ___?" questions. For some children, this distinction may be too difficult to develop at this stage. If the child does not demonstrate progress, you may settle for object requests ("I want ___") and address "Where" questions at a later time.

- Most children will be unable to ask questions on demand ("Say...Where is it?") until they are proficient with "Say versus do" (#65, #66).

#58   Requesting From 2nd Person

Purpose	• To teach the child to request information from a second person when the first person is unable to provide it.
Set up	• Practice this exercise in the child's natural environments with known objects. • This exercise requires two instructors.
Procedure	• Tell the child to get an object ("get the X"). The child should search for the object and bring it to you. Then tell the child to get another object. He searches for the object, but it is unavailable (i.e., hidden). • The child approaches you and asks; "Where is X?" Or alternatively "I want__" (see "considerations" in "Blocked Response" #57). • You say "Mommy has it," or "ask Mommy." • The child should then travel to the designated person, ask for the object and bring it back to you.
Considerations	• The child must be able to ask "Where" questions (see "Blocked response" #57). • If the child is unable to ask "Where" questions, settle for "I want__" statements and reintroduce "Where" questions at a later time (see "Blocked Response" #57, for considerations) • This exercise is highly complex and demands that the child make several pragmatic decisions. For greater scaffolding, use "Sequential Matching: Interrupted Chain" (#56) as the antecedent condition. • For relevant commentary see Lovaas 1977 pp. 77, 163 ('Giving and seeking information').

#59   Managing Listener's Responses

Purpose	• To teach the child to respond to a variety of situations when requesting an object.
Set up	• This exercise involves interrupted chains and should be practiced in the child's natural environment. • This exercise requires two instructors.
Procedure	• When the child requests a missing item (e.g., in the context of an interrupted chain) you may: • Provide the requested item (the child says "thank you").

- Ask: "Do you want this?" (present an item) (the child says "yes" or "no" accordingly) (see #146).
- Point to location and say, "It's over there."
- Present two objects of the kind requested (i.e., two different cups), and ask: "Which one?" (The child should point to one of the items and say "this one").
- Tell the child where it is ("It is in the drawer").
- Tell the child to ask someone else (i.e., "Daddy has it") (see "Requesting from Second Person," #58).

Considerations	• Some of the above situations require separate exercises/isolated practice. For instance, answering yes/no may need to be taught in a different setting before incorporating it in this exercise.
Additional steps and permutations	• Additional obstacles could eventually be added to this routine. For example, if the child is directed to an item on a top shelf, he might then need to request help to get it down.

Integrating Basic Learning Skills

#60	**Naming to Requesting (contrived)**

Purpose	• To 'connect' naming and requesting so that when learning a name of an object there is a direct transfer to requesting. Thus, if the child has learned to name objects through direct instruction, the child should be able to request them under appropriate conditions without explicit teaching.
Set up	• "Sequential Matching: Interrupted Chain (# 56) and novel items (pictures and objects).
Procedure	• Teach the child to name a novel item (target) using direct instruction (#47). • Implement "Sequential Matching: Interrupted Chain (#56) where the target is missing. • The child requests the missing item. • If the child is unable to request the missing item (i.e., forgot the name), discontinue the segment and practice "Expressive Naming 1" (step 1). • Return to step 2.
Considerations	• This exercise takes considerable time to run and may require many repetitions. • Bridging naming and requesting is imperative in order to move to advanced language exercises. • This exercise may be implemented when the child begins to identify and name things with relative ease. Occasionally, the exercise can be implemented successfully from the very outset of language intervention.

#61	**Requesting to Naming**

Purpose	• To connect requesting and naming so that learning the former transfers directly to the latter. Thus, if a child learns to request an object through direct instruction, the child will be able to name the object without explicit teaching.
Set up	• "Sequential Matching: Interrupted Chain (#56) and novel items (pictures and objects).
Procedure	• Arrange "Sequential Matching: Interrupted Chain" where novel items are missing. When the child approaches you to request the missing item, prompt

the correct response (provide the name in the prompted request), deliver the item, and reintroduce "Sequential Matching: Interrupted Chain." If the child requests the target item independently on this second trial, afford the child a short break, then ask the child to name the object ("What is it?").

Considerations	• This exercise demands considerable memory since the time delay between prompting (time of request) and new response opportunity is often a matter of minutes. Extensive practice may be necessary.
Troubleshooting	• A number of things could happen when a child approaches an instructor to request the novel item; (a) the child may stall (since the child has no name for the missing item), (b) the child may point to the picture of the novel item, (c) the child may invent a name for the missing item (e.g., use a name of an object with similar physical features), (d) discontinue the task (give up), or (e) cry or tantrum. In all cases, prompt the correct response and ensure that the child completes the task.

#62   Receptive-Expressive Correspondence

Purpose	• To connect receptive identification and naming so that learning one modality yields the other. Thus, if you teach the child to identify an object receptively, he will be able to name it without direct instruction.
Set up	• The child and instructor sit at a table containing a few familiar items and one novel item.
Procedure	• Teach the child to identify the novel item receptively or name it. Once the child learns an item in one modality (e.g., receptive), test for the other modality (expressive). • Example 1: Teach "eraser" receptively, then probe naming when the child discriminates it from other known objects. • Example 2: Teach "tissue" expressively, then when the child remembers the name in expanded trials, probe receptive identification.
Considerations	• Bridging these modalities is imperative in order to move towards more advanced language exercises. • Typically, it is easier for children to go from expressive to receptive than the other way around.
Additional steps and permutations	• Gradually increase the time between the teaching trial and test trial. • Receptive-expressive correspondence exercises can be arranged in different ways that would also include natural settings. For instance, tell the child to bring an item for which they have not yet learned the name. Point to the item and tell the child to get it (using the name). When the child returns,

follow-up with asking the child "What's this?").

#63	**Receptive to Requesting**

Purpose	• To connect receptive identification and requesting so that learning one modality yields the other. Thus, if you teach the child to identify an object receptively, the child will be able to request this item without direct instruction.
Set up	• "Sequential Matching: Interrupted Chain" (#56) and novel items (pictures and objects).
Procedure	• Teach the child to identify a novel item receptively. • Implement "Sequential Matching: Interrupted Chain" where the target item is missing. • If the child is unable to request the missing item (i.e., forgot the name), discontinue this segment and practice receptive identification (step 1). • Return to step 2.
Considerations	• In order to implement this exercise successfully, the child should show some progress with "Receptive-Expressive Correspondence" (#62).

#64	**Matching, Receptive and Naming**

Purpose	• To teach the child to shift flexibly between different instructions and modalities. The child will learn to shift between instructions such as "Do this" while pointing to a picture ("Selection-Based Imitation), "find one of these" / "find this one" (searching), "What is this?" ("Naming"), and "Point to the ___" ("Receptive Identification").
Set up	• The child is at a desk about six-seven feet away from the wall (or a large board). Place an array of known pictures on the desk and attach corresponding (and non-corresponding) pictures to the wall; place objects corresponding to the instructor's pictures around the floor.
Procedure	• Present one of the following instructions: "Do this" / "find this one" (while pointing to a picture on the wall) "What is it? (pointing to a picture on the wall), "point to the ___" [one of the child's pictures], "bring me a __ [referring to one of the objects on the floor]. An assistant prompts from behind.
Considerations	• Shifting flexibly between different instructions may be challenging to some children. Difficulties may be compounded if the child has been exposed to extensive "compartmental teaching" (i.e., one kind of 'program' at a time).

#65   Say versus Do (1)

Purpose	• To teach the child to differentiate between the instructions "Say [name of the object]" versus "Point to/Where is [name of the object]?" • Example: "Say cup" versus "Point to the cup."
Set up	• Sit face to face by a table with familiar items.
Procedure	• Randomize the instructions "Say [name of the object]" and "Point to/Where is [name of the object]?"
Considerations	• This exercise involves *conditional instructions* (Say the word only if you hear the word "say," otherwise point to the object corresponding to the word). These "if-but-not-otherwise" conditions may be quite difficult to learn and will often require additional practice before the ability solidifies see "Receptive Colors: Conditional Discrimination" (#116). • Mastery of "Say versus do" is necessary in order to address complex language abilities such as asking questions or using pronouns.

#66   Say versus Do (2)

Purpose	• To teach the child to discriminate between following; the direction to 'say the action word' vs 'perform the action.' Example: "Say clap" versus "clap."
Set up	• Sit face to face
Procedure	• Randomize the instructions "Say [action]" and "[action]"
Considerations	• As with "Say versus Do (1), this exercise involves *conditional instructions* (say the word only if you hear the word "say," otherwise perform the corresponding action). • This "if-but-not-otherwise" condition tends to be more difficult than "Say [object name]" versus "Point to the [object]." • Without the ability to discriminate these conditions, the child will not be able to move beyond labeling and rote responding. This is a "bottleneck" that the child must get through.

#67	Naming by Exclusion

Purpose	• To teach the child another way to learn names for things.
Set up	• Same as sequential naming (#52). • One of the pictures in the field is new to the child, i.e., the child has not learned its name.
Procedure	• Same as sequential naming except that when the child encounters the picture for which the child has not learned the name, prompt the child to say "What is it?." Provide the child with the name, then ask the child to name it, i.e., you say, "What is it?" and the child names it. Repeat the sequence, this time to determine if the child has acquired the name. If so, the child should simply name the new item. If the child 'asks' again, continue to repeat the sequence until the child no longer 'asks' but simply names the new item.
Considerations	• It is essential that the child is fluent with "say vs do" discriminations (see say vs. do #65, #66). Otherwise, when the child is prompted to say "what is it?" the child may attempt to 'answer' the question. • We are hesitant to refer to this exercise as one in which the child is "asking." Asking presupposes several things: 1) an interest/desire to know, 2) a self-reflective experience in which one recognizes that they "know" or don't "know" something, 3) apprehension that the answer is 'out there,' and 4) seeking a likely source for the answer. • Helping children understand the terms "who," "what," and "where" are addressed in later sections. These later exercises should serve as a starting point for a basic understanding of "wh" terms.

#68	Tracking/Naming Hybrid

Purpose	• To teach the child to follow instructions involving a receptive component (name of the object) and tracking. • To increase joint attention acuity.
Set up	• Spread across the floor several sets of familiar objects. There should be at least two different items of each kind (e.g., two different cups, balls, dolls, etc.).
Procedure	• Point to an item and say: "Give me *that* cup." The child should distinguish the target cup from other cups in the vicinity.
Considerations	• This exercise is an extension of previous tracking exercises. • In order to respond correctly, the child has to integrate two cues of different modalities; visual (pointing) and auditory (object label). • The child should be fluent with basic tracking (see Section 1).

| Troubleshooting | • It is not uncommon for children to respond to only one of the cues (i.e., responds to the word "cup," but fails to track the pointing or vice versa). It is often necessary to build this skill gradually, starting with two sets of objects placed near the child. |

#69   Retrieving by name and tracking-combined

| Purpose | • To teach the child to follow instructions involving receptive identification and tracking. |

| Set up | • Spread several familiar objects across the floor. |

| Procedure | • Say: "Give me the [object]…and that" (pointing to another object). The child gathers the two objects.
• The order of these modalities should be reversed once the child begins to respond correctly to receptive-point relation ("give me the [object] and that one"). |

| Considerations | • Before implementing this exercise, the child should be fluent with more basic tracking exercises including multiple step tracking (#42).
• The child must be able to respond correctly to any combination of these modalities (receptive/pointing and pointing/receptive). |

| Troubleshooting | • Children often over-select on one of these cues (i.e., respond to the word "cup," but fail to track, or vice versa). It is often necessary to start by separating the instructional components, Deliver one instruction ("give me the cup"), wait for the child's response, then deliver the second instruction ("…and that," pointing to an object). |

Expanding Basic Naming

70   Receptive Locations

Purpose	• To teach the child to identify locations within familiar environments (e.g., home, school, yard). • Expanding vocabulary and teaching environments.
Set up	• This exercise can be practiced in all environments.
Procedure	• Determine a starting point (initially it should be close to the target location). Tell the child to "go to [location]," then guide the child to the destination and back to the point of origin. Repeat the instruction and fade prompting over successive trials. • As the child acquires a few locations, extend the distance from the point of origin to the location.
Considerations	• This exercise is initially highly contrived. As soon as the child acquires this skill, exercises must be less contrived (e.g., go to location and get things, put things in locations, go to location and engage in activities). • As the child acquires a few locations, vary the starting points.

#71   Receptive Location and Action

Purpose	• To teach the child to follow two-step directions that involve a location and an action. • To strengthen working memory and inhibition.
Set up	• This exercise can be practiced in all environments.
Procedure	• Determine a starting point. Tell the child to go to a location and perform an action ("Go to [location] and [action]"). Guide the child to the target location, prompt correct action, and guide the child back to the point of origin. Repeat the instruction and attempt to provide less guidance. Continue until the child is able to perform the action at the location. Introduce new location/action combinations until the child is able to do novel combinations.
Considerations	• This exercise has two main functions. First, it is designed to teach the child to inhibit the second part of an instruction until another situation occurs (arriving at a location). This ability is essential and will be extended

further (e.g. see "Basic Rule-Following (#166). Second, it establishes the conditions for teaching other skills such as "Reporting Locations" (#74), and verb tensing.

- Being able to describe and track sequenced events is a precondition for addressing causal relations between object-object, object-person and person-person (who did what to whom) and a precondition for a rudimentary understanding of "What happened?"

#72   Naming Stationary Objects

Purpose	• To teach the child to name stationary objects. • To expand vocabulary.
Set up	• Travel all around the house or other locations.
Procedure	• Walk with the child to various objects in the house; point to them and ask: "What is it?" • Prompt correct response; Leave area and return later to check for acquisition.
Considerations	• This exercise usually goes smoothly if the child acquires object names with ease and demonstrates proficiency with tracking.
Additional steps and permutations	• "Naming Stationary Objects" and "Receptive Locations" • (#70) should be merged into one lesson as soon as the child demonstrates success (see also "Reporting locations 1" #74).

#73   Naming Locations

Purpose	• To teach the child a rudimentary understanding of the concept of "Where" as it relates to his current whereabouts.
Arrangement	• Walk with the child to various locations/rooms in the house (or other places).
Procedure	• Walk with the child to various locations/rooms in the house. Stop at specific locations and ask; "Where are you?" • Prompt correct response; go for a short walk, return to the target location and repeat the question.
Considerations	• A "location" can be a quite abstract notion, and it is often difficult for children to know where a room begins and ends. It is often a good idea to start with concrete items such as door, window, and book shelf (see "Naming stationary Objects," #72), before extending to less concrete locations such

as living room, kitchen, bathroom, and hallway.

- Success with this exercise is a precondition for teaching how to report recent activity (e.g., "Where did you go?") and declaring ongoing activity ("Where are you going?").
- When conducting this exercise is it important to intersperse "Where" questions with other demands and instructions such as "What is it?" while displaying or pointing to objects.
- Naming locations or accounting for where you are involves the use of various prepositions including "in," "by," and "at" (e.g., "in the kitchen" versus "at the bookshelf"). Proper use of prepositions in novel situations requires experience with multiple situations.

#74   Reporting Locations (1)

Purpose	• To teach the child to report recent whereabouts.
Set up	• This exercise can be practiced in all environments. • This exercise is a direct extension of "Receptive Locations" (#70).
Procedure	• Tell the child to go to a location. • When he returns to the point of origin, ask: "Where did you go?" and prompt the correct response. The response may be "I went to the [location]" or simply "to [location]." • Repeat the instructional segment and introduce additional location when the child masters the first one.
Considerations	• This exercise complements "Naming Locations" (#73), and these exercises may be implemented simultaneously. • Once this exercise is implemented it may no longer be necessary to continue "Receptive Locations" (#70).

#75   Reporting Locations (2)

Purpose	• To teach the child to report actions. • *Self-observation* is a critical target of this exercise.
Set up	• This exercise can be practiced in all environments; start with familiar locations. • This exercise is a direct extension of "Reporting Locations 1" (#74).
Procedure	• Tell the child, "Come with me" and walk with the child to a familiar location. Use known locations only. • At the destination, ask the child "Where are you?" • When the child answers return promptly to the point of origin and ask: "Where did we go?" Prompt correct response (e.g.

"To the kitchen," or "the kitchen") and repeat the segment. Fade prompts over successive trials.
- When child is proficient, omit the question "Where are you?" at the target location (see "Considerations" for clarification).

Considerations
- This exercise replaces "Naming Location" (#73). Thus, new locations should be taught in this format.
- This exercise is often more difficult than "Reporting Location 1" (#74) as it *does not involve a verbal instruction*. When a specific verbal direction is omitted, the child is required to observe where he is.
- This lesson has the child traveling 'through' or 'past' other locations. Therefore, the correct answer may be unclear. In order to highlight the right answer, it is often necessary to spend time at the target location (e.g., perform a simple activity).
- This exercise tends to be more difficult as distance increases.

#76   Declaring Destination (1)

Purpose
- To teach the child to declare where he is going.

Set up
- This exercise can be practiced in all environments

Procedure
- Tell the child to go to a familiar location
- While in transition, another instructor asks: "Where are you going?"
- Prompt correct answer ("I am going to the ___," or simply "to the___")
- When the child answers, the assistant ensures that the child continues to the designated location and then returns to the point of origin.
- Repeat the instructional segment and fade prompting over successive trials.

Considerations
- Common error: Children do not continue to the destination after answering "Where are you going?" Multiple successive trials are often necessary in order to establish this routine.
- In order to reduce the child's tendencies to stall and wait for a question, it is important to intersperse this lesson with trials in which the child is *not* asked, "Where are you going?"

#77   Declaring Destination (2)

Purpose
- To teach the child to declare where he is going based on spontaneous transitions.

Set up
- This exercise can be practiced in all environments at unstructured times.

Procedure
- When the child travels from one location to another under the child own

volition (i.e., not requested to go) ask: "Where are you going?" This exercise is to be implemented during unstructured time as soon as "Declaring Destination (1)" (#76) is mastered.

Considerations	<ul><li>Common problem: Initial lack of "say-do" correspondence. For instance, the child may answer "to the bathroom" while traveling to the child's bedroom. Extensive practice is often needed, and it may be necessary to correct correspondence errors by gently placing the child a few feet from the location and then let the child proceed if the report is accurate.</li><li>Make sure to assess the errors properly, i.e., is it a lack of correspondence or does the child confuse names of things? (e.g., calling the bathroom "bedroom").</li><li>It may be necessary to strengthen "say-do" correspondence in general (see #65).</li></ul>

ACTIONS

#78   Expressive Actions (1): Following an Instruction

Purpose	• To teach the child to name what he is doing. • This exercise has *some* commonality with "Expressive Naming 1 (objects)" (#47), and the two exercises may be introduced at the same time.
Set up	• This exercise can be practiced in all environments using common objects.
Procedure	• Instruct the child to do something (e.g., "clap"). While the child is doing it, ask; "What are you doing?" and prompt correct answer (i.e., "clapping"). • Use conventional discrete trial instruction.

#79   Expressive Actions (2): Following a Model

Purpose	• To teach the child to name what he is doing. • To disentangle naming from the 'cue' of the verbal antecedent.
Set up	• This exercise can be practiced in all environments using common objects.
Procedure	• Instruct the child to imitate what you do (e.g., say "Do this" and then). While the child is doing it ask, "What are you doing?" and prompt correct answer (i.e., "clapping"). • Use conventional discrete trial instruction.
Considerations	• The difference between this and the previous exercise is subtle but profound. Here, the child has to recognize what he is doing without access to an antecedent verbal 'cue.'

#80   Expressive Actions (3)

Purpose	• To teach the child to name simple actions he or others are doing.
Set up	• This exercise can be practiced in all environments.
Procedure	• Do something simple (e.g., wave) and ask: "What am I doing?" • Use conventional discrete trial instruction.

| **Considerations** | • Once the child is able to name a few actions, "Expressive actions (1)" (#78), "Expressive Actions (2)" (#79), and "Expressive Actions (3)" (#80) may be combined. |
| | • For many children, it may be strategic to avoid pronoun use until there is progress with nominative pronouns (see pronouns section). |

| **Next steps and permutations** | • Generalization training should include: (1) practice in less contrived environments involving other people ("What is she doing?" while pointing to another person) (2) naming (describing?) actions in pictures and motion pictures, (3) shifting attention between two simultaneous performances ("What is he doing?" → pointing to person 1, "What is he doing?" → pointing to person 2). |

#81   Progressive Actions (1)

| **Purpose** | • To help the child apprehend transitive verbs and actions identified by intent or outcome. "Coloring the picture," "building a tower," and "looking for Mom" are all examples of actions-in-progress defined by intended outcome. |

| **Set up** | • This exercise can be practiced in all environments. |

Procedure	• Instruct the child to get an object from a short distance; "Get the ___." While he carries out the task, ask: "What are you doing?" Prompt the correct response ("getting the ___") and ensure that the child completes the action.
	• Stay with "get" instructions until the child identifies the object accurately.
	• Introduce actions such as *"putting away," "building," "packing," "looking for,"* etc.

Considerations	• This exercise concerns *transitive verbs* - verbs that require a direct object. Thus, when a child is required to "get the cup", while the child is walking towards it, you ask: "What are you doing?" the answer is "getting the cup," not just "getting." Nor is it a matter of referring to a current segment/stage of the action. For instance, the answer to "What are you doing?" is not "walking" or "standing."
	• In this exercise, the child describes an 'action' that has not yet been completed by referring to the goal. This kind of teleological expression is more intricate than simply naming current or past actions.
	• The action "getting" is merely a convenient starting point in addressing "multi-step-actions-in-progress." Other simple transitive actions include *building* (e.g., "building a tower"), *Putting away/putting on* (e.g., "putting away the book," "putting on shoes"), *packing* (e.g., "packing the bag"), and *looking for* (e.g., "looking for Mommy").
	• "Multi-step-action-in-progress" often requires complex grammatical

constructions such as *"giving the cup to Mommy," "putting plates on the table,"* and *"opening the door for Daddy."* These complex actions may be addressed once the child makes substantial progress with simpler kinds of transitive actions.
- Naturally, descriptions of more complex actions are only feasible when a youngster demonstrates fluency with linguistic elements such as pronouns and prepositions.

#82   Progressive Actions (2)

Purpose	• To teach the child to describe progressive actions of others.
Set up	• This exercise requires two instructors and common objects.
Procedure	• With the child present, tell another instructor to get an object nearby ("get the ___").
	• While the assistant carries out the action, ask the child; "What is [person] doing?"
	• Prompt correct answer ("getting the ___"). Repeat the instructional segment and fade prompting over successive trials.
Considerations	• Continue with "get" instructions until the child reports accurately.
	• It's necessary for the child to be aware of the pre-conditions in order to describe another person's action. For instance, the child would not be able to identify someone else's action as "getting the cup" unless the child had witnessed the other person receiving an instruction or he can discern from the context (e.g., the person wants something to drink during snack and gets up to get a cup).
	• This exercise should eventually be extended to include past tense ("Tense Discrimination of Progressive Actions," #87).

#83   Past Tense Actions (1): Following Instructions

Purpose	• To learn the distinction between present and past tense verbs.
Set up	• This exercise can be practiced in all environments.
Procedure	• Tell the child to perform an action (to do something simple?) (e.g., "clap"). When the child has done it, ask: "What did you do?" and prompt the correct answer ("clapped"). Repeat the segment and fade prompts over successive trials.
	• When the child begins to master past tense, begin mixing present progressive (#81, #82) and past tense questions; "What are you doing? → What did you do? (#87) for a description of this exercise).

| Considerations | • The use of verb tenses involves an understanding of the temporal dimensions of actions as well as projected actions (e.g., "going to ___," "will ___"). The child has to discern when an action is in progress and when it has ended (past) which is not always perfectly clear. |
| | • The nominal objective of this exercise is to teach the child to use the morpheme –*ed*, when the question involves the word "*did.*" Mastery of this skill is not an indication that the child understands verb tenses; it is merely a starting point for achieving such understanding. |

#84 Past Tense Actions (2): Following a Model

| Purpose | • To teach the child the distinction between present and past tense actions. |
| | • To further strengthen abilities in visual observation and shifting modalities. |

| Set up | • This exercise can be practiced in all environments. |

| Procedure | • Instruct the child to <u>imitate</u> what you do, "Do this" (e.g., clap). When the child has done it, ask: "What did you do?" and prompt the correct response ("clapped"). |
| | • When the child shows reliable progress, begin mixing present progressive (#81, #82) and past tense questions: "What are you doing?" → "What did you do?" |

| Considerations | • In "Past Tense Action 1" (#83), the child responds to a verbal instruction; in the present exercise, the child does not have the benefit of a verbal instruction. |
| | • As the child masters the current exercise, extend to less contrived settings (i.e., ask: "What did you do?" when the child has carried out an action on his own initiative). |

| Additional steps and permutations | • Perform an action (e.g., clap) and ask: "What did I do?" |
| | • Generalization should include (1) practice in less contrived environments involving third persons ("What did she do?" while pointing to a person) and (2) describing actions in motion pictures. |

#85 Past Tense Actions (3): Location and Action

| Purpose | • To expand the child's ability to use past tense. |

| Set up | • This exercise can be practiced in all environments. |
| | • This is a direct extension of "Receptive Locations and Action" (#71). |

Procedure	• Determine a starting point. Tell the child to go to a location and do something ("Go to [location] and [X]"). When the child returns, ask: "What did you do?" Prompt correct response, repeat instruction, and fade prompts over successive trials.
Considerations	• This arrangement is often implemented as a way of teaching children to discriminate "What" and "Where" questions. While this may work for some children, for most others we urge caution since very often the same response can be used in both cases. This conceals the possibility that the child may not understand the difference between the two questions. Thus while "Going" to a location is an <u>action</u> and serves as a basis for answering "what did you do?" it also serves as an appropriate basis for answering "Where" questions. For instance, when the instructor asks: "Where did you go?" The child may say: "I went to the door," but may answer the same thing when asked: "What did you do?" The concept of "Where" is elusive and for many children, and this may not be an optimal entry into teaching this concept.

#86   Tense Discrimination

Purpose	• To teach the child to discern present and past tense.
Set up	• This exercise can be practiced in all environments.
Procedure	• Instruct the child to do something (e.g., "clap") or imitate what you do ("do this"). While the child is doing it, ask; "What are you doing?" and prompt correct answer (i.e., "clapping"). When the child stops, ask: "What did you do?" Prompt correct answer ("clapped").
	• Instruct the child to observe what others are doing and ask, "What is __ doing?" and "What did __ do?"
Considerations	• This program is highly contrived and merely designed to help the child make (a) a distinction between what's ongoing (present progressive) and what's been discontinued (b) express this linguistically in terms of the morpheme "ing" and "ed."

#87   Tense Discrimination of Progressive Actions

Purpose	• To teach the child to discern present and past tense of the progressive verb "to get."
	• To increase abilities in observing and tracking other person's actions.
Set up	• This exercise can be practiced in all environments with familiar objects, and requires two instructors.

Procedure	• This exercise is essentially the same as the "Tense Discrimination" exercises (#86) but introduces items from "Progressive Actions" (#81, #82).
	• Tell the child to get an object from a short distance; "Get the ___." While he is in route, ask; "What are you doing?" The child answers: "Getting the ___," while continuing the action. When the child returns and delivers the item, ask; "What did you do?"
	• Third person: Tell another instructor to get an object from a short distance; "get the ___." While the assistant is in route, ask; "What is ___ doing?" the child should answer: "getting the ___". When the assistant returns with the object, ask; "What did [person] do?" The child should answer: "got the cup."
Considerations	• This exercise places considerable demands on observation and tracking other person's actions.
	• This exercise will also aid in development of "say-do" correspondence.

#88   Tense Discrimination: Reporting Observations

Purpose	• To teach the child to report observed scenarios using correct verb tenses with respect to "see," "is," and "have."
Set up	• Place a familiar object on the table, chair or in a container. Other persons are holding familiar objects.
Procedure	• Ask the child to label what the child sees on the table or in a container: "What do you see?" Prompt the child to say: "I see [object]." Then cover the object or turn the child away and ask: "What did you see?" Prompt the child to say: "I saw [object label]."
	• Place an object on a chair or in a container away from the child's visual field. Bring the child over and ask: "What is on the chair?" / "What is in the container?" Prompt the child to use full sentences: "A(n) [object] is on the chair." Guide the child back to the point of origin and ask: "What was on the chair?" Prompt the child to use full sentences: "A(n) [object] was on the chair."
	• Bring the child to another person so the child can observe that person. Ask the child "What does [person] have?" or "What does he/she have?" (while pointing). If the child has mastered "Expressive Action (3) (#80), this should be easy to establish. Bring the child back to the point of origin and ask: "What did [person] have?" prompt the child to use full sentences: "[person] had a(n) [object]"
Considerations	• These exercises are highly contrived and are designed to get the skill "off the ground."
	• This exercise requires that the child is able to formulate long sentences ("A cup was on the chair"), and thus implementation should be postponed until the child is fluent with five- to six-word utterances.

FUNCTIONS

#89   Functions of Objects: Problem Solving by Tool Use

Purpose	• To teach the child to use objects to achieve specific outcomes.

Set up	• Everyday activities that include the use of objects to achieve certain outcomes. • Examples: Carrying items in a container, wiping the table with a paper towel, eating cereal with a spoon, coloring a picture with a crayon, hanging up art on the wall using tape, using a stool to reach an object, getting a chair to sit down at a table, getting water from the faucet.

Procedure	• Teach the child to carry out everyday tasks (manual guidance, repeated practice). Once the child is able to carry out the task, begin giving instructions such as "bring these over here," "Let's hang this up," "Clean that up please," or simply expose the child to the tasks. • Example: The child must find a container to carry building blocks from one place to where the activity will take place.

Considerations	• Teaching functions must be based on salient *experiences and actual use* of objects. Practical problem solving and use is imperative to successful development of these abilities and their corresponding linguistic tokens. Consequently, the teaching environment must encompass abundant practical tasks that child must complete independently. • Use a variety of items with the same/similar function. For instance, crayons, pencils, and markers are for writing; tape and Velcro are for hanging things up. • "Functions of objects" is a pivotal component with respect to "superordinate categorization" (see #177-180). • The practical use of everyday tools establishes conditions for eventually addressing (1) causal formulations and reasons, e.g., "Why did you use/ do you need the scissors?" (2) answering how questions and describing a process (How did you hang it up? / What did you use to clean it up?).

#90   Functions of Objects (Demonstration)

Purpose	• To teach basic understanding and language concerning the function (purpose) of common objects and events. • To teach the child that common objects can be referred to or classified in terms of how people use them.

Set up	• Sit across or next to the child and ensure easy access to known objects.
Procedure	• Ask; "Show me what this is for" while pointing to one of the objects. Guide the child to demonstrate the proper function (e.g., cup/drinking, spoon/eating, hat/wearing, ball/bouncing).
	• As the child begins to learn the task, use alternative instructions (e.g., "What do you do with this one?").
Considerations	• Only use items that the child uses independently in everyday life (e.g., spoon, cup) or items the child has observed being used on a regular basis.

#91   Functions of Objects: Receptive (1)

Purpose	• To teach basic understanding and language concerning the function (purpose) of common objects and events.
	• To teach the child that common objects can be referred to or classified in terms of how people use them or how they are intended to be used.
Set up	• Sit across or next to the child with easy access to known objects. Use items the child has mastered in "Functions of objects ("Functions of Objects: Demonstration" #90).
Procedure	• Display known objects and ask: "Which one is for drinking/reading/cutting, etc.?" Prompt the child to point to or otherwise identify the pertinent object. Fade prompts over successive trials.
Considerations	• "Function of Objects: Receptive (1)" and "Functions of Objects (Demonstration)", (#90) can be taught simultaneously or the order of introduction may be reversed.
	• Introduce objects that are used daily. Target multiple objects with the same function (e.g., fork and spoon are for eating, tape and glue are for attaching things). See "Functions of Objects: Multiple Examples" (#95) for elaboration.
	• 'Functions of objects' is a fundamental abstract concept and may be introduced alongside other fundamental abstract concepts such as colors (Receptive Colors: Conditional Discrimination, #116, and Naming Colors, #118-124).

#92	Functions of Objects: Receptive (2)
Purpose	• To teach the child to refer to an object in terms of different properties such as proper name, function and color.
Set up	• Display an array of known objects.
Procedure	• Display known items and ask the child to point to an item by referencing its (a) name ("Point to the cup"), (b) function ("Point to the one that is for drinking"), or (c) color ("Point to the yellow one"). Randomize these questions and alternate the field of objects.
Considerations	• The child must be fluent with "Receptive Colors: Conditional Discrimination" (#116) before introducing this exercise.

#93	Functions of Objects: Naming (1)
Purpose	• To teach the child to describe objects by their functions.
Set up	• Same as "Functions of Objects (Receptive 1)."
Procedure	• Ask the child to identify objects receptively ("point to the cup"). Once the child does, hold it up and ask: "What is it for?" Prompt the child to say: "It is for [drinking, eating, etc.]," or just "For [drinking, eating, etc.]." Fade prompting over successive trials.
Considerations	• This exercise may be introduced when the child has acquired three to four items in "Functions of Objects: Receptive (1)" (#92) and "Naming Colors (2)" (#119).
Next steps and permutations	• When the child has acquired at least three items, alternate receptive identification and naming with asking, "What is it for?" without presenting a previous receptive instruction; sometimes present the receptive instruction without a subsequent function question.

#94	Functions of Objects: Naming (2)
Purpose	• To teach the child to understand a variety of semantically identical instructions/questions concerning functions of objects.
Set up	• Same as "Functions of Objects (receptive 1)."
Procedure	• Display familiar items and present instructions and questions in a randomized

fashion: "What do you do with this?" / "What is a(n) [object] for?" / "What is for drinking?" / "Which one is for drinking?" / "Give me the one you drink with?" (Additional instructions/questions may be introduced).

Considerations	• The child may display grammatical difficulties. For instance, in response to: "What is a cup for?" the child may say: "drinking is for cup." It is important to identify grammatical error patterns so interventions can be designed to address them.
Troubleshooting	• If the child makes frequent errors, it may be useful to restrict the question to "What is a ___ for?" Once the child reliably responds correctly (i.e., "A __ is for ___" or "for ___"), the question may be reversed: "What is for _____?" When the child is successful with both kinds of questions, additional questions may be introduced gradually ("What do you do with this?", "What is this for?" etc.).

#95   Functions of Objects: Multiple Examples

Purpose	• To teach the child that several objects may have the same function (e.g., fork and spoons are for eating, cup and straw are for drinking, shoes and hats are for wearing).
Set up	• Display an array of known items including at least two items with the same function.
Procedure	• Display known items and ask: "Which one is for ___?" (E.g., "Which one is for wearing?"). The child responds (e.g., "The hat is for wearing."). Then follow up with the question: "What else is for ___?" (e.g., "What else is for wearing?"). Prompt correct response and fade prompts over successive trials.
Considerations	• The concept of "what else" may be challenging and should be addressed in a number of contexts. • The child may list multiple objects in response to the first question (e.g., "the hat and the shoe are for wearing," or "the hat is for wearing, the shoe is for wearing." While this is an acceptable answer, attempt to design the exercise so the concept of "what else" can be addressed.

#96   Functions of Objects: Answering Questions (1)

Purpose	• To teach the child to describe the functions of objects when the objects are not displayed.
Procedure	• Ask: "What is a __ for?" (e.g., "What is a hat for?"). Prompt correct response

("A hat is for wearing"). Prompts are faded over successive trials. *Note: In this context, the objects are not visible.*

- When the child is able to generate answers in this format, reverse the question ("What is for [function]?"). *Note: You should only use objects the child has learned in previous function exercises. Do not expect the child to generate answers to novel objects.*

Considerations	• This exercise is only meaningful if the child demonstrates proficiency with all previous "functions" exercises.
	• Generally, all exercises involving pure questions-answers should be delayed until the child, (a) demonstrates practical skills concerning the objects/ events in question (practical application/use) and (b) is able to answer different questions concerning the object (see "intraverbal fallacy".)
	• Being able to answer these kinds of questions is bound up with related "why" questions i.e., providing reasons.

#97   Functions of Objects: Answering Questions (2)

Purpose	• To solidify a child's ability to answer questions regarding functions of objects.
Set up	• Display an array of known items including at least two items with the same function.
	• This exercise has two phases: 1) ask function questions in different ways and 2) combine function questions with other questions concerning the object (name) and color.
Procedure	• *Phase 1*: Ask the child to (a) list functions of objects (e.g., "What is a ___ for?"), (b) lists objects based on their function (e.g., "What is for ___?") and (c) identify the function of objects when the instructor points to them (e.g., "What is this one for?").
	• *Phase 2*: Ask randomly: "What is a ___ for?", "What is for ___?", "What is this for?" (while pointing to an object in an array), "What is this?" (displaying or pointing to an object), "What color is this?" (displaying an object), and "What color is the [object]?" (while pointing to an object).
Considerations	• The child needs to have mastered Receptive Colors: Conditional Discrimination (#116).
	• Receptive exercises may also be part of this exercise; i.e., incorporate instructions from "Function of Objects: Receptive 1" (#96), "Receptive Object Identification" (#32) and "Receptive Colors: Conditional Discrimination" (#116).
	• To present questions in this manner is still highly contrived. Efforts should eventually move to applications such as "Get me something to hang this up," "Can you get me something to open this."

- These kinds of questions can and should eventually be folded into the ongoing activities i.e., as the child is eating ("what's that fork for?", What are you using to drink?"); hanging something up ("What are you doing with the tape/Velcro?", "What else can you use?", "What can you use to hang that up?"); drying their hands ("What are you doing with the towel?", "Your hands are still wet, get something to dry them with", "What do you need to dry your hands?") These kinds of situations will eventually serve as platforms for giving reasons e.g., "Why do you need a towel now?"

PARTS AND WHOLE

#98	**Receptive Identification of Parts**

Purpose	• To teach the child to <u>identify</u> salient parts of common objects, and shift attention flexibly between the object proper (gestalt) and its parts.
Set up	• Place several known items in front of the child. • Use objects the child can name, receptive identification, and functions.
Procedure	• Ask the child to identify one of the objects (e.g., "find the dog"). Once the child points to the correct item, pull it away from the array, and ask the child to point to one of the parts (e.g., tail). Prompt correct response and repeat the instructional segment. • Teach a few parts of common objects such as those of a "dog" and then introduce similar kinds of objects to address generalization (e.g., cows, cats). As generalization emerges, address additional salient parts of target objects.
Considerations	• The main objective of is to teach the child to distinguish between the object name (as a whole) and relevant parts. • Address only salient parts of common objects. Be reasonable; the child does not have to be an expert in object dissection. Some objects have *a rich internal structure* (e.g., a person has arms, legs, head, belly, etc.) while other objects are more limited (e.g., a book has pages). Note that *aspect* (e.g., front and back; inside and outside) is somewhat different than parts. • This exercise can be challenging and it may be helpful to start with "Distinguishing Between Parts and Whole" (#99). • The development of receptive part-whole can be supported by other activities. For instance, while engaging in creative activities such as building a car out of Legos, introduce parts such as wheels, roof, and windows.

#99	**Distinguishing Between Parts and Whole**

Purpose	• To teach the child to <u>name</u> salient parts of common objects, and shift attention flexibly between the whole object (gestalt) and its parts.
Set up	• Place several known items in front of the child. • Use objects the child has mastered in naming, receptive identification, and functions.

Procedure	• Present an item and ask: "What is this?" When the child names the object, point to a part and ask; "What (part) is this?" Prompt correct response and repeat instruction.
	• Once the child has mastered a couple of parts, introduce similar kinds of objects (e.g., car and truck have wheels) to address generalization. As generalization emerges, introduce additional parts of target objects.
	• Once the child names parts and generalizes these parts across objects, alternate this exercise and "Receptive Identification of Parts" (#98).
Considerations	• See "Receptive Identification of Parts (#98).
	• The concept of part-whole should eventually be extended to making inferences about an object based on limited visual information (a specific part or segment) of objects. For instance, you may display a part or segment of an object and ask the child "What is it?" and teach the child to provide the name of the object's (identity) as opposed to the displayed part.

#100   Part-Whole Association (1)

Purpose	• To teach the child to name an object given a salient part.
Set up	• Place several known items in front of the child. Use objects that the child has mastered in "Distinguishing between parts and whole" (#99) and "Receptive Identification of Parts" (#98).
Procedure	• Display several known objects and ask: "Tell me something that has a [part]." The child should look at the display and name a pertinent object.
	• As the child acquires this skill learns, you may remove the objects so the child will then state the objects in its absence.
Considerations	• Initially, the child's answer may be limited to the label of the object ("Tell me something that has wheels → "a car"). As the child makes progress, he should learn to use a full sentence ("Tell me something that has wheels → "a car <u>has</u> wheels").
	• Many children struggle with the distinction between *is* and *has* (e.g., a banana is yellow; it does not have yellow – it *has* a peel). The distinction between *parts* and *features* is often difficult to learn, and this difficulty becomes more evident at advanced language levels.
	• As the child makes progress, address the concept of "something else" (i.e., "Tell me something that has wheels → *a car has wheels* → "Tell me something else that has wheels" → *a bike has wheels*) and then "tell me some things that have wheels."
	• In the present context the possessive formulation "has" and the preposition "with" are practically congruent. Thus, the exercises should be designed so that the child will learn to respond to both questions ("Tell me something

that has…"/Tell me something with…").

#101   Part-Whole Association (2)

Purpose	• To teach the child to compare objects by part when given visual information.
Set up	• Place several known objects in front of the child. Use objects the child has mastered in "Distinguishing between parts and whole" (#99) and "Receptive Identification of Parts" (#98).
Procedure	• Pick up one of the objects, point to one of its parts and ask; "Tell me something else that has '*this*' [part]." The child tracks the instructor's focus and names an appropriate item/items.
Considerations	• This exercise demands that the child compare 'objects by part' *when given visual information only*. Consequently, the child cannot rely on simple word-word associations.

#102   Listing Parts

Purpose	• To teach the child to list salient parts of common objects.
Set up	• Place several known objects in front of the child. Use objects the child has mastered in "Distinguishing between parts and whole" (#99) and "Receptive Identification of Parts" (#98). • As the child learns to list parts, remove the objects so that the child lists the parts in their absence. • You may start out by allowing the child visual access to relevant objects. Remove objects as the child makes progress.
Procedure	• Display known objects and ask; "Tell me a part of a ____." • Help the child to orient to the appropriate object (i.e., point to it). If the childdoes not label a part, then point to a part and prompt correct verbal response. Repeat instructional segment until the child is able to state a part. • As the child makes progress and shifts flexibly between objects (i.e., "tell me a part of a car," "tell me a part of a dog," "tell me a part of a house"), remove the objects so the child learns to list parts in their absence. • Eventually combine this exercise with "Part-Whole Association (1)" (#100): Tell me a part of a car → "wheels" → Tell me another part of a car → "doors" → Tell me something else that has a door → "A house" → tell me another part of a house → etc.
Considerations	• This exercise can be implemented once the child makes progress with "Part-Whole Association (1)" (#100).

- The basics of the part-whole concepts involve concrete objects with a rich part-whole structure. Eventually, part-whole should be extended to abstractions such as *activities*, *time frames* (day, week, month, year), and *concepts* such as 'family' and 'sentence.' Such metaphorical extensions are later targets.
- A solid grasp of part-wholes is important to advanced skills such as *descriptions* and *comparing and contrasting*.
- We should note that whole-part structures constitute one aspect of Why questions. Why do cars have wheels/doors have handles/cups have lids, etc.

NAMING BY DIFFERENT MODALITIES

#103	Naming by Touch

Purpose	• To teach the child to name common objects based on tactile information.

Set up	• Place a known object in a box or conceal it some way (under the table, in a bag).

Procedure	• Ask: "What is in the box?" → Guide the child's hand into the box to manipulate the object. Reveal the object (visual access) and prompt the child to name it. Repeat until the child begins to name objects based on tactile information.

Considerations	• Children require strong conventional naming skills (*see-say*) before implementing this exercise.
	• Start with objects that are tactilely distinct (e.g., ball versus fork; Block versus Play-Doh) and are objects with which the child has previously interacted while learning to identify and name.
	• This exercise can be challenging for many children, and a considerable attention span is required. It may be useful to begin this exercise by letting the child see the object before it is concealed. Repeat this reveal-conceal-touch sequence a few times in order to establish familiarity with and understanding of the task.
	• This exercise can be challenging for many children, and a considerable attention span is required.
	• This task is a pivotal component in teaching the child to explore or investigate before answering questions and will be put to use in later exercises related to inference development.

#104	Naming by Taste

Purpose	• To teach the child to name common foods based on how they taste.

Set up	• Blindfold the child and feed the child different kinds of desirable foods.

Procedure	• Ask: "What is it? Give the child a small piece of desirable food immediately. When the child chews and swallows, prompt correct response.

Considerations	• The child should be proficient with "Naming by touch" (#103).

- If the child struggles with this exercise, discontinue the blindfold: Place the food items on the table so child can see them. Pick up an item and put it in the child's mouth while asking: "What is it?" Once the child makes progress, reinstate the blindfold.
- Don't force food if the child doesn't want it. This exercise is NOT about introducing foods.

#105   Distinguishing between Salty, Sweet, Sour

Purpose
- To teach the child to name common tastes such as salty, sweet and sour.

Set up
- Blindfold the child and feed the child salty, sweet and sour liquids or solids (sugar, salt, sour crystals).

Procedure
- Let the child taste the sample (e.g. sugar) and ask: "How does this taste?" Prompt correct response ("sweet"). Present the sample again and fade prompts. When the child answers independently, introduce another target (e.g., salt) and follow the same procedure. Present the two targets in a random fashion until the child distinguish them.
- Give the child a small piece of desirable food immediately. When the child chews and swallows, prompt correct response.

Considerations
- The child should be proficient with "Naming by Touch" (#103).
- If the child struggles with this exercise, discontinue the blindfold: Place the food items on the table so child can see them. Pick up an item and put it in the child's mouth while asking: "What is it?" Once the child makes progress, reinstate the blindfold.
- It is important that taste is disentangled from other sensory features such as texture. For instance, serve the child the different flavors in the same texture form (powder or liquid). Tell the child to "taste this" by pointing to a spoon (with powder) or cup (with liquid). Once consumed, ask: "How does it taste?" Prompt the correct response and repeat the trial.
- Don't force food if the child doesn't want it.

#106   Naming and Identifying Objects by Sound

Purpose
- To teach the child to identify and name objects based on their sound.

Set up
- Use recordings of common sounds (flushing toilet, ambulance, animals, bouncing balls, bell, etc.) and display corresponding pictures. "Sound Lotto" games may be used.

Procedure
- Play a sound and ask the child "What is it?" or "What's that sound?" Prompt the child to point to the picture of the corresponding object.
- As the child begins to master this exercise, remove the pictures and prompt

the child to name the object.

Considerations	• This exercise is essentially the same as "Receptive Object Identification" (#32), with the exception that the sound is not a human voice. • For some children who struggle to learn receptive identification, "Naming by Sound" may be an inroad to acquiring this skill. • Once proficient, take advantage of noises and sounds that occur throughout the day by alerting the child to sounds and ask: "What is that? / What do you hear? / Do you hear that?"

#107   Naming by Inference (Object Permanence)

Purpose	• To teach the child to 'remember' what is in a particular location. • To teach the child to 'search.' • To teach the concept of *"nothing."* • To respond to non-verbal cues. • To enhance memory.
Set up	• This exercise requires common objects and things to conceal them.
Procedure	• Place an object inside a box, under a blanket, in your hand etc. Make sure child observes where the instructor puts the object. Then, prevent visual access (close your hand, cover the box or place something over the object and ask: "What is in the/under the __?"
Considerations	• This exercise may not be successfully implemented before the child demonstrates success with "multiple cue responding:" See "Naming Colors (2)" (#119), "Naming Colors (3)" (#120), Naming Colors (4)" (#121), "Naming Colors (5)" (#122). • To further increase the likelihood of successful implementation, the child should have mastered the basic levels of "Prepositions."
Additional steps and permutations	• This exercise may eventually be extended: a) the child observes the instructor putting an object into a concealed location and answers the question "What is in the __?" The child then observes the instructor take that item out of the concealed location and answers the question; "What is in the __?" ("Nothing"); b) the child observes the instructor putting an object into a concealed location and answers the question "What is in the __?" The instructor immediately puts another item into the same location "What is in the __?" ("object 1 and object 2").

#108 — Locating by Inference

Purpose	• To teach the child to identify the location of an object when it is not directly visible.
Set up	• This exercise requires two objects of considerably different sizes and two blankets.
Procedure	• Place the items under each of the blankets. Conceal the items. The child observes the process. Then ask" Where is the [item 1]?" and "Where is [item 2]?" The child should then identify the location of the items respectively. • Place the items under each of the blankets. This time, the child should not observe the process. Then ask, "Where is the [item 1]?" and "Where is [item 2]?" The child identifies the locations of the items respectively.
Considerations	• The child has to infer the location of an object based on the size of the bulge. This inference may require considerable practice. • Proficiency with "Naming by Touch" (#103) and "Naming and Identifying Objects by Sound" (#106) may facilitate acquisition. • This exercise has much in common with inference based on visual access to parts (see "Considerations in "Distinguishing Between Parts and Whole" #99) and identifying objects based on tactile information (see "Search (Match 1)" #16 and "Search (Match 2)" #17).

TRANSACTIONS AND TURN TAKING

#109	**Turn-Taking: Ball Play**

Purpose	• To teach the child to use statements that match his role in a transaction. • To teach the roles of "giver" and "taker" and to use the phrases "my turn," "your turn," and "thank you" appropriately within a recursive routine.
Set up	• Place a target (e.g., bean bag, ring pole, basketball hoop) a few feet away from the child. Stand next to child. An assistant is available to provide guidance.
Procedure	• Throw an object toward the target. Walk to the target, pick up the object and return to the child. While handing it to the child, say "your turn." The assistant prompts the child to say "thank you." The child accepts the object and throws it toward the target. The assistant then guides the child to pick up the object, return it to the first instructor and say "your turn." After saying "thank you" the first instructor takes another turn, etc. • Use the same arrangement, but when returning to the child with the object, refrain from saying "your turn" and simply wait. After a few seconds or when the child attempts to take the object, the assistant prompts the child to say "my turn" (and reach for the object if the child does not initiate). Say: "here" or "here you go" and hands the object to the child. The assistant prompts the child to say "thank you." At this point the child takes his turn.
Considerations	• Fluency with this exercise will facilitate other exercises concerning personal pronouns."

#110	**Turn-Taking: Delivery**

Purpose	• To teach the child to deliver something to another person while using appropriate language. • To teach the child that when interacting with another person he can use both the person's name and the pronoun "you."
Procedure	• Tell the child to deliver an object to another person (e.g., "Give the cup to Mommy"). When the child locates and approaches the designated person, prompt the child to say "[person's name], this is for you" or "[person], for you", the designated person, says "thank you."

| Consideration | • While this exercise is artificial, it is serves as a useful pre-condition for teaching personal pronouns. |

#111   Turn-Taking: Matching Game

Purpose	• To teach the child simple turn taking. • To establish a context for teaching personal pronouns.
Set up	• Sit across from each other at a table. An assistant sits behind the child. Place a lotto board or spread memory cards face up on the table. Place a stack with matching cards face down within the child's reach.
Procedure	• Say "my turn" and then draw a card from the stack. Place the card on the corresponding one on the table. The assistant prompts the child to say "my turn" and then draws a card from the stack. The child then places it on the corresponding picture on the table.
Considerations	• It is important that the child says "my turn" immediately prior to taking his turn. • If the child does not say "my turn," the instructor may place his finger on the stack to prevent the child from drawing the card until he makes the statement. • This exercise is the first step in more elaborate exercises designed to address personal pronouns and elementary discourse (see #207, #208). • Sometimes it could be helpful to first practice the mechanics (cycle of turn taking) without requiring the accompanying language. Once the mechanics are in place, begin to introduce the language.

#112   Reciprocal Statements 1

Purpose	• To teach the child to make factual statements in response to other persons' statements. • To disentangle the child's verbal statements from direct questions.
Set up	• Sit face to face where you both have access to a pile of common objects. An assistant sits behind the child.
Procedure	• Pick an object from the pile, hold it up and say: "I have a(n) [X]." The assistant helps child select a different object, to hold it up, and to make the same kind of verbal statement ("I have a [Y]").
Additional steps and permutations	• This exercise should eventually be extended to involve two objects ("I

have [object] and [object]"). This extension involves two new components (1) the child must discern when to reciprocate one versus two statements (i.e., differentiate the instructor's behavior), and (2) appropriate use of the conjunction "and." This exercise should also be done in situations when the two objects are the same (e.g., spoons). Thus, child will have to discern when to use a conjunction or the plural (e.g., "I have cups" versus "I have a cup and a doll") (see "Singular-plural (4)" #136).

#113   Reciprocal Statements 2

Purpose	• To further develop the ability to reciprocate factual statements. • To teach the child to attend to other person's statements and shift attention flexibly between different kinds of situations.
Set up	• Sit together on the floor (or somewhere else). Have common objects in reach and distant objects in sight. An assistant sits behind the child.
Procedure	• Point to a distant object and say: "I see [object]." The assistant prompts the child to point to a different distant object and say: "I see [object]." Fade prompts over successive trials. When the child participates successfully, expand to double statements ("I see [object] and [object]"). • Point to something you are wearing and say: "I am wearing [piece of clothing]." The assistant prompts the child to point to or grab a something the child is wearing and say: "I am wearing [piece of clothing]." Fade prompts over successive trials. • Randomize all different kinds of reciprocal exercises (I have __:" I have __, and __;" "I see __," "I see __ and __," "I am wearing__").
Considerations	• "Reciprocal Statement" exercises are quite artificial and are not designed to promote conversational skills. The structure of this exercise has little in common with natural conversations or typical discourse. In fact "conversation" as holistic, dynamic exchanges between two or more people cannot be taught; we can only teach the child elements that are parts of conversation and then offer structured opportunities to apply these components in transactional situations. Conversation involves elements such as perspective taking, comprehensive language comprehension, relevance (staying on topic), inference (interpreting indirect reference), turn-taking, etc. The possible contribution of "Reciprocal statements" to the complex fabric of 'conversation' lies in its potential of promoting attention to what others are saying and the concomitant ability of shifting attention quickly between different kinds of situations.

BASIC ABSTRACT CONCEPTS

COLORS AND SHAPES

#114   Matching Colors

Purpose	• To teach the child to distinguish between colors and to recognize color as a feature of an object as opposed to the object itself.
Set up	• Place three swatches on the table separated by a few inches. The swatches should be solid colors with identical size and shape.
Procedure	• Hand the child a swatch corresponding to one of those on the table. Say "put with same." Upon correct placement, remove the swatch and introduce another trial. Increase the field size gradually as the child is successful. • Once the child matches reliably, shift from "put with same" to "point to same" (display a swatch and the child should point to the corresponding swatch on the table).
Considerations	• Color matching can first be with either identical color matching (same hue of blue, red, yellow, etc.) or matching of different hues… this determination will be child specific. Just be aware that generalization of 'color' requires matching and identification across hues. • Color is a feature of objects and is coded in grammar as "adjective." A basic understanding of color emerges when children apprehend that color is a *general applicable feature*, not a concrete thing. This rarely emerges at the level of matching.
Troubleshooting	• If the child struggles with the above procedure, it sometimes helpful by starting with 'point/find same.' Requiring a 'shift of attention' that may help clarify the task demands.
Additional steps and permutations	• Once the child matches the color swatches reliably, introduce non-identical swatches (different sizes and shapes).

#115   Receptive Color Identification

Purpose	• To teach the child to identify colors receptively.
Set up	• Use identically shaped swatches with solid colors.

Procedure	• Place a minimum of three color swatches on the table. Use instructions such as "Where is [color]?" "Give me [color]" or "Find [color]." Prompt correct response and fade prompts over successive trials.
	• Once the child has made progress with the swatches, switch to objects (identical objects of solid colors).

Considerations	• For some children, it may be possible to teach receptive colors and naming colors simultaneously. As a function of previous exercises, many children have acquired the ability to transfer learning across receptive and expressive modalities (See "Integrating Basic Learning Skills" #60-64).
	• For some children, when first introducing color identification, it may be necessary to say only the name of the color e.g., "blue." See considerations under "Receptive Object Identification", (#32).

#116   Receptive Colors: Conditional Discriminations

Purpose	• To teach the child to follow a two-part instruction involving color and object name ("point to the green triangle").
	• To teach the child to differentiate between the object itself (identity) and its color (feature).

Set up	• A field of objects where each kind of object is represented in two different colors (e.g., green square and yellow square versus green triangle and yellow triangle). This 2 x 2 matrix is a requirement for true *conditional discrimination* as it allows for the possibility of error (Fig. 11).

Procedure	• Say: "point to [color] [object]" (e.g., "red car"). Prompt correct response and fade prompts over successive trials.
	• Once the child has mastered the first color discrimination (e.g., red versus blue), additional colors should be introduced. Consequently, the field size increases proportionally with the number of target colors.

Considerations	• This task involves a "if-but-not-otherwise" contingency (e.g., "point to the cup *but only if it is blue*")
	• When arranging the field, make sure each kind of object is represented in two different colors (e.g., a red car and a blue car; a red plate and a blue plate). Shapes may also be used in (blue square, blue triangle, red square, red triangle, etc.).
	• The step from simple receptive responding (one cue) to two-part instruction is often very challenging and may require considerable practice.
	• Mastery of this kind of conditional discrimination is imperative for advanced language learning. This skill should be considered a significant "cusp."

Troubleshooting	• If the child struggles, it may be necessary to strengthen attention through

other kinds of exercises such as "Two-Step Instructions" (#31), and "Two-Step Receptive Object Identification" (#38). It may also be helpful to practice advanced versions of SBI (#9) in order to curb impulsivity and enhance working memory and attention.

#117   Receptive Colors: "That" Constructions

Purpose	• To teach the child to follow a two-part instruction involving color and object name using a "that" construction (e. g., "show me the car that is red"). • To teach the child to differentiate between the object itself (identity) and its color (feature).
Set up	• Present a field of objects where each kind of object is represented in two different colors (e.g., blue car and red car versus blue cup and red cup). This 2 x 2 matrix is a requirement for true conditional discrimination as it allows for the possibility of error.
Procedure	• Say: "Show me the [object] that is [color]" (e.g. "show me the car that is red"). • When the child understands the instructions, intersperse with instructions from "Receptive Colors – Conditional Discriminations" (#116).

#118   Naming Colors (1)

Purpose	• To teach the child to name colors. • Naming color involves discriminating between answering questions such as "What is it?" (object name) and "What color is it?" However, it is often necessary to first teach the child to name colors before expecting the child to differentiate between these questions.
Set up	• This exercise requires colored swatches and objects with solid colors.
Procedure	• Present a color swatch and ask; "What color?" or "What color is it?" Prompt correct answer and repeat the trial until child responds independently. Once child responds successfully, introduce additional color swatches and use expanded trials. Eventually introduce objects of solid color.
Considerations	• Many children who are proficient with "Expressive Naming (1)" (#47) and "Receptive Color Identification" (#115) usually acquire color names easily. • If the child struggles with object naming (i.e., demonstrates a very slow acquisition rate), it would be premature to introduce color naming. • Once the child is able to name three to four colors, "Naming Colors (2)" (#119) should be considered.

#119   Naming Colors (2)

Purpose	• To teach the discrimination between: "What is it?" (object name) and "What color is it?"
Set up	• This exercise requires familiar objects of solid colors. Shapes may also be used.
Procedure	• Present a familiar solid colored object and ask randomly "What is this?" (or "What is it?") and "What color is this?" (or What color is it?"). Prompt correct response and fade prompts over successive trials.
Troubleshooting	• This task is very difficult for many children and instruction often requires alterations and adjustments.
	• *Problem-solving 1:* Use colored swatches with all basic shapes. Present a swatch and alter the questions "What color?" and "What shape?" When asking the question, place emphasis on the words "color" and "shape." When the child answers these questions, fade the emphasis. Once proficient with that change, add *"is it"* at the end of the questions (i.e., What color is it? / What shape is it?).
	• *Problem solving 2:* Reduce antecedent to just "Color" or "Shape" and pick up procedure from "problem solving 1.
	• *Problem solving 3:* Discontinue the exercise and introduce "Naming Colors (3)" (#120), "Naming Colors (4)" (#121), and "Naming Colors (5)" (#122). When the child demonstrates success with these tasks, reintroduce "Naming Colors (2)."

#120   Naming Colors (3)

Purpose	• To teach the child to differentiate between object and color.
	• The nominal objective is to teach child to answer the question "What color is the [object]?"
Set up	• Present a field of three to four familiar objects of solid colors (e.g., a red car, a blue cup, and a green apple).
Procedure	• Ask: "What color is the car/cup/apple?" and prompt correct response (i.e., "green" or "the apple is green"). Fade prompts over successive trials.
Considerations	• If the child struggles, assist by pointing to the object in question ("What color is the car?" while pointing to the car). Once the child reliably responds correctly, discontinue pointing.
	• Once the child responds correctly, extend the field size and use more colors.
	• Mastery of this exercise may facilitate "Naming Colors (2)" (#119).
	• This is a particularly difficult exercise and requires a routine of *listen,*

remember, scan, find.

#121   Naming Colors (4)

Purpose	• To teach the child to differentiate between object and color. • To teach the child to *identify an object given its color* (i.e., "What is green?" or "Which is green?").
Set up	• Display a field of three to four known objects of solid colors (e.g., a red car, a blue cup, and a green apple).
Procedure	• Ask: "What is [color]?" or "Which one is [color]?" The child names the correct object (i.e., "The car" or "The car is green?").
Considerations	• While a single word answer is acceptable initially, it is important to teach the child to eventually use full sentences (e.g., "the car is green"). Framing the sentence "the [object] is [color]" is fundamental to understanding the difference and relation between objects and features (noun and adjective). • Mastery of this exercise may facilitate "Naming Colors (2)" (#119).

#122   Naming Colors (5)

Purpose	• To teach the child to differentiate between object and color. • To teach the child to shift attention between questions.
Setup	• Display a field of several objects of solid colors.
Procedure	• Randomly ask the questions: "What color is the [object]?" and "What is [color]?" / "Which one is [color]?" The child learns to shift attention between the two questions. • Introduce the question: "What color is this one?" / "What color is this?" (while pointing to an object).
Considerations	• Mastery of this exercise may facilitate "Naming Colors (2)" (#119). • This exercise increases "cognitive load:" shifting attention, tracking, scanning, working memory, switching modalities.

#123   Naming Colors (6)

Purpose	• To teach the child to list multiple objects of the same color when asked the question "What else is [color]?"
Set up	• Arrange a field of several known objects of solid colors including some objects of the same color (e.g., a red car and a red cup, a green apple and

a green sock).

Procedure	• Ask the question "What is [color]?" or "Which one is [color]?" (e.g., "Which one is green?"). The child should name a correct object (i.e., "The apple" or "The apple is green"). When the child answers correctly, ask: "What else is green?" Prompt correct response and fade over successive trials. • Eventually, combine this exercise with "Naming Colors (5)" (#122): Randomize questions (i.e., sometimes the "What color is the [object 1]?" should be followed by "What else is [color]?" and sometimes it should be followed by "What color is the [object 2]?" <u>Sample sequence</u>: *Instructor*: "What color is the car?" – *Child*: "The car is green" – Instructor: "What else is green?" – *Child*: "The sock is green" – Instructor: "What color is the ball?" – *Child*: "The ball is blue?" – *Instructor*: "What color is the spoon?" – *Child*: "The spoon is white" – *Instructor*: "What else is white?" – *Child*: "The napkin is white" – "What color is this?" (pointing to object) – *Child*: "Red" – *Instructor*: "What is yellow?" etc.
Considerations	• If the child struggles with this exercise, reduce the field to three objects: Two of the same color and one different (e.g., a red car, a red sock, and a blue cup). Maintain this arrangement until the child learns to switch to the other object with the same color when asked "What else is [color]?" When proficient, extend the field to four different objects in two different colors. • The concept of "what else" (and "who else") is a general issue and must be extended to all relevant exercises (*functions, parts, categories,* etc.). • Mastery of this exercise may facilitate "Naming Colors (2)" (#119).
Additional steps and permutations	• Once the child proficiently lists additional objects of the same color, the field may include three to four objects of the same color. Consequently, in response to "What else is [color]?" it is more challenging for the child to keep track of which objects he has already named. • This exercise should also address the concept of *"nothing."* In response to the question "What else is [color]?", the child should answer "nothing" or "nothing else is [color]". **See** "Naming by Inference: Object Permanence," (#107). To establish this concept, it may be necessary to scale back to two objects and alternate conditions where the two objects have the same color and where the colors differ. When the child masters this arrangement, the concept should be incorporated in the question sequence described above.

#124   Naming Colors (7)

Purpose	• To teach the child to answer questions regarding object's color when the objects are not present. • To strengthen auditory-visual connection.

Set up	• Sit face to face.
Procedure	• Ask: "What color is a [familiar object]?" Use objects that have a particular color (banana, fire truck, cucumber, lemon, carrot, etc.).
Considerations	• Only use objects with which the child is intimately familiar. This exercise is a matter of enhancing rote memory, which is necessary for expanding fund of general information that will be recruited in later reasoning tasks.

#125   Sorting Shapes

Purpose	• To teach the child to differentiate between common shapes.
Set up	• Use a set of shapes such as circle, square, triangle, rectangle, oval, and heart.
Procedure	• Follow the same procedure as "Basic Identity Matching" (#1).
Considerations	• While "shapes" is a common academic target, it is not critical in order to move language learning forward. As opposed to colors, shapes have a more modest role in natural language. • As opposed to color, shapes often occur as nouns. We often say things like "a square" by referring to a thing, but we do not say "a blue" by referring to something blue. • Acquisition of shapes may help to establish teaching conditions for complex receptive instructions (e.g., "find the big red triangle") and discrimination of factual questions (i.e., "What color?" / "What shape?").

#126   Receptive and Expressive Shapes

Purpose	• To learn the names of common shapes.
Set up	• Use a set of shapes such as circle, square, triangle, rectangle, oval, and heart.
Procedure	• Follow the same procedure as receptive identification and expressive naming (#32, #47). • For expressive shapes, use the instruction "What shape" or "What shape is it?"
Considerations	• Receptive and expressive shapes should not be practiced in isolation for extensive periods. Receptive shapes should be moved quickly to "Receptive Colors – Conditional Discrimination" (#116). Expressive shapes should be incorporated quickly in "Naming Colors (2)" (#119).

Big and Little

#127	**Receptive Big-Little (Identical)**

Purpose	• To teach the child the concepts of big and little when comparing objects.
Set up	• Place two identical objects of different size side by side on the table. The size difference should be apparent. Use a wide range of object pairs (cups, balls, socks, dolls, spoons, etc.).
Procedure	• Present a set of objects and instruct the child to "touch" or "point to" BIG. Prompt correct response and repeat the trial. Switch the set of objects and repeat the procedure. When the child identifies BIG with respect to novel sets of objects, go to the next step. • Present a set of objects and instruct the child to "touch" or "point to" LITTLE (i.e., "point to Little"). Continue until the child responds correctly when presented with novel sets of objects. • Randomize "big" and "little" across sets of objects and introduce novel ones until generalization occurs.
Considerations	• The introduction of one concept at a time (i.e., first big and then little) may not always be effective. Some children are more successful when big and little are randomized from the outset. • Big and little should be practiced across "size levels" and must include levels larger than tabletop items. For instance, socks and cups are "table top size" whereas chairs and trees comprise a larger size level. • As the child acquires the concepts, the size difference could be made less conspicuous. • Big and little (or big and small) is a primary physical distinction, hence one of the most salient "adjectives." • Introduction of "Receptive Big-Little" may be considered once the child demonstrates proficiency with "Receptive Color Identification" (#115). • This section describes the basic aspects of big/little. The concepts are expanded in later sections.
Troubleshooting	• If visual discriminations are difficult, it may be helpful for the child to interact with objects of contrasting size, i.e., get and hold "big" vs "little" / so that the child is prompted to get and hold the large / small items e.g., have identical balls, spoons or balloons of dramatically different sizes. Make sure that items selected do not produce a confound for weight. • Manipulate size; have the child make something "big" then little (e.g. block

structures, drawings, bubbles).

#128   Receptive Big-Little (Non-Identical)

Purpose	• To teach the child the concepts of big and little when comparing objects.
Set up	• Place two different objects of different size on the table (e.g., a car and an apple). The size difference should be quite apparent. Use any combination of objects and make sure that each object will occupy both roles (big and little) during the trials. In other words, if one object (e.g., ball) is big one in one trial, it should be little in a subsequent trial.
Procedure	• Present a set of objects and instruct the child to "touch" or "point to" BIG or LITTLE. Prompt correct response and repeat the trial. Randomize the instruction and alter the set of objects after each trial.
Considerations	• As the child makes progress, intersperse with receptive object identification (occasionally instruct the child to point to an object by reference to its name rather than size).

#129   Receptive Big-Little (Conditional Discrimination)

Purpose	• To teach the child the concepts of big and little when comparing object.
Set up	• Place two sets of identical but different sized objects on the table (e.g., a *big car* and a *little car* and a *big apple* and a *little apple*). Use any combination of objects.
Procedure	• Arrange two sets of objects (big and little X; big and little Y) and randomize the instructions: "point to "big X", "little X", "big Y" and "little Y". • Eventually increase the field size by introducing additional sets of objects (three, four sets of objects).
Considerations	• This exercise is structurally congruent with "Receptive Colors – Conditional Discrimination" (#116). • The step from simple receptive (one cue) to two-part instruction is often very challenging and may require considerable practice. • Mastery of this kind of conditional discrimination is imperative for advanced language learning.

#130	Receptive Big-Little: Name and Feature
Purpose	• To teach the child the concepts of big and little when comparing objects and to distinguish these concepts from object names and colors.
Set up	• Place two different objects of different colors and different sizes on the table (e.g., a blue car and a red apple). Use any combination of objects and make sure that each object will occupy both roles (big and little) during the instructional segment. In other words, if one object (e.g., ball) is "big" in one trial, it should be "little" in a subsequent trial.
Procedure	• Alternate the instructions "point to big," "point to little," "point to [object name]," and "point to [color]."
Considerations	• Once the child is proficient, "Expressive Big-Little (1)" (#131) may be implemented.

#131	Expressive Big-Little (1)
Purpose	• To teach the child to describe objects as "big" and "little" when presented side by side.
Set up	• Place two different objects of different size side by side on the table (e.g. a small cup and a bigger doll).
Procedure	• Alternate the questions "What's big?" and "What's little?" Prompt correct response (e.g., "cup" or "cup is little"). Use any combination of objects and make sure that each object will occupy both roles (big and little) during the instructional segment. In other words, if one object (e.g., ball) is "big" in one trial, it should be "little" in a subsequent trial.
Considerations	• Proficiency with exercises targeting "colors" and "receptive big little" will normally ease acquisition of this skill. • Vary the size difference (considerable to moderate). • Vary the distance between the objects so that eventually, the child is unable to see both objects at the same time (e.g., spread them out on the floor). This will promote the child's ability to hold an object in mind when making a comparison • Eventually this exercise may be extended to different kinds of settings such as "Who has the big ___/little___?" and "Where is the big___/little ___?"

#132	Expressive Big-Little (2)

Purpose	• To teach the child to describe objects as "big" and "little" when presented side by side.
Set up	• Place three or more non–identical objects on the table. One of the objects should stand out from the rest in terms of size (e.g., a big doll, a big shoe, and a cup that is smaller than the first two).
Procedure	• Randomize the combinations of size relations (two or more big objects and one small object, two or more small objects and one big object) and randomize the questions "What's big/little?" Prompt correct response (e.g., "cup and shoe" or "cup and shoe are little").
Considerations	• This exercise requires the child to make a distinction between plural/ singular, which entails application of the verbs "is" and "are." Proficiency with this subtle but critical skill may have to be established separately under more contrived settings (see "Singular-Plural" #133).

Singular-Plural

#133	**Singular-Plural (1)**

Purpose	• To teach the child the distinction between singularity and plurality.
Set up	• Place either several objects of the same kinds (cups, pens, shoes, etc.) or single objects (a cup, a pen, a shoe, etc.) on the table.
Procedure	• Ask; "What do you see?" or "What's on the table?" Prompt correct response ("cups" or "I see cups"). • Alternate between a field of several objects and a single object. For multiple objects the child's response involves the plural-s and no article, for singular objects the child omits plural-s but includes article (e.g., "a cup" or "I see a cup").
Considerations	• The concepts of singular-plural should be addressed systematically when the child demonstrates proficiency with basic object naming. • 'Singular-plural' is complex and is predicated on the concept of "kinds" which involves the principle that objects and events, (but not people) have a generic nature (belong to a class of items). • While the concepts of singular-plural may be addressed receptively first, we find that addressing it expressively is sufficient. • Address only regular plurals at this stage. • In order to promote proficiency, this exercise may be extended to "Self-paced Naming" (#53) using mixed pictures of singular (e.g., a cup) and multiple objects (e.g., cups): Provide the child with a stack of pictures and ask the child to "Name these" or "What are these?" The child picks a picture, names it (e.g., "a cup" or "cups"), puts it down and picks the next, etc.

#134	**Singular-Plural (2)**

Purpose	• The focus of this exercise is to extend the context for singular-plural (see "Singular-plural (1)" #133).
Set up	• Sit face to face with access to common objects.
Procedure	• Give the child two objects (e.g., blocks) and ask: "What do you have?" Prompt correct answer ("blocks" or "I have blocks"). Alternate trials where the child holds one versus two objects ("I have a cup" versus "I have cups").

Additional steps and permutations	• Eventually consider arrangements such as placing a single object in one location (e.g., on a table) and multiple objects in another location (e.g., in a box) (e.g., "What's on the table?" "What's in the box?").
	• These concepts should be combined with numerical concepts e.g., "I have one cup and two balls."

#135   Singular-Plural (3)

Purpose	• To teach the child the application of the verbs "is" and "are" related to distinctions between singularity and plurality.
Set up	• Place two or more objects of the same kind and color and a different object of a different color on the table (e.g., two green cars and a red apple).
Procedure	• Ask: "What's green?" alternating between singular and multiple items (i.e. "What's green? / "What's red?"). For singular objects the answer is: "[object] **is** [color]" (e.g., "the apple is red"), and for multiple objects the answer is: "the [object**s**] **are** [color]" (e.g., "the cars are green").
Considerations	• This is a complex task and will often require considerable time and explicit teaching arrangements.
	• Common problems: (1) children over-use "is" or "are" (i.e., uses either one for both conditions), (2) children pluralize the adjective (e.g., "the cars are green**s**), (3) children use the conjunction "and" instead of pluralizing (i.e., "the car and the car are green"), (4) the child misplaces the conjunction and fails to use correct verb (i.e., "the car and the car **is** green).
Additional steps and permutations	• When the child is proficient, the exercise should eventually be extended: (1) Answering questions such as "Where are the [objects]?" / "Where is the [object]?" → "The [objects] are/[object] is…in the box/on the table," etc.), (2) actions of people (e.g., "Who's sitting on the couch?" → [person] and [person] are/[person] is…sitting on the couch," and (3) features other than color such as size (e.g., "What's big/little (small)?" → "The cup and the ball are small."

#136   Singular-Plural (4)

Purpose	• To teach the child additional applications of the verbs "is" and "are" in relation to the distinction between singularity and plurality.
Set up	• Sit with the child at a table with common objects displayed.
	• _Set up 1_: Two objects of the same kind and same color (e.g. two green balls)

and a different object with a different color (e.g., a blue sock).

- *Set up 2*: Two different objects of the same color (red car and red spoon), and another object with a different color (e.g., a yellow banana).

Procedure	• *Set up 1:* Ask: "What is [color]?" (e.g., What is green/What is blue?" Prompt the child to say; "The balls **are** green" and "The sock **is** blue" respectively. • *Set up 2:* Ask: "What is [color]?" Prompt the child to say; "The car and the spoon **are** red" and "the banana **is** yellow" respectively.
Considerations	• The concept of plurality and singularity is convoluted and difficult to grasp if it does not emerge naturally. Monitor closely for confusion. • Extend to all pertinent future exercises including "Prepositions," "What's missing?" "Same-different," and "Reciprocal statements (1)" (#112).

SAME-DIFFERENT

#137	**Receptive Same-Different (1)**

Purpose	• To teach the basic concepts of "same" and "different."
Set up	• Place two identical objects and one different object on the table (e.g., two spoons and a crayon). Use a variety of sets and make sure that all objects used occupy both roles during the trials (e.g., if cups are "same" in one trial, a single cup should be the "different" object in a subsequent trial).
Procedure	• Say: "Find the same" and prompt the child to touch the matching pair. • Say: "Find different" and prompt the child to use one hand to touch the "different" object. • When addressing "same," it may be useful to prompt child to use both hands to identify the matching pair. Thus, given the instruction "find sam," the child should use both hands simultaneously when identifying the matching objects. Stick with the same kind of objects until the child uses both hands independently, then introduce a new set. Continue multiple exemplar training until the child responds correctly with respect to novel sets. • It may be useful to start with the concept of "same" before alternating "same" and "different." Conduct trials with the instruction "same" until the child reliably identifies the matching objects (any set). When the child responds correctly in the presence of any set (novel combinations), introduce "different." Start the instructional segment with the instruction "find same" and when the child responds correctly, follow up with "find different" (unchanged field). When the child shifts reliably from "same" (two hands) to "different" (one hand), alternate "same" and "different" and randomize the order of instructions.
Considerations	• In developing the concept, we may start with simple arrangements such as "Find the same" and "Find the one that is different" with respect to common objects. The initial objective is to teach the conditional discrimination: *When you hear <u>same</u> → touch the matching objects, when you hear <u>different</u> → touch the object that does not have a match.* It is crucial to address different variants of this simple comparison before moving to more comprehensive language tasks.
Troubleshooting	• The procedures we describe will not work for all children. If a child struggles, you may postpone and reintroduce when the child demonstrates proficiency with "Two-Step Receptive Objects" (# 38), "Answering Factual

Questions," (#146-153) and "Singular-plural."(#133-136).

- Some children learn "Receptive Same-Different (2)" (#138) more easily than "Receptive Same-Different (1)."

| **Additional steps and permutations** | • If the child makes progress with this exercise, change from identical to slightly non-identical objects for "same." |

#138   Receptive Same-Different (2)

Purpose	• To teach basic the concepts of "same" and "different."
Set up	• Place two objects on the table and hold up an object that matches one of them.
Procedure	• <u>Same</u>: Present the instruction "point to same," while holding up an object that matches one of the objects on the table. Prompt the child to point to the matching object. • <u>Different</u>: Place two objects on the table. Tell the child to "point to different," while holding up an object that matches one of the objects displayed on the table. Prompt the child to point to the object that *does not* match. • Alternate "same" and "different."
Considerations	• When the child makes progress, there should be more than one object corresponding to same and different. In the case of *same*, there should be more than one matching object (e.g., two to four cups); and in the case of *different*, there should be two or three non-matching objects (e.g., objects other than cups).

#139   Expressive Same-Different

Purpose	• To teach the child to use the terms "same" and "different" when describing the relation between objects.
Set up	• Place two identical objects and one different object on the table (e.g., two spoons and a crayon). Use a variety of sets and make sure that all of the objects used occupy both roles during the instructional segments (e.g., if cups are "same" in one trial, a single cup should be the "different" in a subsequent trial).
Procedure	• Randomize the instructions "What's same?" and "What's different?" In the case of <u>*same*</u>, the response should involve plural-s (e.g., "cups"); in the case of <u>*different*</u>, the response should be in the singular form (e.g., "cup").
Troubleshooting	• This exercise involves the concept of "kinds" which entails the concepts of

singular and plural. If the child struggles with singular versus plural, teach these concepts in isolation first (see "Singular-Plural").

Additional steps and permutations	• The child's answer should eventually be expanded to a full sentence. In the case of "same," the answer should involve plural-S and the conjunction *ARE* (e.g., "the cups are the same"). In the case of "different" the verbal response should be the singular form with the conjunction *IS* ("the cup is different").
	• If the child makes progress with this exercise; change from identical to increasingly non-identical objects for "same" and introduce the term "alike."
	• Eventually, the concept of "same" should pertain to *superordinate categories* (e.g., cats and cows are the same because they are animals).

#140   Same-Different: Actions

Purpose	• To expand the concept of "same" and "different" to persons and actions.
Set up	• Use pictures of familiar persons performing familiar actions.
	• Arrange the field of pictures so that two persons are performing the same action (e.g., mom and dad are both eating) and a third person is doing something different (e.g., a sibling is sleeping).
Procedure	• Instructions: "Who are doing the same thing?" (or "Who are doing the same?"). Prompt correct answer, which requires naming the appropriate persons (e.g., "mommy" and "daddy"). Continue until the child answers reliably when novel arrangements are presented.
	• When the child answers the question "Who are doing the same thing?" follow up with "Who is doing something different?"
Considerations	• This exercise should be extended to real life situations.

#141   Same-Different: Imitation

Purpose	• To expand the concept of "same" and "different."
Set up	• This exercise can be done in a variety of settings, including one to one instruction, group setting, and circle time.
Procedure	• Perform an action and ask the child to do the same or something different
	• Point to another person and ask the child to do the same ("Do the same as [person]") or something different ("Do something different than [person]").

#142	**Same-Different: Yes and No**

Purpose	• To answer simple "yes" and "no" to questions concerning same and different ("is" and "are" questions).
Set up	• Use familiar objects.
Procedure	• Present pairs of matching objects and pairs of non-matching objects randomly. Ask: "Are these same?" Prompt correct answer (yes and no).
Considerations	• The child needs to have mastered "Yes/No." See "Yes-No" exercises 146-152. • The exercise should eventually be extended to questions such as "Is this the same as this?" "Is this car the same as this one?"

#143	**Same-Different: Possession**

Purpose	• To teach same and different with respect to simple possession.
Set up	• Sit face to face with multiple participants and familiar objects.
Procedure	• Scenario 1: Two instructors each have an object; sometimes, the same kind and sometimes different kinds. Ask: "Do we have the same?" or "Do we have something different?" Prompt correct answer. • Scenario 2: Two persons hold objects; sometimes the same kind of object and sometimes different kinds. The instructor asks: "Do they have the same?" or "Do they have different things?"
Considerations	• This exercise requires fluency with basic genitive and nominal pronouns.

BASIC PRONOMINALIZATION

#144	**Pronominalization: "It"**

Purpose	• To understand the pronoun "it" when used in simple instructions and questions.

Set up	• Use familiar objects.

Procedure	• Display familiar objects on the table, point to one of the objects and ask: "What is it?" When the child answers, point to another object and ask the same question. When the child answers again, follow with the instruction "Give <u>it</u> to me" or the question "What color is it?" Prompt correct answer. Sequence: "What is it?" → "A cup." → "What is it?" → "A shoe." → "Give it to me." → the child hands you the shoe.
	• When the child is able to track "it" back to the correct object, alternate the sequence and questions. For instance, after the child answers the question "What is it?" ask: "What color is it?" and follow up with "Give it to me." Thus, the child will learn that "it" in the last statement still concerns the noun that was mentioned last. Also alternate the time delay between "What is it?" and the follow up statement. The child should be able to respond correctly after a three second delay.

Considerations	• The concept of "it" should be addressed continually as the child progresses with language learning. It is extraordinarily important to avoid the "explicit reference trap."
	• Eventually expand to the pronoun "them" and "they." For instance, "What do you read?" → "Books." → "Where do you keep *them*?"

#145	**Pronominalization: "He/She"**

Purpose	• To understand the pronouns he/she when used in simple instructions and questions.
	• This exercise requires familiar people sitting in a circle or pictures of familiar persons.

Procedure	• *Scenario 1:* Display pictures of familiar persons holding known objects (Mommy holding a cup, daddy holding a ball, etc.). Ask: "Who is it?" When the child answers, point to another person and ask the same question. When the child answers, follow up with the instruction "What does he/she have?"

Prompt correct response. Sequence: "Who is it?" → "Mommy." → "Who is it?" → "Daddy." → "What does he have?" → the child names the object.

- *Scenario 2:* Familiar persons are sitting in a circle, each holding a couple of objects. Ask: "Who is it?" while pointing to a person. When the child answers, follow up with the question "What does he have?" Once the child is proficient, alter the sequence: Sometimes ask: "Who is it? (while pointing) and sometimes ask "Who has a(n) [object]?" When the child answers the latter question, follow up with "What else does he have?"

| **Considerations** | • The nominal objective with the exercise "he," "she," and "it" pronouns is to teach the child to track the pertinent noun, hence to infer what the pronoun stands for. This is of utmost importance for understanding and participating in natural language. Unfortunately, there is a tendency to move away from the use of pronouns towards explicit reference as the child fails to answer questions correctly. In effect, the child shapes the way we ask questions. For instance, if the child does not answer the latter questions in the sequence: "What do you eat for breakfast?" followed by the question, "How do you eat it?" there is a strong tendency to alter the latter question (e.g., "How do you eat cereal?"). This kind of alteration does not solve the problem, but merely avoids a problem that must be addressed in order for natural language comprehension to develop. In fact, this avoidance may worsen the problem by continually de-contextualizing speech acts. This practice in which one sentence never depends on the previous serves simply to exacerbate 'disconnectedness.'
- Expressive use of "he" / "she" can be found in pronouns section. |

ANSWERING FACTUAL QUESTIONS

#146   Yes-No: Desires

Purpose	• To teach the child to answer "yes" and "no" with respect to desired objects and activities.
Arrangement	• Use desired and neutral/undesired items.
Procedure	• Present desired and undesired items in conjunction with the question "Do you want this?" or simply "Want this?" Prompt the correct response. Determination of correct response is based on the child's behavior; if the child reaches for the item prompt "yes" and if the child refuses (pushes item away, turns from item etc.) or ignores prompt "no." • Use random presentations of desired and neutral objects. • When possible expand to activities when the child demonstrates progress with objects ("Do you want to [activity]?").
Considerations	• This exercise is essentially a matter of accepting and rejecting an object by saying "yes" and "no" respectively. • Many children struggle to learn "yes" and "no" with this method and "Yes-No Interrupted Chain" (#147) might be a better starting point.

#147   Yes-no: Interrupted Chain

Purpose	• To teach the child to use "yes" and "no" when offered items to complete a familiar task.
Set up	• The child performs sequential MTS (see "Sequential Matching" #13). Ensure that one of the objects is missing.
Procedure	• When the child encounters a picture that lacks a corresponding object, the should approach you and request it (e.g., "I need a cup"). When the child has made the request, present an object and ask: "Do you want this?" An assistant prompts the correct answer. Randomize pertinent and non-pertinent objects (i.e., sometimes present the object the child requests and sometimes present an irrelevant object).
Considerations	• Expect to run several sequences before the child begins to answer correctly. • Intersperse "yes" and "no" trials with trials in which the requested item is

delivered directly (i.e., when the child requests a missing item, hand it to the child and say "here you go").

Additional steps and permutations	• Introduce alternate conditions (and then randomize all).
	• Ask: "Do you want a (cup)?" without presenting the object
	• Provide the requested item (the child says "thank you").
	• "It's over there" (pointing to location).
	• Tell the child where it is ("it is in the drawer").
	• Tell the child to ask someone else (i.e., "Daddy has it") (In order to proceed with this step, the child must have mastered "Requesting from Second Person", (#58).

#148   Yes-No: Factual Questions (1)

Purpose	• To teach the child to use "yes" and "no" in response to factual questions.
Set up	• Use familiar objects on a table.
Procedure	• Present a familiar object and ask: "Is this a(n) [object label]?" Randomize trials where the label matches the visual object and where there is a mismatch between what you say and the object. Prompt correct answer.
Considerations	• Learning to answer basic factual questions such as "Is this a cup?" is a difficult hurdle for many children. Overcoming this hurdle is necessary for the child to participate in advanced language and cognitive learning objectives.
	• <u>Default strategy</u>: Line up four to five objects (same kind). Point to the first object and say its name (e.g., "block"), a second person prompts the child (from behind) to say "yes." Continue to the next object. When reaching the last object give it a name that does not match the object ("e.g., "banana"). The assistant prompts the child to say "no." Repeat the sequence and fade prompts until the child switches from "yes" to "no" at the appropriate time (Leaf and McEachin, 1999). Continue with the same arrangement but randomize matched and mismatched statements throughout the sequence. When the child is able to identify 'match' versus 'mismatch,' reintroduce the original procedure (i.e., present an object and ask: "is this a(n) [object label]?"
	• If the child continues to struggle, it may be necessary to scale back to exercises such as "Selection-Based Imitation" (#9-11) to strengthen sustained and flexible shift of attention.

#149	**Yes-No Factual Questions (2)**

Purpose	• Extending the child's ability to use "yes" and "no" to answer factual questions.

Set up	• This exercise can be practiced in the child's natural environment with familiar persons, pictures of persons performing familiar actions, and familiar objects.

Procedure	• *Procedure 1:* Travel with the child in familiar environments, point to familiar items and ask "yes" and "no" questions. Intersperse "yes" and "no" questions with other questions such as "What is it?" "What color is it?" "What is [person] doing?" as well as receptive instructions. • *Procedure 2:* Present a picture of a person performing a familiar action and ask: "Is [person] [action]?" (E.g., "Is mommy eating?") Randomize match and mismatch. Extend this exercise to real life situations. • <u>*Procedure 3:*</u> Present objects with solid colors and ask; "Is this [color]?" Eventually, extend this exercise by placing familiar objects on the table and ask" Is the [object] [color]?" (E.g., "Is the car green?").

Considerations	• <u>*Extension:*</u> When the child is proficient, teach the child to make a corrective statement when answering "no" to a question. For instance: "Is the car green → "No…It is red."

#150	**Yes-No: Factual Questions (3)**

Purpose	• Extending the child's ability to use "yes" and "no" to answer factual questions concerning their own activities.

Set up	• This exercise can be practiced in the child's natural environments, based on current activities.

Procedure	• When the child does something the child is able to describe or when en route somewhere, ask questions such as "are you drinking?" "Are you going to [location]?" etc. An assistant prompts correct response.

Additional steps and permutations	• With progress, extend the exercise to (a) possession ("Do you have a ___?" (b) immediate past actions ("Did you go to [location]?"). • Asking "yes" and "no" questions may be incorporated into "Reporting Locations (1)" (#74) and "Reporting Locations (2)" (#75). • When proficient, teach the child to make the correct statement after answering "no" to a question. For instance: "Are you going to the kitchen? No…to the bathroom."

#151   Yes-No: Factual Questions (4)

Purpose	• Extending the child's ability to answer "yes" and "no" to two-part questions.
Set up	• Use familiar items with solid colors
Procedure	• Present an object and ask: "Is this a(n) [color] [object]?" (e.g., "Is this a blue sock?"). The statement may match both features (color and object), one feature (color <u>or</u> object), or none of the features. The assistant prompts correct answer. If the question relates to both features of an object ("Is this a blue sock?") prompt "yes." If the statement matches only one feature or none of the features ("Is this a red sock?" or "is this a red cup?"), prompt "no" + correction statement ("It is a blue sock" or "No, it is a green car"). Make sure to alternate the matching and mismatching feature, e.g., "Is this a blue cup?" (Wrong object) versus "Is this a red sock?" (Wrong color).
Considerations	• This ability is difficult to learn and first requires the child to demonstrate fluency with multi-component receptive instructions.

#152   Yes-No: Factual Questions (5)

Purpose	• To teach the child to use "yes" and "no" to factual questions concerning 'non-visual' facts.
Set up	• This exercise requires only the instructor and child
Procedure	• Ask yes and no questions concerning known facts (no objects in view). Ask about things the child has mastered such as *colors of common objects* ("Is a banana yellow?" – an extension of "Naming colors (7)" #127), *functions* ("Is a car for driving?" – an extension of "Functions of Objects: Answering Questions (1)" #91), and *parts of objects* ("Does a car have wheels?" – an extension of "Listing Parts" #102).
Considerations	• "Yes" and "no" questions should be extended to all concepts and information the child learns.

#153   Yes/No: Correcting Statements

Purpose	• To teach the child to correct inaccurate factual statements and directing instructor's attention to the correct item placed nearby.
Set up	• Place a familiar object on a table. An assistant sits behind the child.

Procedure	•	Point to an item and say, "Is that a fire truck?" The child corrects by pointing to the fire truck and saying "No, that is a (x)... that is a fire truck" The assistant provides prompting from behind. Fade prompts over successive trials.
Considerations	•	This exercise is essentially a matter of strengthening joint attention and directing someone's attention to the object of interest.

Who, What, Where Distinctions

#154   Where: Deixis (1)

Purpose	• To teach the child to point to an object or a person when asked "Where is [the] [object/person]?"
Set up	• Use familiar persons and objects. • This exercise is an extension of "Receptive Object Identification" (#32).
Procedure	• Ask, "Where is the [object]?" An assistant directs the child to orient toward the object, point to it and say "there" or "over there."
Considerations	• Orienting (searching) and pointing to an object at a distance is pivotal in developing a concept of "Where." • The concept of "Where" is linked intimately with the *deictic* "here" and "there." To simplify, "there" is 'any location other than the spot from where the speech act is executed' (that spot is referred to as "here"). Consequently, "Where," "here" and "there" must be taught together. • "Here" and "there" entail *"joint attention."* The child points to an object (or person) and checks back to see if the listener looks in the right direction. Proficiency of this kind of joint-attention is pivotal.

#155   Where: Deixis (2)

Purpose	• To teach the child to point in the direction of an object or person when asked "Where is the [object/person]?"
Set up	• Use familiar people and known objects.
Procedure	• Ask; "Where is the [object]?" → The child orients towards the object, points to it and says, "there" or "over there." When the child has declared the location, say "There?" and point in a different direction →An assistant guides the child to say "No... there" while pointing in the right direction → Point in the right direction and say "There?" → the assistant prompts the child to say "Yes."
Considerations	• The instructor should randomize correct and incorrect pointing (sometimes correct the first time and sometimes after correction). • This is a direct extension of "Yes-No Correcting Statements" (#153).

#156	**Where: Multiple Scenarios**

Purpose	• To broaden conditions under which the child answers "Where" questions.
Set up	• Practice this exercise in the child's natural environment using arrangements from earlier exercises (specification below)
Procedure	• Randomize the following scenarios: (a) Ask: "Where is the [object]?" → The child orients towards the object, points to it and says "there" ("Where: Deixis (2)" #155), (b) Take the child to a location and ask; "Where are you?" ("Naming Locations" #73), (c) Tell the child to travel to a location, when he returns, asks; "Where did you go?" ("Reporting Locations (1) #74), (d) answering "Where are you going?" when in transit ("Declaring Destinations (1)" #76 and "Declaring Destination (2)" #77).
Considerations	• Each time you run this exercise, make sure to involve several of the above scenarios. • While this compound exercise may broaden the child's context for answering where questions, it is typically insufficient to establish the concept of "Where."

#157	**What/Where Distinction (1)**

Purpose	• To teach the distinction between basic "Where" and "What" questions.
Set up	• Use familiar persons and known objects in arrangements from earlier exercises (see below)
Procedure	• Point to a location and ask: "What is over there?" → prompt the child to orient and name the object. This exercise is an extension of "Expressive Naming (1)" (#47) and "Expressive Naming: Multiple Presentation Forms" (#50) • Randomize two scenarios (a) Point to a location and ask: "What is over there?" and (b) ask: "Where is the [object]?" (see "Where: Deixis (2)" #155). • Tell the child to put an object away (e.g., "put this away" while pointing to an object). Prompt the child to place the object somewhere. This task is often difficult since the destination is unspecified. When the child gets the idea (putting objects anywhere), introduce multiple objects: Tell the child to put away object (A) and then object (B). Upon completion, ask the child; "Where did you put the [object]?" "Where is the [object]?" and "What is over there?" (while pointing). • Introduce Yes/No (see "Where: Deixis (2) #155): In the context of Step 3.

#158	**What/Where Distinction (2)**

Purpose	• To teach the distinction between basic "Where" and "What" questions.
Set up	• Use multiple familiar persons and familiar objects.
Procedure	• <u>Step 1</u>: Two to three (or more) persons are scattered around the room. Each person holds an object. Ask: "Where is [person]?" → the child points and says "over there." Follow up with: "What does she have?" • <u>Step 2</u>: When the child is proficient, add the questions "What does [person] have?" followed by "Where is he/she?"
Considerations	• This exercise is an extension of "Pronominalization: He/She" (#145). • What and where questions will eventually be contrasted with "Who" questions (see #159, #160).

#159	**Who-questions (1)**

Purpose	• To establish a rudimentary understanding of the pronoun "Who."
Set up	• Use multiple familiar persons and objects.
Procedure	• Two to three (or more) persons are situated around the room. Each person holds an object. Ask these questions: (a) "Where is [person]?" → the child points and says "over there" and (b) "Who has the [object]?" → The child *points to the person* and says the person's name. • Same arrangement as above. Ask, (a) "Where is [person]?" (→ the child should point and say "over there"), follow with (b) "What does she have?" (the child names the object), (c) Who has the [object]?" (the child points and names the person), (d) "Where is she?" (the child points and says: "over there").
Considerations	• "Who" is a pronoun which stands in for a person or a personified thing (character). • The distinction between persons (or personified objects) and things is often elusive for children with ASD. • "Who" questions are intimately linked to other pronouns such as the personal pronouns I, you, my, your. The concept of "Who" cannot fully emerge without these pronouns. The current exercise merely gets the concept "off the ground."

#160   Who-Questions (2)

Purpose
- To establish a rudimentary understanding of the pronoun "Who."

Set up
- Use multiple familiar persons and objects

Procedure
- Two to three (or more) persons are situated around the room or sit around in a circle.
- One person holds an object. Tell the child to give an object to the other person. When the child complies, ask: "Who has the [object]?" and "What does [person 1 or 2] have?"
- When proficient with (a), tell the child to give one object to person 1 and another object to person 2. When the child complies, ask: "Who has the [object]?" and "What does [person 1 or 2] have?"
- Same arrangement as above. Ask the questions "What did you give to [person 1 or 2]?" → when the child answers, then ask ,"Who did you give the [object] to?" (or "Who did you give the object to?") → The child should point to the person and state their name using the proposition TO (i.e., "to Mommy).

#161   Who-Questions (3)

Purpose
- To establish a rudimentary understanding of the pronoun "Who" in the context of "Where" and "What."

Set up
- Two to three (or more) persons are situated around the room or sit in a circle. Familiar objects are placed around the room.
- This exercise is a combination of previous exercises

Procedure
- Randomize (a) "What is over there?" (b) "Where is the [object]?" (c) "Is the [object] over there?" (d) "Where is [person]? followed by (e) "What does she have?" (f) Who has the [object]?" followed by (g) "Where is she?" (h) "Who is over there?" (i) "Is [person] over there ?" (points), (j) "What did you give to [person 1 or 2]?" (see "Who Questions (2)", #160), (k) "Who did you give the [object]?" (or "Who did you give the object to?") see "Who Questions (2)" #160
- Same arrangement as above. Add the question: "Where is the [object]?" when someone is holding the object. The child should answer, "[person] has [it]" rather than "over there." Randomize questions about objects in someone's possession ("[person] has it") and not in someone's possession ("over there").

#162 — Expressive "Who/What"

Purpose	• To introduce a rudimentary understanding of when to use pronouns, "who" vs. "what."
	• To introduce 'child-as-teacher' as an instructional format.

Set Up
- Sit across from the child. Place a stack of cards containing pictures of persons and things for which he knows the names. An assistant stands behind the child.

Procedure
- Step 1: The child draws a card from his pile. Child looks at the card, then shows it to you (he needs orient it so that you can clearly see it) and says, "Who is it" or "What is it" accordingly → you answer → The child is prompted to provide feedback, e.g., "that's correct."
- Step2: Once the child learns when to use "Who" vs "What" in Step 1, alter your responses so that they are either correct or incorrect. If your answer is correct, the child provides praise, if incorrect, the child is to correct you and say something like "No, that's x."

Considerations
- The 'attentional' and pragmatic considerations in this exercise are many;
    - The child needs to first look at his card in order to know which pronoun to use.
    - The child then needs to orient the card so that you can easily see it. (perspective taking)
    - The child needs to carefully attend to what you say and adjust his responses based on yours.
- Child needs to be proficient with "Say vs Do" (#165) and "Yes/No Corrective Statements (#153). Standard strategies for intoducing asking "who" and "what" questions can be found in Leaf and McEachin, 1999 p. 277.
- This 'child as teacher' format has broad utility and is especially useful for strengthening social acuity.

CORE EXERCISES (3)

Complex Receptive Instructions

#163   Three-Component Instructions (1)

Purpose	• To teach the child to respond to a three-part instructions concerning features of objects.
Set up	• Present a set of eight familiar objects that vary according to kind, color and size. For instance (1) a big yellow square, (2) a little yellow square, (3) a big yellow triangle, (4) a little yellow triangle, (5) a big green square and a (6) little green square, (7) a big green triangle and (8) a little green triangle (BYS, LYS, BYT, LYT, BGS, LGS, BGT, LGT) (Fig. 12)
Procedure	• Ask the child to point to one of the objects (e.g., "big blue ball"). Prompt correct response. Randomize instructions. • Alternate the field of objects, but make sure that each arrangement encompasses all the variations.
Considerations	• The child must be proficient with "Receptive Colors- Conditional Discrimination" (#116). • When the child is proficient, increase distance to strengthen working memory (i.e., the child is required to travel to an area containing the objects) • This exercise expands the "if-but-not-otherwise" contingency (see "Receptive Colors: Conditional Discrimination" #116).

#164   Three-Component Instructions 2

Purpose	• To teach the child to respond to a three-part instructions involving "that" constructions.
Set up	• Present a set of eight familiar objects that vary according to kind, color and size. Same set up as in "Three-Component Instructions (1)."
Procedure	• Ask the child to point to one of the objects using "that" constructions (e.g., "point to the big square that's green," "point to the green triangle that's big"). Prompt correct response. Randomize instructions. • Alternate the field of objects, but make sure that each set up encompasses all the variations.
Considerations	• While "Three-Component Instructions (1)" (#163) and "Three-Component

Instructions (2)" (#164) have different forms (structure), they mean the same thing (have the same referent). Children often do not recognize that different structures have the same meaning and forming such equivalence may require explicit teaching.

- "That" constructions are central to the development of complex declarative sentences and "propositional attitudes" such as "I think that [the door is open]."

#165   Three Step Instructions

Purpose	• To expand the child's ability to follow multiple step instructions. • In "Three-Component Instructions" (#163, #164), the verbal instruction is complex, but the child's response is singular (i.e., pointing to an object) and is the same every time (points or retrieves). In contrast, three-step instructions require that the child does three distinct things.
Set up	• This exercise should be practiced in the child's natural environment.
Procedure	• Expand on earlier multi-step exercises including "Two-Step Instructions" (#31), "Receptive Location and Action" (#71). • "Three-Step Instructions" should also include delivering two objects to a person ("Give [object] and [object] to [person]"). This is an extension of "Two-Step Receptive Object Identification" (#38).

#166   Basic rule following

Purpose	• To teach the child to follow instructions in which the condition for responding is not immediately present ("When I stand up, you get the cup"). • This exercise is central to developing the concept of "When."
Set up	• Face the child and place an object within his reach. An assistant stands behind the child.
Procedure	• Instructor: "When I [action], you get the cup." The assistant prevents immediate responding. • After 2-3 seconds, the instructor performs the designated action (claps) and the assistant guides the child to pick up the cup). • This particular sequence is practiced until the child responds reliably to the instructor's action (clap) rather than the verbal instruction. • When the child responds reliably, alter the action but keep the child's response the same (e.g., shift from "When I clap, get the cup" to "When I stand up, get the cup"). When the child is able to follow these two instructions in a randomized fashion, continue to change actions while the child's response remains the same. Continue to introduce new actions until

the child responds correctly to novel instructions.

- When the child responds correctly to novel instructions, begin to alter the child's response (e.g., shift from "get the cup" to another action such as "get the ball"). Randomize the two actions until the child performs proficiently.
- When the child performs proficiently, randomize actions (e.g., "get the cup" versus "get the ball"), introduce additional actions (*multiple exemplar*) until the child performs reliably to any novel instruction.

Considerations	• As the child becomes more language able, rule governed behavior may be extended in terms of complexity, time delay, re-stating rules, generating rules, describing discrepancies between rules and other's actions, etc.

DEMONSTRATIVES

#167	**Demonstratives (1)**

Purpose	• To teach the child to understand and use demonstratives including "this" and "this one."

Set up	• Step 1: Display a field of several objects of solid colors. • Step 2: Display a field of several _unknown_ objects of solid colors.

Procedure	• Step 1: Ask: "What color is this one?" / "What color is this?" (while pointing to an object) (This step is identical to "Naming Colors (5) #122, step 2). • Step 2: Ask: "Which one is [color]?" Prompt the child to point to the item and model: "this one." Ask about another color and provide prompting. Continue while fading manual and verbal prompting over successive trials. • Step 3: Same as step 2, but add yes/no questions: point to an item and say "Is this [color]?" and prompt the child to say "yes" or "no" accordingly. This is an extension of "Yes-No Factual Questions (2)" (#149).

Considerations	• Demonstratives (or deixis) is very challenging for most children and will often require considerable time and practice in all kinds of settings. • Intervention that does not require the child to attend to the speech partner (e.g., conventional expressive and receptive naming) will very likely obstruct development of even rudimentary understanding of demonstratives. • Fluency with tracking and basic "Yes-No" may facilitate acquisition of demonstratives.

#168	**Demonstratives (2)**

Purpose	• To teach the child to understand and use demonstratives including "this," "that," "(over) here," "there."

Set up and procedures	• _Set up:_ Display a field of several objects of solid colors. • _Procedure:_ Ask: "What color is this one?" or "What color is this?" while pointing to an object (this is identical to "Naming Colors (5)" #122, step 2). • _Set up:_ Display a field of several _unknown_ objects of solid colors. • _Procedure:_ Ask: "Which one is [color]?" Prompt the child to point to the item and to say "this one." Ask about another color and provide prompting. Continue and fade manual and verbal prompts over successive trials.

- *Set up:* Display a field of several <u>known</u> objects on a table or, the floor. All objects should be within the child's reach.
- *Procedure:* Ask: "Where is the [object]?"; prompt the child to point to the item and say "here." Move the object considerably outside the child's reach and ask: "Where is the __?" or "Where is it now?" (the latter requires fluency with pronominalization). Prompt the child to point in the direction of the object and model "there" or "over there." Randomize "here" and "there." Fade manual and verbal prompting over successive trials.
- *Set up*: Display a field of several <u>known</u> objects on a table or the floor. The objects should be within the child's reach. Mix in a couple of unknown objects of solid colors. Make sure these colored objects do not have the same color as the known objects. For instance: A red and blue shoe (known), a transparent plastic cup (known) a metal fork (known), a green Jones plug (unknown), and a yellow wug (unknown).
- *Procedure*: Mix steps #2 and #3

#169   Demonstratives: Matching (1)

Purpose	• To teach the child to understand and use demonstratives including 'this,' 'that,' 'here,' and 'there.'
Set up	• Sit side by side at a table. A lotto board is placed in front of you and a stack of corresponding pictures is placed next to the lotto board. • An assistant sits behind the child.
Procedure	• Pick a card from the stack, display it to the child and say: "Where does this go?" The assistant models the response: says "Here" while pointing to the correct spot on the board. Place the card accordingly, pick another, display it to the child, and ask: "Where does this go?" The assistant may (a) model again, (b) provide partial manual guidance and verbal prompting (say: "Here"). Fade prompting over successive trials.

#170   Demonstratives: Matching (2)

Purpose	• To teach the child to understand and use demonstratives including "this," "that," (over) "here," "there."
Set up	• Same as "Demonstratives: Matching (1)" (#167).
Procedure	• Same as "Demonstratives: Matching (1)" (#167). • In addition: When the child points to the right spot and says "here," you point to a different spot and say "here?" (with questioning intonation). If you point to the correct spot, the assistant prompts "yes," and you put the picture down. If you point to an incorrect spot, the assistant prompts "no,"

then prompts the child to point to the right spot and to say "here."

| **Considerations** | • | Fluency with "Yes/No: Correcting Statements" (#153) may facilitate this exercise. |

Complex Abstract Concepts

#171	**Receptive Negation (1)**

Purpose	• To teach the child to follow instructions involving the exclusion "not."
Set up	• Display known objects of different colors (e.g., a yellow crayon and a green sock).
Procedure	• Alternate "inclusion" instructions: "point to the one that is yellow" (or "where is the yellow one"), and "exclusion" instruction: "point to the one that is <u>not</u> yellow." Change the objects from trial to trial and randomize the order of inclusive and exclusive instructions.
	• When the child is proficient, involve multiple objects of the same colors (e.g., a yellow crayon, a yellow car and a green cup). Both inclusion and exclusion instructions should sometimes involve two objects. For instance, "point to the ones that are not yellow" (i.e., green cup) versus "point to the one that is not green" (crayon and car).
Considerations	• If the child struggles with this arrangement, abbreviate the instruction to "not [color]" and introduce full sentence when he makes progress.
	• It may be useful to sometimes use object names rather than 'color' in the initial stage of this exercise: place two known objects on the table and randomize inclusive instructions ("point to [object name]") and exclusive instructions ("not [object name]").
	• When the child masters this exercise, involve all known features and properties such as shapes (e.g., not a circle), size (not big/little), categories (e.g., not an animal), and persons (not Daddy).
	• This exercise may be extended directly to "Expressive Negation" (#174)

#172	**Receptive Negation (2)**

Purpose	• To teach the child to follow instructions involving *but not* and *only* clauses.
Set up	• Display several of the same kind of objects but with different colors (three yellow crayons and one red, four yellow crayons and two red, etc.).
Procedure	• Instruction 1: "Give me the crayons **but not** the red ones."
	• Instruction 2: "Give me **only** the red crayons."

Considerations	• This exercise should be extended to all acquired concepts and situations such as shapes, size (big/little) and functions.
	• This exercise covers merely a fragment of speech acts involving *but*, *but not*, and *only*. It is important to continue to develop these concepts throughout intervention. For instance, comprehension of speech acts such as "only you can have a cookie," "only fish can swim in the water," "John only has one," "A car has wheels but not wings," "Everybody has a crayon but not I," must be addressed explicitly as the child acquires more complex language and concepts.

Additions and Permutations	• As the child advances, you can consider more complex formulations such as "Give me all **but** the red crayons," "give me the crayons **but only** the green ones," and "give me the crayons **but only** the ones that are green."

#173   Expressive Negation (1)

Purpose	• To teach the child to answer questions involving the exclusion "not."
Set up	• Display known objects with different colors (e.g., a yellow crayon and a green sock).
Procedure	• Alternate "inclusion" questions: "What is yellow?" and "exclusion" questions: "What is not yellow?"
Considerations	• This exercise is an extension of "Receptive Negation (1)" (#171).

#174   Expressive Negation (2)

Purpose	• To teach the child to follow instructions involving different kinds of negation.
Set up	• Display known objects and pictures.
	• This exercise may be practiced with a group of familiar people.
Procedure	• *Does not 1:* Display objects mastered in "Part-Whole Association (1) #100." Randomize the instructions: "Which one does <u>not</u> have a [part]?" and "Which one has a [part]?"
	• *Does not 2:* Group of people holding objects. Randomize the instructions "Who has an [object]?" and "Who does not have an [object]?"
	• *Is not:* Use things the child has easily identified by function. Randomize instructions: Which one is for cutting/not for cutting.
	• *Is not:* Display pictures of people performing simple actions. Randomize

the instructions: "Who is [action]" and "Who is <u>not</u> [action]." Extend to real life situations (group of people performing simple actions).

- *Are not 1:* Display objects with different colors. Randomize instructions: "Which ones are <u>not</u> [color]" versus "Which ones are [color]." Extend the exercise beyond colors (e.g., "Which ones are/are not big/little"). Alternate plural (are/are not) with singular (is/is not).
- *Are not 2:* Display pictures of persons performing simple actions. Randomize the instructions: "Who are [action]?" and "Who are <u>not</u> [action]?" Extend to real life situations (group of persons performing simple actions).
- *Did not:* Gather a group of persons. (1) The instructor hands out an object to each participant with the exception of one person and asks: "Who got a [object]?" and "Who did not get a [object]?" (2) The instructor gives the group an instruction (e.g., go to the door) and all but one person responds: "Who went to the door?" or "Who did go to the door?" and "Who did not go to the door?"

Considerations	• Negation should be extended to use as when using categories, prepositions (what is/isn't on/under/in, etc.) and personal pronouns (who has/does not have, who is/isn't, can/can't etc.).

#175 What's Missing? (1)

Purpose	• To teach the child to recognize that objects are missing from a field. • To enhance the child's working memory. • To teach the child to remember observed situations and recognize changes. • To teach the child to compare a situation at two different times and identify differences.
Set up	• Up to four familiar objects and/or pictures are placed in a row. The child faces the row.
Procedure	• Point to the table, and ask: "What do you see?" or "What are these?" The child points to each object while naming them (see "Sequential Naming" #52). • Cover the objects and remove one of them. Then uncover them and ask: "What is missing?"
Considerations	• The child should be proficient with "Sequential Naming" (#52). • This exercise involves naming an absent object, which entails the capacity to see a new scenario in relation to a previously one; Not two separate scenarios, but **one** changed scenario. For many children with autism, this leap of imagination – *construing the present as a changed past* – is quite challenging, but it is a fundamental cognitive ability that must emerge in order to address more complex forms of inference, deduction and social abilities. • As the child make progress, this exercise may be conducted in less

contrived manners.

Additional steps and permutations	• "What's missing?" should eventually be expanded to concepts such as "What's been added?" and "What's changed?" (e.g., leaving the same kind of objects on the table, but change the colors of one of them). The latter demands higher order linguistic ability (e.g., "the cup is blue instead of red") thus it is not an immediate extension of "What's missing?" • What's missing should eventually be expanded to "parts."
Troubleshooting	• If the child struggles, it may be necessary to scale back to two items and remove one after the child names them. • This exercise places great demand on working memory and it may be necessary to teach the child to rehearse observed objects before introducing the question "What's missing?" Rehearsal may involve presenting three objects to the child and ask: "What do you see?" When the child has labeled them, cover them up and ask: "What did you see?" If the child is unable to recall all the objects, present them again and repeat the procedure. Reintroduce "What's Missing" when the child recalls proficiently.

#176   What's Missing? (2)

Purpose	• To teach the child to recognize that objects are missing from a field. • To expand the concepts of "and" and "nothing" to a "What's missing?" scenario.
Set up	• Use up to four familiar objects and/or pictures placed in a row. The child faces the row.
Procedure	• Point to the table, and ask: "What do you see?" or "What are these?" When the child has named them (see "Sequential Naming" #52), cover the field of objects and remove one, two, or none of them. Then uncover them and ask: "What is missing?" The child answers accordingly ("the __ is missing" / "the __ and the __ are missing" / "nothing is missing"). • The concepts of two objects missing and nothing missing may have to be taught separately.
Considerations	• This is often very difficult, and may be postponed until the child is fluent with other memory-based exercises and abstract concepts.

Categorization

#177   Receptive Categorization

Purpose	• To teach the child to assign higher-order descriptions (category names). • To teach the child to accept that a single object can be referred to by its proper name (basic-level) and a category name (superordinate level); that each object has a unique name (cookie) as well as a name shared by other objects with similar function (food).
Set up	• Use objects the child can name. Start with two distinct and salient categories (e.g., food and clothing). • Display one object of each kind on the table.
Procedure	• Select two different kinds of objects (e.g., cookie and shoe) Vary the instructions: "Point to the [object name]" and "point to the [category name]."
Considerations	• Expand to other pertinent categories (e.g., furniture, food, animals).

#178   Naming Categories (1)

Purpose	• To teach the child to assign higher-order description (category names) to objects. • To teach the child when to use basic description and when to use higher order description.
Set up	• Use "category containers" with three or more items of the same category. For instance: Animals (dog, sheep, cow), clothing (hat, shoe, mitten), and food (cookie, pizza, hot dog).
Procedure	• *Step 1*: Present three category containers with three or more examples in each. Point to a container and ask: "What is in here?" Prompt the child to say the category name (e.g., "animals"). Point to the next container, etc. Vary the items and position of the containers. Teach to proficiency. • *Step 2*: Present three containers with three or more examples in two of them and a single item on one of them. For instance: Animals (dog, sheep, cow), clothing (hat), and food (cookie, pizza, hot dog). Point to a container and ask: "What is in here?" If the container has several objects (dog, sheep, cow), prompt the child to say the category name ("animals"). If the container has one single item (cookie), prompt the child to name the item

("cookie"). Point to the next container, etc. Vary the items and position of the containers. Alternate single item containers and category containers. For instance, if *cookie* was the single item container in one trial, it should be in a category container in the next (cookie, pizza, hot dog). Vice versa, a category container in one trial (e.g., "animals") should be dismantled in the next ("dog").

• *Step 3:* Three category containers with three or more examples in each. Point to a container and ask: "What is in here?" The child says the category name (e.g., "animals"). Pick up a single item from one of the containers (this may include the container he just named) and ask the child: "What is this?" Prompt the child to say the proper name (e.g., "dog"). Point to the next container, etc. Alternate questions about category containers and single objects.

Considerations	• If the child struggles with this strategy, it may be necessary to begin by using standard approaches (See Leaf and McEachin, 1999 p. 241).

#179   Naming Categories (2)

Purpose	• To teach the child to assign higher-order description (category names) to objects. • To teach the child when to use basic description and when to use higher order description.
Set up	• Use three "category containers" with one example in each. Place several "category items" on the table outside of the bin.
Procedure	• *Exercise 1*: Point to on object on the table and ask: "What is it." When the child names it, instruct the child to "put it with the same" (or "Where does it go?") and prompt the child to place it in the right category container. Continue to fill up the containers. When a category container has more than one item, you may alternate the instructions "put with the same" and "put with the [category name]" (e.g., "put with the food") • *Exercise 2*: Ask the child to identify an object on the table. When the child does, instruct the child to "put it with the same" (or "Where does it go?") and prompt the child to place it in the right category container. Continue to fill up the containers. When the child is proficient, intersperse with questions from "Naming Categories (1)" (#178), steps 2 and 3.

#180   Reciprocal Categories

Purpose	• To teach the child to alternate appropriately between higher-order naming (category naming) and basic level naming.
Set up	• Sit face to face where you both have access to a pile of common objects. An assistant sits behind the child.
Procedure	• *Step 1*: Pick two objects of the same category from the pile (e.g. cracker and a piece of cheese), hold them up and say: "I have food." The second instructor guides child to select two objects of a different category (e.g. a dog and a bear), hold it up, and reciprocate by using the appropriate category name ("I have animals").
	• *Step 2:* Pick two items from different categories and say ("I have [object name] and [object name]"). The child reciprocates by picking two items from different categories and say "I have [object name] and [object name]." The instructor then puts the items down and picks two items from the same category (e.g. cracker and a piece of cheese), holds them up and says: "I have some food." The assistant guides child to select two objects of a different category (e.g. a dog and a bear), hold them up and reciprocate by using the appropriate category name ("I have some animals"). Alternate between these two conditions until the child discovers the language game.
Additional steps and permutations	• This extension involves two new components (1) the child must discern when to reciprocate one versus two statements (i.e., differentiate the instructor's behavior), and (2) appropriate use of the conjunction "and." This exercise should also be done in situations when the two objects are the same (e.g., spoons). Thus, child will have to discern when to use a conjunction or the plural (e.g., "I have cups" versus "I have a cup and a doll").

#181   Describing Kinds

Purpose	• To learn the meaning of "kind."
Set up	• Place several objects from different categories on a table in front of the child.
Procedure	• Step 1: Ask: "What kind of animal do you have?" / "What kind of food do you have?" etc. Prompt the child to apply the appropriate category name.
	• Step 2: Same as step one, but ask additional relevant questions such as "Where is it?" and "What color is it?" Thus, when the child answers "What kind of [category name] do you have?" Follow up with "Where is it?" (the child points and says "here") and/or "What color is it?" etc.

#182	**Sorting Category Items**

Purpose	•	To decide which things go together.
Arrangement	•	Place three items from three different categories on the table (e.g., a dog, a sandwich, and a coat).
Procedure	•	Hand the child an item corresponding to one of the categories (e.g., a cat, pizza slice, and pants). Instruct the child to "put with same" and place the item in the right spot.

Prepositions

#183	**Basic Receptive Prepositions (1)**

Purpose	• To teach the child to follow instructions involving the simple locatives *on* and *in*.

Set up	• Sit together at a table on which is an opaque container (e.g., bin) (the base object) and a smaller object such as a block or puzzle piece (ambulant objects).

Procedure	• *Step 1*: Place a bin right side up in front of the child, hand the child an object and say "put in". Prompt correct response and repeat trial. When the child does it independently, present the base object upside down while maintaining the same instruction. Consequently, the child must turn the base object right side up in order to carry out the instruction ("put in"). When the child is successful, randomize the presentation of base object (sometimes right side up and sometimes upside down).
	• *Step 2*: Continue the same procedure but expand and alternate base objects and the ambulant objects. Use different kinds of objects until *generalization*.
	• *Step 3*: Place two different base objects side by side (e.g., a bin and a bowl). Hand the child an ambulant object and randomize the instructions "put in bin" and "put in bowl." (Fig. 13.2). Prompt the child to distinguish between the base objects. When the child acquires this distinction, maintain the same arrangements (two base objects) and (a) randomize the prepositions "in" and "on" and (b) randomize the orientation of the base objects; they should sometimes be presented upside down and sometimes right side up. Consequently, the child must identify whether the target base object is oriented correctly or must be changed.

Considerations	• While "in" and "on" are two of the most salient and versatile prepositions, they may not necessarily be the best starting point for all children (see "Basic Receptive Prepositions (2)" #184).
	• The above arrangement is merely a starting point, representing prototypes (best examples) of the prepositions "in" and "on." For example, the prototype of "on" can be defined by three characteristics (a) above a base object, (b) contact with a base object, and (c) supported by a base object. Not all of these characteristics are present in many common usages of "on." For instance "the picture is on the wall" lacks the feature of *"supported by"* and "mommy is on her way" lacks all the features and will only makes sense if we construe the event as a "source path goal schema" and mommy as a trajectory moving from one place (source) to another (goal) on an

imaginary line stretching between these places (Lakoff and Johnson, 1987). In other words, "on" is a radial concept with many related applications; some of which are idiomatic or vividly metaphorical ("he is on fire") while, some are more clearly related to an extension of a prototype. Consequently, an intervention must take the nature of this concept into consideration and arrange systematic learning contingencies that extend uses from the prototype; the physical features of each must be traced out in detail and established as an explicit exercise.

#184   Basic Expressive Prepositions (1)

Purpose	• To teach the child to describe relations involving the simple locatives *on* and *in*.
	• The main targets of this exercise are to teach the child (a) to use simple prepositional statements (preposition-object), (b) to distinguish between different questions regarding objects (*Where* versus *What*), and (c) generalizing pronominalization ("it," see #144).
Set up	• Sit together at a table on which is an opaque container (e.g., bin) (the base object) and a smaller object such as a block or puzzle piece (ambulant object).
Procedures	• *Step 1*: Place the ambulant object (e.g. block) *on* or *in* the base object, (the bin) and ask: "Where is the block?" Prompt correct answer ("in" or "on") and randomize the positions. Fade prompts over successive trials.
	• *Step 2*: Place two different base objects next to each other, place an ambulant object in or on one of them, and ask: "Where is the block?" Prompt correct answer "in/on the [base object]." Fade prompts over successive trials and randomize all possibilities (in/on both base objects).
	• *Step 3*: Place two different base objects next to each other, place a different ambulant object (e.g., block and spoon) in or on both of them (Fig. 13.3) and ask; "Where is the block?" versus "Where is the spoon?" Prompt correct answer "in/on the [base object]," e.g., "in the bin." Fade prompts over successive trials and randomize all possibilities (in/on both base objects).
	• *Step 4*: Same as step 3, but introduce additional factual questions such as "What color is the X?" (see #120), and "What color is this?" (while pointing to an object) (see #122). Consequently, the child must discriminate "What" and "Where" questions in the context of a "preposition arrangement." Make sure to present as many different variations as possible and include pronominalization (see #144). For instance, point to the block and ask: "What is it? When the child answers, point to another object and ask: "What is this?" When the child answers, change its position (e.g., into a cup) and ask: "Where is it?
Considerations	• Step 4 requires that the child is fluent with pronominalization (#144).

#185   Basic Receptive Prepositions (2)

Purpose	• To teach the child to follow instructions involving the locatives *on, under, behind, next to, in front of.*

Set up	• Large base objects (e.g., chair, table) and smaller ambulant objects. The child sits on a chair across from the base object three to four feet away.

Procedures	• *Step 1*: Hand the child an ambulant object and tell the child to put it in a position relative to the chair (e.g. "put on"). Guide the child to get up from his chair, step forward to the base object and place the object in the right position. Provide feedback and guide the child back to his chair. Repeat the instruction and fade prompts over successive trials. Introduce the next position (e.g., "under") and follow the same procedure. Randomize the two positions ("on" and "under") until the child differentiates. When the child acquires this skill, introduce a third position (e.g., behind), and randomize it with acquired positions. Continue to add positions until the child differentiates between *on, under, behind, next to*, and *in front of.*
	• *Step 2*: Introduce additional base objects (one at a time) and assess for generalization of the various locations acquired in step 1. Continue introducing new base objects until the child is able to apply all locations to novel base objects.
	• *Step 3*: Place two different base objects next to each other, hand the child an ambulant object, and tell the child where to put it (e.g., "put on chair" or "put under table").
	• *Step: 4*: Place two different base objects next to each other and place objects next to the child. Tell the child to place an ambulant object somewhere (e.g., "put the car next to the chair"). The child must select the correct ambulant object and place it in the right location.
	• *Step 5:* Place two to three different base objects around the room and spread several objects on the floor. (a) Point to an object on the floor and provide an instruction (e.g., "put this/that next to the table" see #41). The child must identify the correct ambulant object and then put it in the right place. (b) Point to a base object and ask the child to put an ambulant object somewhere relative to it. Do not say the name of the base object (e.g., "put the crayon behind that/this one."). (c) Point to a base object and say "put this on that" (or "that on that/that one") while pointing to a base object (see #41 for description of tracking).
	• *Step 6*: Same arrangement and procedures as in steps 4 & 5, but include additional instructions and questions unrelated to prepositions such as "give me the [object]," "What color is the [object]?"

Considerations	• Step 4 requires that the child is able to follow three-step directions (see #165). • Practice incidentally in extra-teaching settings using any base object and any ambulant object ("put the pillow on the table"/Put the pillow on *that* table" (while pointing).

#186	**Basic Expressive Prepositions (2)**

Purpose	• To teach the child describe relations involving the simple locatives *on* and *under, next to, behind,* and *in front of.*

Set up	• A large base object (e.g., chair) and a smaller ambulant object. The child faces the base object.

Procedure	• *Step 1*: Place the ambulant object (e.g. block) in any position relative to the base object, (a chair) and asks: "Where is the block?" Prompt correct answer ("on," "under," etc.) and fade prompts over successive trials. (a) Introduce additional locations one at a time. When introducing a new location, always randomize it with acquired ones. (b) Vary the ambulant object. (c) Intersperse expressive and receptive trials. • *Step 2*: Introduce additional factual questions such as "What color is the __?" (see #120), "What color is this?" (while pointing to an object) (see #122), and questions involving pronominalization (see #144). For instance, point to the block and ask; "What is it?" When the child answers, move it to a location (e.g., under the chair) and ask; "Where is it? • *Step 3*: Place two different base objects next to each other and an ambulant object (e.g., spoon) relative to one of them. Ask: "Where is the spoon?" Prompt correct answer (e.g., "it is <u>under</u> the <u>chair</u>") and fade prompts over successive trials. Place the spoon in another location and repeat the procedure. Continue until the child discriminates between all locations with both base objects. When accomplished introduce additional factual questions (see step 2). • *Step 4*: The instructor places two different base objects next to each other and an ambulant object in each of the possible locations (a total of 10 locations). Asks: "Where is the spoon?" "Where is the cup?" etc. The child answers using prepositions and location (e.g., it is <u>under</u> the <u>chair</u>") and fade prompt over successive trials. When the child scans and answers fluently, "reverse" the question; "What is [preposition] [location]?' (e.g., "What is on the chair?"). Prompt correct answer (e.g., "a cup" or "the cup"). Randomize "What" and "Where" questions and fade prompts over successive trials. When acquired, introduce additional questions unrelated to prepositions (see step 2).

Considerations	• The child may point to the location of an object in cases when you want the child to tell you. In such instances, simply ask the child to tell you where it is. If this becomes a habit, modify your instruction so that you say, "Tell me where the (object) is."

#187	**Self-Referential "Behind" and "In Front"**

Purpose
- To teach the child the locative "in front of" and "behind" relative to the child.

Set up
- The child stands in the middle of the floor with an object in front of the child and another behind the child.

Procedure
- Step 1: Ask: "What is in front of you?" or "What is in front?" (see 'Considerations' below). Prompt the correct answer (e.g., "the cup") and fade prompts over successive trials. Switch objects frequently.
- Step 2: Ask: "What's behind you?" or "What is behind?" (see 'Considerations' below) Prompt the correct answer (e.g., "the cup") and fade prompts over successive trials. Switch objects frequently.
- Step 3: Randomize the questions "What's in front?" and "What's behind?"
- Step 4: Same as Step 3, but when the child answers one or both of the questions, turn the child around and ask: "Now, what is in front?" and "What is behind?"

Considerations
- In the current setup we advise against asking the question "Where is the [object]?" since prompting a prepositional statement ("in front of me" or "in front") may suppress acquired pragmatics (see "Where: Deixis 1 and 2, #154, #155).
- If this exercise is implemented before the child has acquired personal pronouns (see section for "Personal Pronouns"), it may be confounding to include "you" in the question. While omitting it from the question is artificial and contrived, it may be more constructive in the long run.

#188	**Self-Positioning**

Purpose
- To teach the child to follow instructions in which the child positions himself relative to objects.
- To extend the understanding of the prepositions *in, on, under, behind, in front* and *next to*.

Set up
- This exercise can be practiced in the child's natural environments. Use large objects such as boxes, and tables, chairs.

Procedure
- Instruct the child to position himself somewhere (e.g., "go under the table," "go in/inside the box," "go on the chair." (Prompt using full physical guidance and fade over successive trials).

Considerations
- The primary focus is to teach the child to follow simple practical directions. Self-positioning may be extended to answering questions such as "Where are you?" in which the child is taught to report "prepositional proximity" (on the chair, under the table). However, this could undermine acquired

pragmatics (see "Reporting Locations (2)" #75).

#189   "Behind" and "In Front Of" Others

Purpose	• To teach the child the locative "in front of" and "behind" relative to another person.
Set up	• A person stands in the middle of the floor with an object in front of themselves and another behind themselves. The child observes the person from the side, from behind and when facing the person.
Procedure	• Step 1: Ask: "What is in front of [person]?" Prompt the correct answer (e.g., "the cup") and fade prompts over successive trials. Switch objects frequently. • Step 2: Ask: "What's behind [person]?" Prompt the correct answer (e.g., "the cup") and fade prompts over successive trials. Switch objects frequently. • Step 3: Randomize the questions "What's in front? [person]" and "What's behind [person]?" • Step 4: Same as Step 3, but when the child answers on or both of the questions, the person turns around and the questions are asked again.
Considerations	• Teach both locatives from one vantage point at a time (e.g., first the child observes the person from the side, then from behind and finally when facing her). • When the child is proficient with all vantage points, include more than one person. Consequently, the child will have to shift attention across persons.

#190   "Front" and "Back": Aspects of Objects

Purpose	• To teach the child the aspects "front" and "back" in preparation for teaching the prepositions "in front" of and "behind" relative to object's fronts and backs (see "Object Relative in Front and Behind" #191).
Set up	• Use base objects with a distinct front and back such as dolls, cars, and chairs.
Procedure	• Place an object in front the child and ask: "Show me the front/the back" or "Where is the front/back?" • You may teach one aspect (e.g., in front) using multiple exemplars before introducing the second (back) or teach both front and back simultaneously across multiple exemplars.
Considerations	• Objects with fronts and backs vary considerably in terms of distinctness of these features. For instance, while some 'objects' such as people and certain animals have intrinsic front and backs, other objects require an

understanding of their use. For instance, the front and back of a book requires an understanding of how it is used and the front and back of a T-shirt requires an awareness of how it sits on your body.

#191   Object Relative "In Front" and "Behind"

Purpose	• To teach the child the locative "in front" of and "behind" relative to objects with intrinsic fronts and backs.
Set up	• Use base objects with a distinct front and back such as dolls, cars, and chairs and a variety of ambulant objects.
Procedure	• *Receptive*: Give the child an object and instruct the child to put it in front and behind a base object. Vary the child's position with respect to the base object (i.e., the child approaches the object from different places). • *Expressive:* Place ambulant objects in front and behind base objects and ask the child "Where is the [object]?" Vary the child's point of view.

#192   Asking "Where" Questions

Purpose	• To teach the child to ask "Where" questions when the child is unable to locate an object. • *Note*: This is an extension of "Requesting from Second Person" (#58).
Set up	• Use base locations, ambulant objects, and an assistant to provide verbal prompting.
Procedure	• *Exercise 1*: Tell the child to retrieve objects from the immediate vicinity (see "Bring me" #36). The objects should be easy to locate. When the child has retrieved two or three objects, request an object that is out of sight but in a position relative to a base object (see, and "Basic Receptive Prepositions (2)" #185). When the child stops searching for the object, the assistant guides the child to you and prompts the child to say "Where?" or "Where is it?" You provide the information (e.g., "behind the shelf") and the assistant guides the child to the object so he can retrieve it. Repeat the segment and fade prompting over successive trials. • *Exercise 2*: Same as above but when the child asks: "Where is it?" point in the direction of the object ("Tracking" #___). Alternate verbal (prepositional) information and pointing. • *Exercise 3*: Same as Step 2, but when the child asks "where," instruct the child to ask another person (e.g., "ask Mom"). When the child requests the object, the person provides the information. Sequence: Instructor: "Get me the fire truck." → Child searches and asks: "Where is it?" → Instructor: "Ask Mom." → Child asks Mom: "Where is the fire truck?" → Mom

answers: "Under the box." → Child: Retrieves the object and brings it back to the instructor. In this exercise the child must (a) change from reflexive pronoun "it" to the proper noun when asking the second person, and (b) return with the object to the right person (instructor). Thus, this represents a two-factor process of pragmatics (adjusting grammar) and taking a detour to achieve a goal (executive function).

Considerations	• The child must be fluent with basic prepositions ("Basic Receptive Prepositions (1) #183, and "Basic Prepositions (2)" #184) and must be able to discriminate between "say" and "do" (#65).
	• Mastery of TPSM (#13) may facilitate this exercise.
	• This exercise exemplifies the interdependence of abilities and the inherent complexity of exercises at this stage. Thus, it is important to recognize the conceptual and pragmatic plurality of Exercise 3; not only does it teach the child to ask "Where" questions, it also requires that he take into consideration what other people know. When the child asks the instructor for information the reference is shared so the reflexive pronoun "it" will suffice. On the other hand, when the child asks someone who does not know what he is looking for he must explicate (i.e. name) the referent. The child must thus *know* what various communication partners knows and do not know and adjust his utterances accordingly. Such apprehension of other people's 'frame of attention" is a core element of social cognition.
	• Additionally, this exercise addresses the distinction between 'task' and 'process'; one of many core deficits of autism. The exercise requires that the child decipher what the task is (what it consists of) in order to get it done properly and efficiently. The *task* in this case is to fulfill the instructor's request (to bring the fire truck to the instructor) and the *process* is to request it from another person. As such, the, distinction between task and process is addressed in an unambiguous way.
	• While "Where" questions are subsumed under the broader heading of prepositions, we are moving beyond the common practice of addressing (teaching) only one thing at a time as we are incorporating acquired skills into a larger and more complex nexus of core programs. As described above, we are incorporating tracking into a framework originally designed to address prepositions and as described in Exercise 3 (just above), we are addressing a core component of social understanding. This skill confluence – the adduction of skills acquired individually is a defining characteristic of "intrinsic program coherence."

Personal Pronouns

#193	**Genitive Personal Pronouns (1)**

Purpose	• To teach the child to respond correctly to instructions involving the genitive (possessive) pronouns "my" and "your."
Set up	• Child and instructor sit face to face.
Procedure	• Tell the child to touch one of your body parts ("touch my knee") and the child's corresponding body part ("touch your knee"). These instructions are randomized and manual guidance is faded over successive trials. • Alternatively, ask: "Where is my/your [body part]?" and prompt the child to point in conjunction with saying "here." An assistant prompts the child from behind. This is a less direct approach (question versus instruction). For some children the latter is a more appropriate starting point. It should eventually be introduced when children do well with the more direct approach.
Considerations	• The child should be fluent with basic conditional discriminations such as "Receptive Colors: Conditional Discrimination" #116) and comparative terms such as "Receptive Big and Little" #127, #128, #129). • For children who struggle with this exercise, it may be helpful to omit words such as "touch" or "point to" (simply present the pronoun in conjunction with a body-part). • Some children are more successful when there is a short delay between the pronoun and the body part (e.g., "my… knee"). • Initially, target one body-part and expand when as the child successfully distinguishes between "my" and "your." Eventually, randomize all body-parts and use different ones when switching from "my" to "your" and vice versa (e.g., "my knee," "your shoulder," "your head," "my elbow," etc.). • Eventually this exercise may be extended to include possessions other than body-parts (clothing, personal items). This change to unattached belongings can be quite challenging since the possessions are conceptual rather than concrete. • For children on the autism spectrum disorder, the very concept of "possession" is elusive and accentuates their difficulties with genitive pronouns. Importantly, "possession" in terms of external belongings is an *idea* based on an unspoken "social contract," not something that can be discerned in terms of physical links or connections. The property of "belonging to" does not have any physicality, as opposed to colors, size and

prepositions which do. As such, genitive pronouns stand apart from other concepts we have discussed so far.

- The development of even rudimentary apprehension of the concept of "possession" is a challenging task and often requires diverse exercises.
- If the child does not demonstrate progress, other exercises should be considered (see "Turn Taking").

#194   Genitive Personal Pronouns (2)

Purpose	• To teach the child to use "my" or "your" when asked "Whose [body part]?"
Set up	• Sit face to face. Another person provides prompts.
Procedure	• Touch one of child's body parts (e.g., knee) and ask "Whose [knee]?" Conversely, touch one of your own body-parts (in an obvious fashion) and ask: "Whose [body part]?"). A second person prompts the child to say "My/your [body part]" respectively (e.g., "my knee," "your head," etc.). Randomize instructions and fade prompts over successive trials.
Considerations	• This is difficult for most children and requires a great deal of practice.

#195   Genitive Personal Pronouns (3)

Purpose	• To teach the child to switch between receptive and expressive personal pronouns (my/your).
Set up	• Sit face to face. Another person provides prompts.
Procedure	• Tell the child to touch one of your body parts ("touch my knee"). When the child responds accurately, point to the body part the child just touched and ask "Whose [knee]?" Randomize instructions of "my" and "your." Sometimes omit the first instruction ("touch my [knee]") and simply point to a body part and ask "Whose [knee]? This omission of the first instruction will ensure that the child does not develop rote response patterns.
Considerations	• The requirement to transform receptive to expressive pronouns is very difficult for most children. This is when many children begin to "reverse pronouns." Thus, what had been "my," is now called "your" and vice versa. Names are no longer fixed. The difficulty of assigning names based on shifting environmental events (context) is a fundamental challenge for most children with autism. In order to assist, it may be useful to pare down the instructions so that when alternating expressive receptive "my/your", simply state the pronoun for receptive e.g., say "my" or "yours" and for the expressive, simply say "whose?" It is imperative that the prompt be

immediate.

#196   Nominal Personal Pronouns (1)

Purpose	• To teach the child to use nominal pronouns "I" and "You."
Set up	• Have the child hold an object (e.g. cup) and you hold a different object (e.g. ball).
Procedure	• Ask the child, "Who has the X?" (e.g. cup) vs "Who has Y?" (e.g. ball). • Prompt correct responses according to who is in possession of each object, i.e., "I have the X/Y" or "You have X/Y." • Make sure to switch possession so that the child will not memorize responses. • It is imperative that when working this and all other pronoun exercises that a "say" instruction is used when prompting, i.e., **Say**, my nose." (See "Say vs Do" #65). Otherwise, you end up saying "my nose," when referring to the child's nose, which is factually incorrect and only confuses an already very complicated learning process.
Considerations	• Sometimes it helps to have only one object that is switched between you and the child. Make sure the child tracks the switch and be sure to prompt quickly.

#197   Nominal Personal Pronouns (2)

Purpose	• To teach the child to use nominal pronouns "I" and "You" when asked "What do I/you have?"
Set up	• Have the child hold an object (e.g. cup) and you hold a different object (e.g. ball).
Procedure	• Ask the child "What do I have?" and alternate with "What do you have?" • Prompt correct responses according to who is in possession of each object, i.e., I have the X/Y or You have X/Y. • Make sure to switch possession so that the child will not memorize responses.
Considerations	• This is another point where children reverse pronouns since "I" had earlier referred only to the child, now it refers to the instructor and vice versa. • As earlier, it may help to have only one object which is switched between you and the child. Make sure the child tracks the switch and be sure to get the prompt in quickly • Be careful that if you use behavior specific praise, that you avoid reversing the pronoun, i.e., such that if the child is asked "Whose nose?" and the

child says "My nose," you don't say "good, that's your nose". Rather say something like, "Yes, you said my nose" or to play it safe, avoid behavior specific praise at this early stage.

#198 Nominal Personal Pronouns (3): Combining "what" and "who" questions.

Purpose	• To further the child's understanding of nominative pronouns "I" and "You."
Set up	• Have the child hold an object (e.g. cup) and you hold a different object (e.g. ball).
Procedure	• Ask the child "What do I/you have" and alternate with "Who has the "X/Y?" • Prompt correct responses according to who is in possession of each object, i.e., "I have the X/Y" or "You have X/Y." • Make sure to switch possession so that the child will not memorize responses.

#199 Nominal personal pronouns (4): Shifting speakers

Purpose	• To teach the child to use nominative pronouns "I" and "You," combined with proper names.
Set Up	• Three or more persons are required. • Have the child hold an object (e.g. cup) and you and an assistant each hold different objects. You and the assistant rotate asking.
Procedure	• *Step one*: You and assistant rotate asking, "Who has the X?" (e.g. cup) vs "Who has Y?" (e.g. ball), "Who has Z?" (e.g. spoon). When you ask questions regarding the assistant, the child refers to her by name. When you are the spectator and the assistant is asking questions, the child will refer to you by your proper name and the assistant as "you." Of course, the child always refers to themselves as "I" and when you are asking to "you" as "you." • *Step two*: You or the assistant ask the child "What do you have?" "What do I have?" "What does (person/proper name have?" • Prompt correct responses according to who is in possession of each object, i.e., "I have the X," or "You have Y," "[Proper name] (Sally) has Z". This is more difficult than step one because it requires transforming the pronoun. • Make sure to change what each of you is holding so that the child will not memorize responses.
Considerations	• This exercise is not only matter of answering questions. It entails personal deixis; *the right answer depends on who is asking*. The primary goal is to teach the child to say "you" when the speaker asks the child what the speaker is holding, to say "I" when the speakers asks about what the child is holding

and to use a proper name when the child is asked about what any other person is holding (if that person is not the speaker). This discrimination requires considerable practice.
- If the child struggles with these arrangements, segment instruction into smaller 'switched' sequences as described in step 3 of "Assigning Pronouns to Pictures of Persons (1)" (#203).

#200   Nominal personal pronouns (5)

Purpose	• To teach the child to use nominative pronouns "I" and "You," "We," and "They."
Set up	• The child sits with other persons at table or in a circle. • *Step one*: Instruct the child and another/other persons to do something (clap). Say as one statement, "(Child), (Susan), and (Billy) clap." Ask the child "What did you, Billy, and Susan do?" Prompt "We clapped." • *Step two*: Alternate asking the child individually "(Child's name, clap") and child with others (as in step one) to do something (e.g., clap); "What did you do?" "What did you and Billy do?" Prompt correct responses accordingly, "I clapped," "We clapped." • *Step three*: This time, instruct others as in step one, but do not include the child (your student) "Billy and Susan, clap"; "What did Susan and Billy do?" Prompt correct response, "They clapped." • *Step four*: Randomize all steps.
Considerations	• This should also be taught without using proper names i.e., use a gesture (point) and the designation "You" for whoever is to be included. • Teaching "he," and "she" (expressively) can be addressed using a similar strategy.

#201   Combining Nominal and Genitive Personal Pronouns

Purpose	• To teach the child to assign two pronouns (nominal and genitive pronouns) when both basic nominal personal pronouns (I, you) and genitive personal pronouns (my, your) are required.
Set up	• Child and instructor sit face to face. Another person provides prompts.
Procedure	• *Exercise 1*: Touch one of child's body parts (e.g., knee) and ask "Who has your [knee]?" Conversely, touch your own body part (in an obvious fashion) and ask; "Who has my [body part]?"). A second person prompts, "You have my knee" or "you have your knee" respectively. • *Exercise 2*: Guide the child to touch one of your body parts or one of his own body parts (e.g., knee) and ask "Who has your [knee]?" or "Who has

my [knee] A second person prompts the child, "I have my knee" or "I have your knee" respectively.

- *Exercise 3*: Combine exercises 1 and 2.

Considerations	• This is very difficult for most children. Nonetheless, the ability to track and report 'who is doing what to whom' is basic in language. These kinds of constructions need to be perfunctory.
	• Use of "he," "she," "his," and "her" combined also with proper names (e.g., Billy has her arm, He has her arm, I have her arm, etc.) can be taught using these formats. These uses should be further developed when the question is changed, e.g., "What did you do?" → "I touched her arm," "He touch my head," "You touched his arm," etc.).

#202   Assigning Pronouns to Pictures of Persons (1)

Purpose	• To teach the child to use "you" and "me" in response to questions regarding pictures of persons.

Set up	• Sit with the child at a table. Display pictures of familiar persons. The display should include pictures of the child and the instructor. An assistant prompts the child from behind.

Procedure	• *Step 1*: Present a picture of a familiar person and ask: "Who is it?" and the child answers (see "Expressive Naming (3)" #49). Then hold up a picture of the child and ask: "Who is it?" The assistant prompts the child to say: "Me." Repeat this segment and fade prompts over successive trials. Randomize pictures of the child and other persons. The instructor should <u>not</u> present pictures of herself at this stage. When the child is proficient, go to step 2.
	• *Step 2*: Display a picture of yourself and ask: "Who is it?" The assistant prompts: "You." Randomize pictures of yourself, the child, and other familiar persons. Fade prompts over successive trials until the child answer "you," "me," and the names of third persons correctly.
	• *Step 3*: Present pictures and ask questions. The pictures include yourself and the assistant who is present at the table. When you present pictures of the assistant, the child refers to her by name. When the instructional segment ends, the child gets a short break. When he returns to the table you and the assistant change roles (i.e., you are now a spectator and the assistant is asking questions). The child will now refer to you by your proper name and the assistant as "you." Continue this 'break and switch' until the child learns this language game.
	• *Step 4:* Present pictures and ask questions. After presenting a picture of yourself and the child answers correctly ("you"), hand the picture to the assistant who then asks: "Who is it?" Now the child must refer to you by your proper name. Continue this role switch until the child is proficient.
	• *Step 5*: Display pictures of familiar persons on the table. The display should

include pictures of the child, you, and the assistant who is present at the table. Point to a picture and ask: "Who is it?" The child answers: "You," third person's name, or "me" accordingly. The assistant then points to a picture and asks: "Who is it?" The child answers: "You," the third person's name, or "me" accordingly. You and the assistant alternate asking questions. The child must always take into consideration the person who is asking the question.

| Considerations | • | The primary goal is to teach the child that when the person in the picture is the same as the person asking, he should say "you" and when the person in the picture is someone else he should use her proper name. This discrimination requires considerable practice. |
| | • | This exercise is not only matter of answering questions. It entails person deixis; *the right answer depends on who is asking.* |

#203   Assigning Pronouns to Pictures of Persons (2)

Purpose	•	To broaden the child's understanding of "I" and "you" in response to questions involving pictures.
Set up	•	Sit with the child at a table. Display pictures of familiar persons. The display should include pictures of the child and the instructor. An assistant prompts the child from behind.
Procedure	•	*Step 1*: Direct the child's attention to the display of pictures and say: "Where are you?" An assistant prompts the child to point to his own picture. Prompts are faded over successive trials and when the child answers independently, intersperse with questions of other persons ("Where is Mommy?" "Where is Daddy?" Etc.) You should <u>not</u> include your own picture at this stage.
	•	*Step 2*: Direct the child's attention to the display of pictures and say: "Where am I?" The assistant prompts the child to point and say "here." Prompts are faded over successive trials and when the child answers independently, include pictures of other persons ("Where is Mommy?" "Where is Daddy?" Etc.) The instructor should <u>not</u> include the child's picture at this stage.
	•	*Step 3*: Combine Steps 1 and 2 (all pictures included).
Considerations	•	Switching from using personal pronouns expressively to using personal pronouns receptively to identify persons in pictures is very difficult for most children. Extensive practice is often necessary.

#204	**Assigning Pronouns to Pictures of Persons (3)**

Purpose	• To broaden the child's understanding of "you," "I," and "me" in response to questions involving pictures.
Set up	• Display pictures of familiar persons on the table. The display should include pictures of the child and the instructor. An assistant prompts the child from behind.
Procedure	• Step 1: Direct the child's attention to the display of pictures and ask randomly: "Where are you?" Questions of other persons ("Where is Mommy?" "Where is Daddy?" Etc.) "Where am I?" The assistant prompts the child to point and say "here." • Step 2: Combine with "Assigning Pronouns to Pictures of Persons (2)" (#203) randomize questions.

#205	**Pronouns Combined with Yes-No**

Purpose	• To broaden the child's use and response of "you," "I," and combined with yes-no questions.
Set up	• Sit face to face.
Procedure	• Step 1: Perform some simple action (e.g., clap). Ask one of the following questions, "Did I clap ?" "Did you clap?" Prompt the appropriate response. "Yes, you clapped" or "No, you didn't clap." • Step 2: Ask the child to perform some simple action, (e.g., clap). Ask one of the following questions, "Did I clap ?" "Did you clap?" Prompt the appropriate response, "Yes I clapped," "No, I didn't clap."
Considerations	• This is extremely tricky and helps to solidify appropriate assignment of these pronouns. Fluency with previous exercises is recommended before initiating this exercise
Additions and Permutations	• See "Personal Pronouns: Turn Taking (3)" (#208). •

#206	**Personal Pronouns: Turn-Taking (1)**

Purpose	• To advance the child's basic understanding of "my," "your," "I," and "you" in the context of a turn taking routine.
Set up	• Sit across from the child at a table. An assistant prompts from behind. Place

a lotto board or spread memory cards face up on the table   Place a stack with matching cards face down within the child's reach. (ILLUSTRATION)

Procedure	•	The procedure consists of several elaborations of one basic routine. The first step establishes the routine and each subsequent step adds complexity.
	•	*Step 1*: Say: "my turn," and then draw a card from the stack and place it on its match. When done, the assistant prompts the child to say: "My turn," and to draw a card from the stack and match it. This routine is maintained until the child is proficient and takes his turn at the right time.
	•	*Step 2*: This time when the child draws a card, ask immediately: "What do you have?" The assistant prompts the child to name the picture and prevents the child from matching until he answers. The child must use a full sentence: "I have a(n) [object]." (see #112, #113 for pre-requisites). This routine is practiced until the child is proficient.
	•	*Step 3*: This time when you draw a card, the assistant prompts the child to ask: "What do you have?" You answer before you match the picture. This routine is practiced until the child is proficient.
	•	Step 4: This time when it's your turn, delay drawing a card. After 3-4 seconds, the assistant prompts the child is to say, *"your turn"* while pointing to you. You then say *"my turn"* and pick a card and the routine continues.
	•	See Appendix for additional description and ILLUSTRATION of the entire routine.
	•	(WILL you be using pics from the article or do we need additional pics?)

Considerations	•	If this exercise proves difficult for the child, it may be helpful to strengthen and elaborate more basic turn-taking routines (see "Transaction and Turn Taking").
	•	The child must be able to ask questions when instructed to do so ("say… what do you have?" see "Say vs. Do" #64).

#207   Personal Pronouns: Turn-Taking (2)

Purpose	•	To advance the child's understanding of "my," "your," "I," and "you" in the context of a turn taking routine.

Set up	•	Sit at a table, across from the child while an assistant sits behind the child.
	•	Use two picture boards with 4 or more pictures on each. The pictures on each board are of the same things (dolls, balls, cars, etc.) but are not identical. Place one board in front of the child and the other in front of you. Thus, you and the child have a set of the same kind of pictures but with different exemplars. Matching cards are placed in a stack face down on the table.

Procedure	•	This exercise presupposes proficiency with "Personal Pronouns: (#193-201).
	•	*Step 1:* Say *"my turn,"* and pick a card from the stack. The child asks: "What do you have?" You answer (e.g., "I have a doll"), scan the boards and

place the card on the exact match (e.g., doll). The child then says "my turn," picks a card and you ask: "What do you have?" The child answers (e.g., "I have a ball"). Before the child matches, follow up with the question "Whose ball do you have?" The assistant prompts the child to scan the boards. If the corresponding card is on the child's board the assistant prompts the child to say: *"I have my ball"* and match it. If the corresponding card is on the instructor's board the assistant prompts the child to say: *"I have your ball"* and match. The assistant prompts as needed and fades out assistance over successive cycles of turns.

- If the corresponding card is on the child's board the instructor says *"your flower"* and matches it. If the corresponding card is on your board say *"my flower"* and match it. The child now says, *"my turn"* and picks a card. You ask: *"What do you have?"* The child scans the boards to locate the exact match. If the corresponding card is on the child's board he says *"my ball"* and matches it. If the corresponding card is on your board say *"your ball"* and matches. The assistant prompts as necessary and fades over successive cycles.

- *Step 2:* This time, when you say *"my turn,"* pick a card. The assistant prompts the child to ask: "What do you have?" You answer (e.g. "I have a flower"). The child then asks: "Whose flower do you have?" Scan the boards to locate the corresponding picture. (e.g., flower). If it is on the child's board, say: *"I have your flower"* and match it. If the corresponding card is on your own board say: *"I have my flower"* and match it. Upon completion, the child says *"my turn"* and picks a card. You ask: "What do you have?" The child scans the boards to locate the corresponding picture. If the corresponding picture is on the child's board he says: *"I have my ball"* and matches it. If the corresponding picture is on your board he says: *"I have your ball"* and matches.

- **NOTE:** In response to the question "What do you have?" the child may say "I have a(n) [object]" or "I have my/your [object]." In the event of the former, follows up with the question "Whose [object] do you have?"

- *Step 3:* Same as the previous step, but alternate conditions where you answer: (a) "I have a(n) [object]" thus evoking the child's response: "Whose [object] do you have?" and (b) "I have my/your [object]" thus setting the occasion for the child refraining from asking a further question. Say *"my turn"* pick a card and say *"I have my flower"* or *"I have your flower"* and match it. The child says *"my turn"* picks a card and says *"I have my cookie"* or *"I have your cookie"* and matches it.

- *Step 4:* Say: *"my turn"* pick a card then show the card to the child and ask; *"Whose butterfly do I have?"* The child answers, *"you have my butterfly"* or *"you have your butterfly."* The child says *"my turn"* picks a card and says *"I have my cookie"* or *"I have your cookie"* and matches it.

#208   Personal Pronouns: Turn-Taking (3)

Purpose
- To advance the child's understanding of "my," "your," "I," "mine," "yours," and "you" in the context of a turn taking routine.

Set up
- Same as "Personal Pronouns: Turn-Taking (2)" (#207).

Procedure
- *Step 1:* Pick a card and delay matching, conceal the card and state: *"I have a butterfly."* The child asks: *"Whose butterfly do you have?"* Show the card to the child and ask: "Whose butterfly do I have?" and the child answers: "You have my butterfly" or "You have your butterfly" correspondingly. Once the child answers the question, he takes his turn and the routine is reinstated.
- *Step 2:* Pick a card and delay the matching, conceal the card and state: *"I have a cookie."* The child asks; *"Whose cookie do you have?"* Show the card to the child and ask; *"Do I have my/your cookie?"* The child will respond in a yes/no format using a full sentence (e.g., *"yes, you have my cookie," "no, you have my cookie," "yes, you have your cookie," "no, you have your cookie"*). Once the child has responded, match the card. When the child takes his turn, he repeats step 5.
- *Step 3*: Rather than ask "Whose (picture) do I have?" show the child the card and say, "Whose is this?" to which the child is prompted to answer, "(It's) Mine" or "(It's) Yours" and he takes his turn.

#209   Personal pronouns: Turn-Taking (4)

Purpose
- Increase the child's understanding of personal pronouns.

Set up
- Level 4 incorporates steps 3-4 from Level 2 with an additional person. You and the other person ask the child questions from steps 3-4 outlined in Level 2 and take turns asking questions and being the third person. For instance, person 1 asks *"Whose butterfly do I have?"* and the child answers *"you have his butterfly"* while pointing to person 2. In the subsequent trial person 2 asks the child *"Whose car do you have?"* and the child answers *"I have his car"* while pointing to person 1. Questions should be arranged to elicit as many combinations as possible. Figure 2 illustrates the possible combinations.

Procedure
- Same as above procedure, except with three persons and three set of cards/boards with similar but discrete pictures.

REFERENCES

Koegel, R. L., & Koegel, L. K. (1995). *Teaching children with autism: Strategies for initiating positive interactions and improving learning opportunities.* Paul H. Brookes Publishing Co. Inc.

Leaf, R., & McEachin, J. (1999). *A work in progress: Behavior management strategies and a curriculum for intensive behavioral treatment of autism.* New York: DRL Books.

Lovaas, O.I. (1977). *The autistic child: Language development through behavior modification.* New York: Irvington Publishers, Inc.

Lovaas, O.I. (1981). *Teaching developmentally disabled children: The me book:* Austin, TX, Pro-ed.

Lovaas, O.I. (1987). Behavioral treatment and normal educational and intellectual functioning in young children with autism. *Journal of Consulting and Clinical Psychology, 55,* 3-9.

Lund, S. K. (2001). Content and contingencies: Considerations regarding curriculum development for young children with autism. *The Behavior Analyst Today, 3,* 187-191.

Lund, S. K. (2004). Selection-based imitation: A tool skill in the development of receptive language in children with autism. *The Behavior Analyst Today, Vol. 5, No 1,* 27-36.

Lund, S. K., & Eisenhart, D. (2002, May). Establishing icon-based communication in children with autism and severe cognitive delay. Poster presented at the *28th Annual Convention of the Association for Behavior Analysis,* Toronto, Canada.

Maurice, C., Green, G., & Luce, S. (1996). *Behavioral intervention for young children with autism: A manual for parents and professionals.* Pro-ed, Austin, Texas (181-194)

Miller, G. A., Galanter, E., & Pribram, K. H. (1986). *Plans and the structure of behavior.* New York: Adams-Bannister-Cox.

Niemann, G. W. (1996). The neurodevelopment of autism: Recent advances. ACCP Occasional Papers, No. 13, Advances in the assessment and management of autism. Schreibman, L., & Pierce, K. (1993). Achieving greater generalization of treatment effect in children with autism: Pivotal response training and self-management. *The Clinical Psychologist, 46,* 184-191.

Sundberg, M. L. & Partington, J. W. (1998). *Teaching language to children with autism or other developmental disabilities.* Pleasant Hill, CA: Behavior Analysts. Sundberg, M.

L., & Michael, J. L. (2001). The benefit of Skinner's analysis of verbal behavior for children with autism. *Behavior Modification, 5*, 698-724.

Taylor, B.A., & McDonough, K.A., (1996). Selecting teaching programs. In C. Maurice, G. Green, & S. Luce (Eds.), *Behavioral intervention for young children with autism: A manual for parents and professionals* (pp. 63 - 177). Austin, Texas: PRO-ED.

Thompson, T. (2005). Paul E. Meehl and B. F. Skinner: Autitaxia, Autitypy, and Autism. *Behavior and Philosophy, 33* 101-131.

Wittengenstein, L. (1953). *Philosophical investigations*. New York: Macmillan

APPENDIX

Figure 1

Figure 2

Figure 3

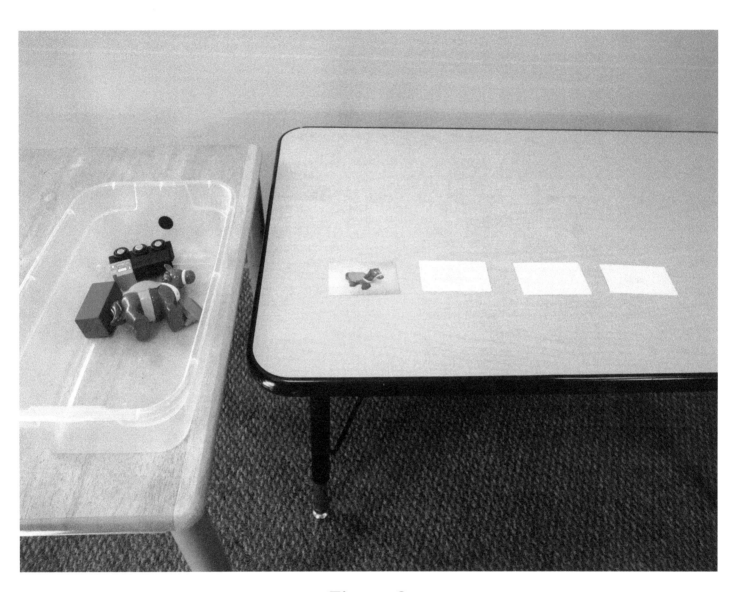

Figure 3

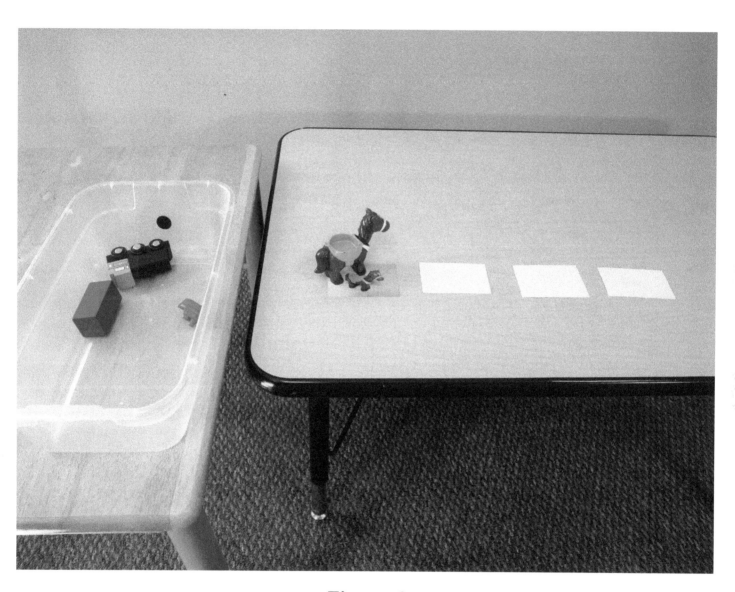

Figure 4

Figure 5

Figure 6

Figure 7

Figure 8

Figure 8

Figure 9

Figure 10

Figure 11

Figure 12

Figure 13

Figure 14

Figure 15

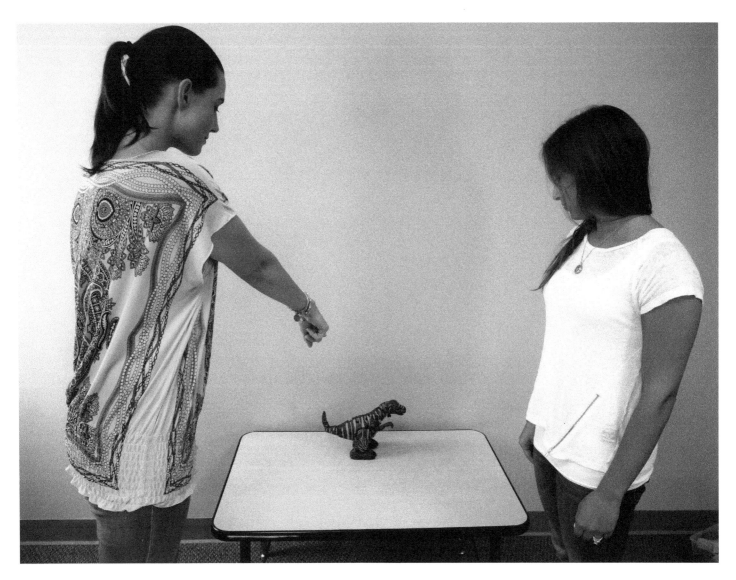

Figure 16

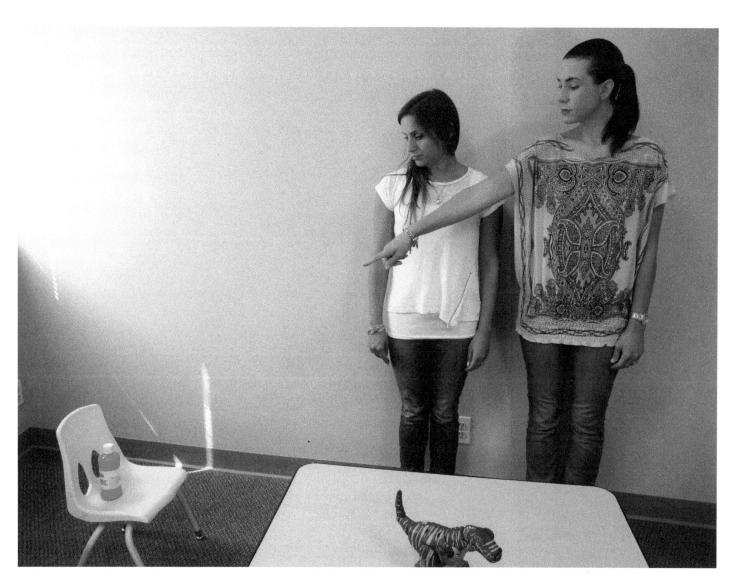

Figure 17

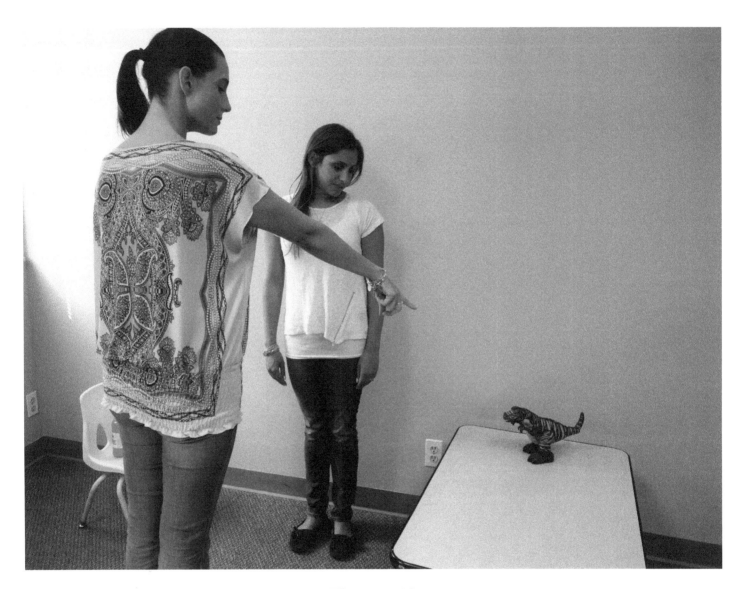

Figure 18

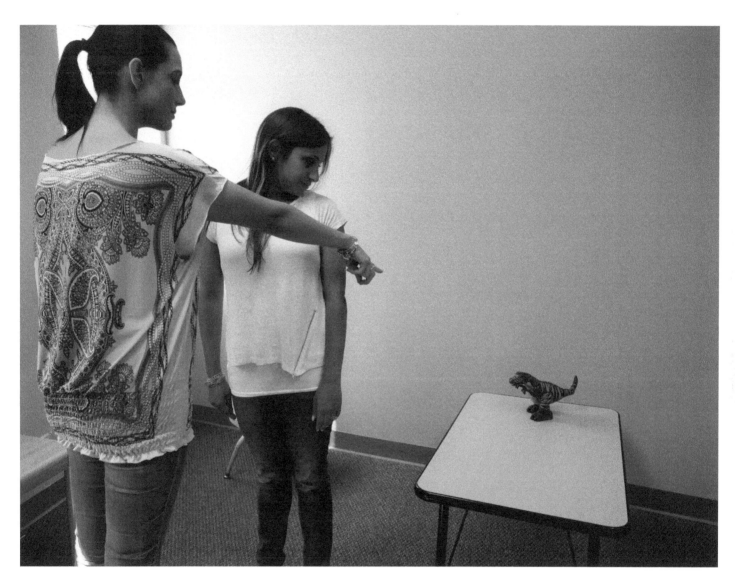

Figure 19

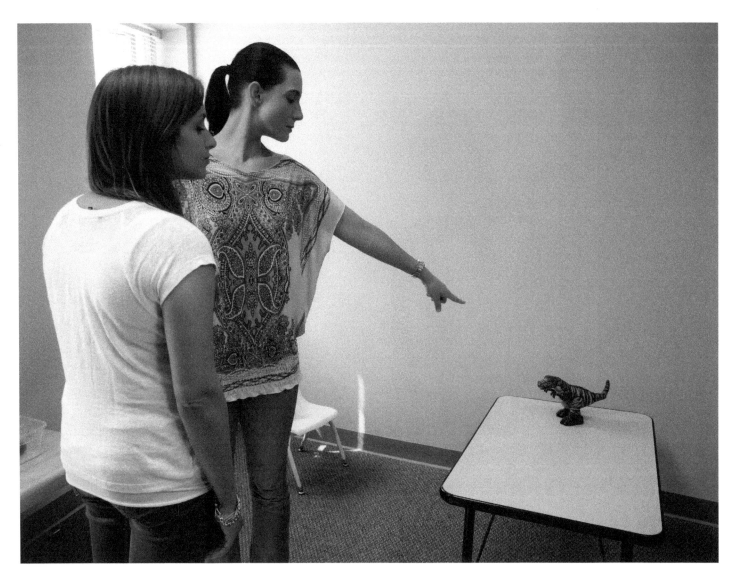

Figure 20

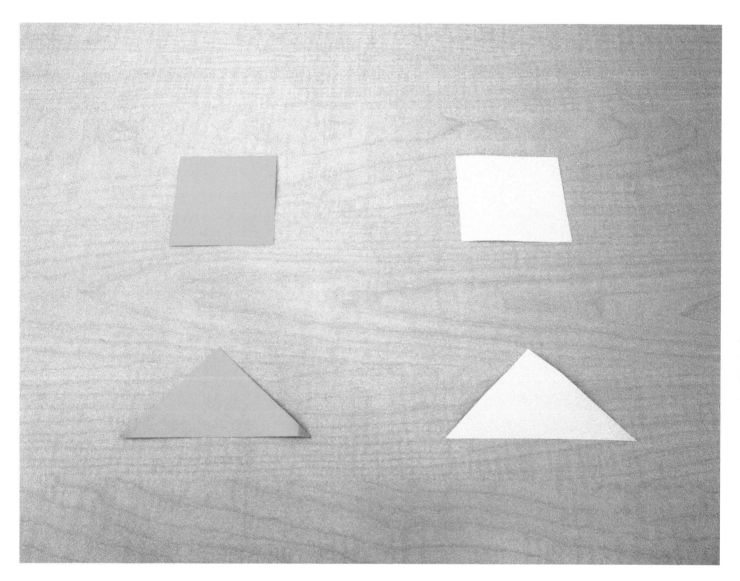

Figure 21

Figure 22

Figure 23

Figure 24

Figure 25

Figure 26

(Footnotes)

1   Lund, S. K., & Eisenhart, D. E. (2002, May). *Establishing icon-based communication in children with autism and severe cognitive delay*. Poster presented at the 28th Annual Convention for the Association for Behavior Analysis. Toronto, Canada.

The islands' lifeline

Miles Cowsill • Colin Smith

NorthLink

Ferry Publications

Published by: Ferry Publications, PO Box 33, Ramsey, Isle of Man IM99 4LP
Tel: +44 (0) 1624 898445   Fax: +44 (0) 1624 898449   E-mail: ferrypubs@manx.net   www.ferrypubs.co.uk

Contents

Produced and designed by Ferry Publications trading as Lily Publications Ltd
PO Box 33, Ramsey, Isle of Man, British Isles, IM99 4LP
Tel: +44 (0) 1624 898446   Fax: +44 (0) 1624 898449
www.ferrypubs.co.uk   E-Mail: info@lilypublications.co.uk

Printed and bound by DW Jones, Wales
© Ferry Publications 2016

Foreword

by Stuart Garrett

The 5th July 2012 saw the transfer of the Northern Isles contract to Serco Ltd, with the safe custodianship of the fleet and service delivery transferring at 15.00 hrs that day.

It is an honour to lead the team, both ship and shore, who deliver the 'North Boats' service and we all feel the responsibility of maintaining the connectivity, both on the Pentland Firth and between Aberdeen and the Northern Isles as has existed for almost 200 years.

To see our house flag, a close match to the original pennant of the North of Scotland & Orkney and Shetland Steam Navigation Company dating from 1873, flying on our port side in harbour, proudly proclaims our presence. Our new livery, introduced at dry dock 2014, however, also shows that bold creativity has its place and has allowed a distinct characteristic to evolve over the last four years that exhibits the subtle differentiation of service delivery and operating environment alliances which we have worked to cement.

Our core values of Trust, Care, Innovation and Pride are obvious and visible in the delivery of our lifeline services: we work closely with the Scottish Ministers' civil servants in fulfilling the contractual obligations inherent in our relationship, ever mindful of the needs of the communities we serve and the particular nuances of the routes and ports to and from which we operate.

Finally I would like to reflect on the service given to the contract, most recently by a number of our Masters. The responsibilities of command are many and varied, but operating over our route network we face, at times, particularly challenging conditions. The professionalism and dedication of all our colleagues is acknowledged, but ultimately those in command of the vessel carry the most significant accountability.

Since 2012 Captain Nigel Barnes, Captain Willie MacKay, Captain David Wheeler and Captain Gordon Cameron have retired and we lost the services of our late colleague Captain Stewart Gunn. The contribution of all is acknowledged in this foreword. Their successors carry on the long

Above: **Stuart Garrett**

lineage of appointment as Master.

So to all my colleagues, key contractors and Port Authorities my thanks for your support in enabling us to deliver the Northern Isles service and to those who are reading this, please enjoy and reflect perhaps on all that has been and continues to be done to maintain these historic routes.

Stuart Garrett
Managing Director
Serco NorthLink Ferries

John,

with best wishes

Stuart—

Above: The *St. Magnus* (IV) prepares to leave Kirkwall for Aberdeen with the *St. Rognvald* (III) ahead of her loading livestock for her 21.00hrs sailing. (Bruce Peter collection)

Below: The *St. Clair* (V) leaves Lerwick on her evening passage to Aberdeen. (Colin J. Smith)

Introduction

During 1999 Ferry Publications published *The North Boats*, the work of the late Alastair McRobb, which offered a full account of the ferry and passenger shipping operations to the Orkney and Shetland Islands, for which he had a great passion and followed for many years. Alastair had the advantage of a career at sea, serving in ships of the North of Scotland, Orkney and Shetland Shipping Company Ltd – the North Company which motivated him to follow the marine operations of the company in great detail for over 50 years. The publication proved to be an over-whelming success, selling not only in Shetland and Orkney but also worldwide, as there has always been great interest in the historical and fascinating ships that have served these islands.

In 2002 NorthLink took over the ferry routes to the islands from P&O Scottish Ferries. A major shift and modernisation in the operations was to take place with the introduction of three new purpose-built ships to serve Orkney and Shetland. NorthLink not only offered an enhanced style and standard of service, but the introduction of their new ferries has opened new markets and has generated substantial growth of tourist traffic to the islands. In addition to improving the passenger operations, two freight ships were acquired to enhance the frequency of sailings for the commercial traders in the Northern Isles.

Those who travel on the services to the islands as 'locals' will know that the shipping operations play a vital role in their everyday life for provisions and trade. The 'Island Lifeline' operated by NorthLink has to be maintained 52 weeks of the year and the current fleet has proved to be very reliable in this role. For those who travel as visitors to Orkney and Shetland it is a fascinating journey to two distinctive island groups, both fiercely independent in their own way from each other and from mainland Scotland, with each island in each group offering its own charm and individual experience. In this edition, Captain Willie Mackay, an Orcadian by birth, describes the journey as master from Aberdeen to Lerwick, via Kirkwall.

Also in this new edition we bring the history of the 'North Boats' up to date, following the appointment in 2012 of international services company Serco Ltd, to run the operations. Since the re-organisation the fleet now appears with their striking logo and Viking Norseman 'Magnus' on their ships. In 2016 the company won the 'Best Ferry' award in the 'Guardian and Observer Travel Awards'.

We hope that this updated and revised edition provides a fascinating read for everyone who has a passion for the Northern Isles and for the ships that have served them today and in the past.

We would like to thank Stuart Garrett, Managing Director, NorthLink for all his help and encouragement with this book. The following should also be thanked for going that extra mile for us with photos and information for the title: Sarah Young, Sara Donaldson, Bruce Peter, Lawrence MacDuff, David Parsons, Willie Mackay, and all of the crew members and staff at NorthLink.

Miles Cowsill, Isle of Man &
Colin Smith, Glamis, Scotland

September 2016

Chapter one

From Sail to P&O Scottish Ferries

Setting the Scene – The Sailing Ship Era

The formation of P&O can be traced back as far as 1790 and the Leith & Clyde Shipping Co (L&C). Thirty-two years prior to the opening of the Caledonian Canal, and with the company possibly only offering a service between Leith on the Firth of Forth and the Clyde, all vessels had to travel via the Pentland Firth, a notorious stretch of turbulent water separating Orkney from the Scottish mainland. The vessels employed at that time were probably small sailing smacks and the service frequency is unlikely to have been better than weekly.

In 1820 the L&C amalgamated with the Aberdeen, Dundee & Leith Shipping Co., to become the Aberdeen, Leith, Clyde & Tay Shipping Co. The positioning of 'Aberdeen' at the beginning of the company title presumably reflected Aberdeen's position as head office and premier port of call, something which has continued until the present day. The word 'Tay' was soon dropped as it was perhaps an area which did not figure greatly in the company's activity, and the name that came to be used for some 50 years was the Aberdeen, Leith & Clyde Shipping Co., which was certainly in use by 1824. This was normally shortened to AL&C and in the 1960s it was still possible to find saloon silverware embossed with their mark. Examples are on display in the Aberdeen Maritime Museum.

Little is known of the early vessels, but we do know that the *Glasgow Packet* was built in 1811

and the *Edinburgh Packet* (simply *Edinburgh* in some accounts) in 1812. Both were built by A. Hall & Co. of Aberdeen, renowned builders of the Aberdeen clippers. The *Glasgow Packet*, at about 82 tons, was somewhat larger than other ships. This early pair presumably operated on the routes signified by their names. For the first three decades of its existence the AL&C operated only sailing vessels and a further four decades elapsed before sail finally disappeared from the scene.

By 1824 the AL&C had four main routes and a fleet of eight ships: three each allocated to the Leith and Glasgow routes and one each to the Liverpool and Rotterdam routes. The frequencies for sailings were 4/5 days, weekly, monthly and six-weekly respectively. Known vessels in the fleet at this time were the *Clyde*, the *London* (or *London Packet*) and the *Marquis of Huntly* serving Leith, the *Rotterdam Packet* and the *Liverpool Packet* serving their namesake ports, and the *Edinburgh*. Fares in the cabin were 15/- , 21/- , 2.5 Gns. and 3 Gns. respectively, which were substantial amounts at the time.

The Liverpool service ceased around 1830/32, while the Glasgow route continued for at least another 12 years, and these services may have latterly operated via the Caledonian Canal after its opening in 1822. The Rotterdam service has not been traced after 1835, but in 1843 there were still seven smacks trading to Leith and Glasgow and, curiously, the *Belmont*, recorded as serving Grangemouth. One of the Glasgow traders was apparently the *Glasgow Packet* (II), or at least her listed tonnage was quoted as less than before, suggesting a replacement vessel of the same name had been introduced at some stage.

Some 17 sailing vessels have been identified as belonging to the AL&C, but there were possibly others. While sail and steam overlapped in the fleet for some 40 years (1821–1860) the earliest steamers did not operate in the winter months, with the Leith route reverting to sail during the winters up to 1937/38 and the long vulnerable Lerwick route up to 1860. Lerwick was served by the *Marquis of Huntly* (formerly serving Leith) in 1828, the *Aberdeen Packet* in 1838/39 and 1843, the

Early Steam Days

Henry Bell's *Comet* is universally acknowledged as the precursor of powered vessels in UK waters and became the first Clyde steamer when she introduced sailings in 1812 between Glasgow, Greenock and Helensburgh, though she did make one foray that year to the West Highlands via the Crinan Canal. The other great Scottish estuary, the Forth, also introduced steamer sailings between Grangemouth and Newhaven (Edinburgh) in 1813, again with the *Comet* which had transferred to the east coast. When she

The *St. Magnus* (I) was built as the Waverley in 1864 for the Silloth-Belfast route of the Northern British Railway. Some three years later she joined the Aberdeen, Leith and Clyde fleet and became both the first vessel to be given the 'Saint' name and their first paddle-steamer. (Ferry Publications Library)

William Hogarth between 1848 and 1852 and the *Fairy* from 1852 to 1860. This last named was probably the largest sailing vessel in the fleet, a topsail schooner of 150 tons and approximating in tonnage to the first two steamers in the fleet.

eventually returned to the west coast in 1819 she became the first West Highland steamer. The Tay was the next area to feel the influence of steam when the *Union* commenced plying on the Dundee to Fife (Woodhaven or Newport-on-Tay) ferry crossing in 1821.

All major Scottish estuarial and island areas had steamer services, if in some cases very minimal, in place within nine years of the introduction of steam navigation and, in the case of the Clyde, some 42 steamboats had been built to work that area by 1820. Open seas were a rather different matter, but in 1821 the Leith & Aberdeen Steam Yacht Co. (L&ASY Co.) placed the *Tourist* on the route linking the two named ports, her maiden voyage taking place on 24th May. The *Tourist* called at eight

period. She arrived in Aberdeen on 2nd July 1821 from the Clyde and made her maiden voyage two days later to Leith. The terminal used was actually the Stone Pier at Newhaven, which was about one mile from the harbour at Leith. Both competing companies' steamers always appear to have berthed at Newhaven but the smacks normally berthed in Leith.

The *Velocity* made the passage south on Mondays, Wednesdays and Fridays, returning on Tuesdays, Thursdays and Saturdays,

The distinctive-looking *Queen* (II) at Victoria Pier, Lerwick. She was the first screw steamer in the fleet, entering service in 1861 and replacing the wrecked Duke of Richmond. (Ferry Publications Library)

intermediate calling places and took around 12/13 hours for the passage, departing from the terminal ports on alternate days.

The AL&C at this time were operating two trips weekly between Aberdeen and Leith with their vessels and, anticipating a loss of trade to the steamer, ordered a paddle steamer for their operations. This was the *Velocity*, built by Denny's of Dumbarton and engined by the Greenhead Foundry. The *Velocity* was 149 gross tons and 112 feet long (deck) and was bigger than nearly all the Clyde steamers of the

departing at 6am daily and calling at Stonehaven, Montrose, Arbroath, Crail, Anstruther, Elie and Dysart. The *Tourist* operated on a similar basis, but always sailing in the opposite direction to the *Velocity*. Both companies appear to have charged similar fares for their steamers of 21/- cabin and 12/- steerage for the single passage, considerably more than on the ships, while intermediate ports were charged on a pro rata basis. At none of the intermediate ports did the steamer go alongside, passengers being transferred by a small boat, a procedure which must have been exciting, if not actually perilous, on occasions.

The L&ASY Co. ordered a second vessel for the trade from the yard of James Lang of Dumbarton. It was intended that she would supplement the *Tourist*'s sailings and continue on to Inverness via intermediate ports. The new vessel, the *Brilliant*, was launched on 9th June 1821 and was 10 gross tons larger and 13 feet longer (deck) than the *Velocity*. Her maiden voyage commenced from Newhaven at 5am on 21st August and appears to have been a direct sailing to Aberdeen before continuing to Peterhead where she lay overnight. The following day calls were made at Fraserburgh, Banff, Portsoy, Cullen, Lossiemouth, Findhorn, Nairn, Cromarty, Fortrose and Fort George, arriving at Inverness at 8.30pm. The return voyage was made in two similar daily passages on 24th/25th August.

The *Brilliant* probably made a further trip to Inverness the following week, after which both companies terminated operations for the season. For many years services operated during the summer only, from about April to early October. The AL&C always substituted their smacks on the service during the winter months, but also kept some of them operating alongside the *Velocity* during the summer to maintain cargo services.

Whichever way the L&ASY Co. had intended to operate their two ships, the *Tourist* was withdrawn for refitting at Leith on 7th August 1821, after which she took up the Leith–London service in mid-September. She appears to have operated thus for a further year, after which she was sold to the London & Edinburgh Steam Packet Co. who maintained that service thereafter.

The *Velocity* and the *Brilliant* both re-entered service in April 1822 after having improvements made to their accommodation. Services had been curtailed to two round trips by each vessel per week and the Inverness visits were not attempted that year as possibly the services previously offered had been unduly generous. Dysart had been dropped from the schedules but both ships were billed to make the Aberdeen to Newhaven passage every Friday, one of the few occasions when they were offering a concurrent service.

The L&ASY Co. altered their schedule at the end of May operating their two Aberdeen trips within the period Monday to Thursday and inaugurating a return Newhaven to Dundee service, outwards on Friday and returning on Saturday. The AL&C possibly saw an opportunity here, for they reintroduced a three-trip weekly schedule for the *Velocity* at the beginning of June, which reverted to the usual two trips in the first week of September. The *Brilliant* came off service in mid-September, being chartered by the Government, and the *Velocity* was withdrawn in early October.

The succeeding years saw similar schedules operated, the 6am start being a regular feature for a considerable period. There were no further experiments as both companies stuck to their twice-weekly service between Aberdeen and Newhaven. However, in 1825 both companies attempted territorial expansion, the L&ASY Co. operated a fortnightly Inverness service during July and August, and both companies made one trip to Wick, presumably to test the market.

Service Extended to Kirkwall

In February 1826 the *Brilliant* was offered for sale due to the expiry of the agreement between the owning partners. The AL&C stepped in and bought her, probably to forestall any further competition (since then, until modern times, the company has never experienced any serious major competition). Only the basic service was operated in 1826, while in 1827 the *Brilliant* made two trips to Inverness and one to Wick. The service to Inverness was organised on a permanent basis in 1829, operating weekly during the summer period. Wick still had an occasional steamer but received a permanent service in 1833, but only fortnightly initially and only during the summer. The Wick steamer this year also extended her run to Kirkwall on a permanent basis after having made a test run the previous year.

The company was now operating the three services (Newhaven, Inverness and Wick/Kirkwall) with the two original steamers and the provision of additional tonnage was becoming imperative. In 1836, therefore, the *Sovereign* appeared, at 378 tons she was more than twice the size of the earlier pair. The *Sovereign* introduced the system of giving the ships names with a monarchical flavour; a system that was to be employed for the next 25 years. The year 1836 was significant in that the Wick/Kirkwall service became a weekly one and was also extended to Lerwick, initially on an alternate week basis. After a decade cautiously experimenting in northern waters and gradually increasing services, 1836 marked the origins of P&O Scottish Ferries' service pattern, before NorthLink took over the operations to Orkney, a service little altered until 2002. In 1838 the company obtained the mail contract and have continued to provide mail services ever since.

Eventually, trade justified keeping the service running in the winter months. This probably commenced with the Aberdeen to Newhaven service in 1838, as an additional vessel, the *Duke of Richmond*, slightly larger than the *Sovereign*, was built that year. Winter services were introduced in 1848 for Inverness, in 1850 for Wick and in 1858 for the islands. Earlier, in 1840/41, the Edinburgh terminal had been moved from Newhaven to Granton, about a mile further west.

Services were basically unchanged in the period 1836 to 1859, although there were a number of fleet changes. The *Brilliant* was lost when wrecked on the North Pier at Aberdeen in 1839 and replaced by the three-year-old *Bonnie Dundee* in 1840. The *Velocity* was sold in 1844 and replaced by the *Queen* (I), which had been built for the company. The fleet was maintained at four vessels most of this time but two additional vessels were acquired in 1849. The first was the two-year-old *Newhaven* from the Brighton & Continental Steam Packet Co. (a thinly disguised 'cover' name for the London Brighton & South Coast Railway Co., who operated a cross-Channel service), but she was only retained for a year and a half and then sold in 1851. The other vessel was the *Hamburg*, built for the company as their first iron ship, but she was herself sold in 1852. Generally, services could be maintained by three vessels, so a fleet of four was probably adequate to cover overhaul etc. and so an increase to six in the years between 1849 and 1852 appears curious.

After 13 years with the company the *Bonnie Dundee* was sold in 1853, thus reducing the fleet once again to three vessels. It appears that it was in this year that Aberdeen to Granton sailings ceased as a separate service; the northern sailings invariably commenced at Granton, with Aberdeen being effectively an

The *St. Magnus* (I) (ex Waverley) at Lerwick. (A. Deayton collection)

intermediate port of call. It is unclear when the places between Aberdeen and Granton ceased to be called at and as the section between Arbroath and Aberdeen was finally rail-connected in 1850 they probably fell victim to this new mode of transport at that time. The ports along the Fife coast section were progressively rail-connected between 1863 and 1883, but by the early 1850s there were other competing steamboat owners operating in the Firth of Forth and they had probably taken over the local traffic by then. For most, if not all, of the period between 1821 and around 1850 the intermediate calling places on the east coast remained as Stonehaven, Montrose, Arbroath, Crail, Anstruther and Elie. Johnshaven (between Stonehaven and Montrose) was employed from 1824 to around 1831, and possibly later, and Largo (west of Elie) was mentioned in 1853. Dysart may have been dropped at the end of the first (1821) season but was also mentioned in 1853. One other vessel joined the fleet in 1847, the smallest ever owned by the company. This was the tug *Victory* and her main function appears to have been to tender to the other vessels, as and when required. She was stationed in Aberdeen and apart from tendering to vessels lying in the harbour she apparently also carried out this function on occasions when AL&C vessels lay off Aberdeen instead of entering, presumably when tidal conditions or commercial considerations so dictated.

From 1850 an additional sailing was provided to Wick, which was extended to Scrabster in 1852. This was the start of the Caithness route, a service which operated for over 100 years. On its introduction it was usual for Wick to be dropped from the 'indirect' steamer's itinerary during the winter months. 'Indirect' in this context referred to the Aberdeen–Wick–Kirkwall–Lerwick route as opposed to the 'direct' Aberdeen–Lerwick route which only commenced in 1891. For virtually all its existence the Caithness steamer left Granton on a Monday or Tuesday, calling at Aberdeen the same day, and after making the north calls returned to Granton on Thursday evenings.

The very early steamers were in the 150 to 400 ton range but the *Duke of Richmond* was around 500 tons and the *Hamburg* was almost 700 tons. Apart from the coastal east coast sailings, the usual pattern up to 1859 saw departures from Newhaven/Granton on Mondays for Caithness, Tuesdays for Inverness, the usual calling ports (thought not necessarily every trip) being Banff, Cullen, Lossiemouth, Burghead, Cromarty, Invergordon, and Fort George. The Friday sailing was to Wick, Kirkwall and Lerwick and normally all sailings called at Aberdeen in both directions. The Inverness service was terminated in 1859, no doubt due to the fact that Aberdeen and Inverness were rail linked in 1858, but strangely it was reintroduced in 1874 for one year only.

The *Queen* (I) was lost when she struck the Carr Rock off Fife Ness on 19th April 1857 and the *Duke of Richmond* was another loss on 8th October 1859 when she became stranded on the Aberdeenshire shore about one-and-a-half miles north of the River Don. To compensate, the new *Prince Consort* joined the fleet in March 1858 while the *Hamburg* was re-purchased from her Grimsby owners in 1860. However, the fleet was down to two vessels for much of the period 1857 to 1860 and a number of chartered vessels were employed to assist, this being the first occasion that chartering was recorded. They included the *Commodore* (1857/58); the *Earl of Aberdeen* (1857/58); and the *Duke of Rothesay* (1858). All three came from the Aberdeen Steam Navigation Co. who operated the Aberdeen to London service.

To reinstate the fleet to four vessels the *Queen* (II) was built in September 1861 and was effectively a replacement for the *Duke of Richmond* which had been lost two years earlier. The *Queen* (II) was noteworthy in that she was the first screw steamer in the fleet. The *Hamburg* was wrecked on Scotston Head in October 1862 and the *Prince Consort* was seriously damaged in May 1863 when she struck the North Pier at Aberdeen. She was sold in that condition, the purchaser reconstructing her and selling her back to the AL&C later the same year. Initially the *Dundee* was chartered from the Dundee, Perth & London Co. to provide cover, as this mishap had reduced the fleet to two vessels. Another paddler, the *Vanguard*, was later purchased from the Steam Packet Co. of Dublin to temporarily fill the gap

The *St. Clair* (I) entered commercial service in 1868. (Bruce Peter collection)

and she brought ship strength up to three initially, and to four once the *Prince Consort* rejoined the fleet. Unfortunately the *Prince Consort* was herself wrecked on the Altens Rock, a couple of miles south of Aberdeen, on 11th May 1867 and as this left the AL&C with only two vessels once again, the *Princess Alice* was chartered from the Aberdeen & Newcastle Shipping Co. until a replacement could be found, while the *Dundee* was also on charter during April and May. The following two decades were loss-free and the AL&C appears to have been more unfortunate than most in that four vessels, the *Queen* (I), the *Duke of Richmond*, the *Hamburg* and the *Prince Consort* had all been lost through marine peril in the decade 1857 to 1867.

The New Dawn

While the geographical extension of services had followed a slow continuous pattern over the years, the links with the outlying areas and Aberdeen/Leith, with the possible exception of Wick, had invariably been on the basis of a weekly call at best. All this was to change in 1866 when a second ship was allocated to the 'indirect' route, known as the 'secondary indirect' vessel. The basic schedule was Granton (Tuesday); Aberdeen (Wednesday);

Kirkwall (Wednesday/Thursday); Lerwick (Thursday/Friday); Kirkwall (Friday); Aberdeen (Saturday); Leith (Saturday). The *Queen* (II) was the first to be allocated to this route. This service appears to have operated only during the summer, although this was modified after 1937 and was continued in one form or another until 1966. The replacement for the *Prince Consort* was the *Waverley*, the first of that name, originally built in 1864 for the Silloth–Belfast route of the North British Company. Early in 1867 she was overhauled and fitted out on the Tyne and entered north service at the end of that year. She was renamed *St. Magnus* (I), commencing a style of nomenclature still in use some 130 years later. She was also noteworthy in that she was the last paddler to join the fleet, and the only two-funnel vessel ever owned (until the introduction of the ro-ro vessels). She was of similar size to the *Hamburg*, the *Prince Consort* and the *Vanguard* and was generally employed on the 'indirect' route. Presumably to minimise stress on her paddle wheels, she appears never to have done any winter work in her long career and would normally appear in service between mid-March and mid-April and would then be laid up from about the end of October.

In 1868 the *Vanguard* was sold for breaking

up and was replaced the same year by the new *St. Clair* (I), the second screw steamer in the fleet. Although slightly greater in tonnage than the *St. Magnus* (I) she was 20 feet shorter and initially operated the Caithness service, commencing in March of that year.

From 1821 to 1867 some 13 steamers had joined the AL&C and of them six had been second-hand purchases, each averaging nine years with the company. New vessels in that period had averaged 15 years in company service. The introduction of the *St.Clair* (I) in 1868 must have marked a major turning point in the company's economic circumstances as for the next 45 years all vessels built for the AL&C arrived new from the builders. It was only the outset of the 1914–18 war that reversed this trend.

The *St. Clair* (I) was followed in 1871 by the *St. Nicholas*, the only time this name was ever used and one of the few occasions when a 'Saint' name has never been repeated. The *St. Nicholas* took over the Caithness service and she and the *St. Clair* (I) largely shared the route between them until the turn of the century. These vessels were clipper-bowed and were difficult to tell apart, their sterns being their most differentiating feature.

By this time there was a fleet of four ships. The *St. Nicholas* was the largest, while the *Queen* (I) was the smallest. It was an exceptionally modern fleet in 1871: the *Queen* (10 years old), the *St. Magnus* (7 years), the *St. Clair* (3 years), plus the new *St. Nicholas*. The average age profile of five years was never to be attained again.

The North Company

In June 1875 the Aberdeen, Leith & Clyde Shipping Co. became the North of Scotland & Orkney & Shetland Steam Navigation Company – usually abbreviated to the 'North Co.'.

In 1881 it was decided that Shetland would receive a third weekly sailing and this was inaugurated by the *Queen* (II) as a seasonal summer sailing that year. There was one major alteration, in that after leaving Aberdeen she proceeded to Stromness and Scalloway, rather than Kirkwall and Lerwick, thus servicing the western side of the two island groups. Due to

the difficulties in road travel in Shetland, this service also called at various west coast ports including Spiggie, Walls, Brae, Voe, Aith and Hillswick, generally fortnightly in summer and monthly in winter. Hillswick, where the company opened their own St. Magnus Hotel in 1900, was served weekly during the summer. Occasional calls were also made at Reawick or Ronas Voe (an important fishing station during the season) but these did not appear in the timetables. Orkney was not totally neglected as the southbound steamer normally called at St. Margaret's Hope fortnightly after leaving Stromness.

A Decade of Growth (1882–1892)

From 1836 until 1881 the fleet had always remained at three or four vessels, this sometimes including one or two on charter. The next decade saw the fleet size increase to seven by 1887 and nine by 1892, thereafter it remained at nine or ten until the Second World War. This decade of expansion saw the introduction of a number of new routes and to some extent mirrored the expansion of the Shetland fishing trade.

For about 500 years there has been a ferry crossing between Caithness and Orkney, and it was in 1856 that a locally owned Stromness vessel commenced a steamer service between Stromness and Scrabster, then in 1874 the Highland railway reached Wick and Thurso. In 1877, with the steamer service having obtained the mail contract, it commenced operating the route, with this being seen as a logical extension to the northern main line. When Scapa Pier (two miles from Kirkwall) was opened in 1880, this became the Orkney terminal, Stromness being relegated to a twice-weekly call. The route was apparently not profitable and in 1882 the North Company took it over, building the *St. Olaf* specially for the route. This was the shortest route ever operated by the company and on a daily Monday–Saturday basis. The North Company reinstated Stromness as the home port and Scapa Pier became a daily call in each direction for the uplift and delivery of mail. Hoxa, a headland near St. Margaret's Hope, was a calling place, although not always on a daily

The *St. Rognvald* (I) was built in 1883. She was the first AL & C's ship over 1,000 gross tons and was to inaugurate the Norwegian Fjord cruises in 1886. (Bruce Peter collection)

basis, where passengers were ferried ashore in a small boat.

The *St. Rognvald* (I) joined the fleet in 1883 and at just over 1,000 tons was the largest vessel. She spent most of her career on the main indirect route, and she was the first vessel used following the inauguration of the Norwegian cruise programme in 1886, a series of ten-day cruises from Leith and Aberdeen, between 24th June and 24th August. This was such a success that the company built the *St. Sunniva* (I) in 1887, specifically for this role; her appearance being that of a large imposing steam yacht. The *St. Sunniva* was the first purpose-built cruise vessel in the world and the first company vessel to be built with the relatively new triple expansion engine. Thereafter the subsequent steamships built for the company were fitted out with the same engines.

The Norwegian cruising season usually operated from late May until mid-September and encompassed the Norwegian coast and fjords between Stavanger in the south to Trondheim to the north. A steam launch was used to take ferry passengers ashore at the various ports of call and on certain shore excursions it allowed passengers to re-embark at a different location from their landing point. The *St. Sunniva* cruises were so popular that

the *St. Rognvald* had to be enlisted to take the overflow for the two July cruises in the first year. Henceforth, the *St. Rognvald* was incorporated into the advertised cruising programme every year, apart from in 1890, but her absence from the regular routes meant that the North Company had to charter another vessel for their own domestic services. The *Ethel* (from MacBrayne's) was employed during July/August 1889 and the *Quiraing* (McCallum & Co.) from June to August 1891. The summer tonnage shortage was only cured when the *St. Giles* (I) joined the fleet in 1892.

There was further expansion in the Norwegian cruising in 1888 when the *St. Sunniva* and the *St. Rognvald* were rescheduled for the summer season. The earlier 10-day cruises were extended to 12 days duration and allowed for a regular fortnightly departure from Leith/Aberdeen and weekly when both vessels operated. The *St. Rognvald* had a slightly shorter season than the *St. Sunniva*. This eventually allowed for Saturday departures from Leith/Aberdeen to Stavanger with Tuesday departures from Bergen 10 days later for the return voyage. The first sailing for the 1888 season was for a 21-day North Cape cruise undertaken by the *St. Rognvald* and the final sailing advertised for the *St. Sunniva* was for a Baltic cruise, which did not operate. In subsequent years the programme included one cruise to each of these destinations and in 1898 both vessels made a Baltic cruise, the *St. Rognvald* in May/June and the *St. Sunniva* in August/September. An unusual feature of the cruising programme was that passengers could break their journey at any of the ports of call, returning by the following or any subsequent sailing.

Back in 1877, a company called the Shetland Islands Steam Navigation Company had been formed to provide a steamer service with the *Earl of Zetland* (I) between Lerwick and the Northern Isles of Shetland. Fifty per cent of this company appears to have been owned by the North Company and was fully absorbed by them in 1890. This brought another route into the North Company's operations as inter-island sailings continued as before, with the small *Earl of Zetland* being the baby of the fleet.

Direct Services to Shetland

The next, and final, new route to be introduced to the company's schedules was the 'direct' route from Leith/Aberdeen to Lerwick, with no intermediate calls. This was inaugurated by the *St. Nicholas* in the summer of 1891 and was virtually unique to the main services. It operated twice-weekly departing Aberdeen on Mondays and Thursdays and leaving from Lerwick on Tuesdays and Saturdays, spending the weekends in Leith. During the winter months the route was reduced to one round trip weekly. Perhaps due to the winter overhaul programme, the route was covered by the chartered *Argyll* (Argyll Steamship Company) during the first winter. The *St. Giles* (I), the smallest of the main service liners, was built in 1892 and appears to have been used solely for this route during her short career of 10 years.

The *St. Olaf* also had a very short career on the Pentland Firth route from 1882–1890 and, reputedly underpowered, was sold to Canadian interests. For two years a variety of vessels serviced the route with the *John o' Groats* (McCallum & Co.), the *Argyll* (Argyll Steamship Co.), the *Express* (G. Robertson) and the company's own *Queen* (II) also taking spells of duty. The final vessel during this decade was

the *St. Ola* (I) which commenced service on the Pentland Firth route in 1892. It should be noted that *St. Ola* is the Orkney variation of the *St. Olaf*, hence the change in the ship's name.

Around this time two ships were converted to the relatively new triple expansion engines to increase fuel efficiency, the *St. Olaf* in 1890 and the *St. Nicholas* in 1891, but strangely the *St. Rognvald* (I) was not included even though fuel savings could have been much greater in her case. By 1892 the nine ships in the fleet included four that were no more than nine years old, although the other five ranged between 15 and 31 years old, giving an average of 15 years overall. The routes operated provided a pattern which was to exist, albeit with some adjustments, until 1956 when the Caithness service ceased, or 1975 if the Shetland North Isles routes are taken as the cut-off point. The present ro-ro routes retain recognisable similarities with those other services operated over a century ago.

Consolidation

This next period of change by the North Company was their withdrawal from the Norwegian cruise trade and the replacement of older ships with others that were larger and equipped to a higher standard, improving facilities for passengers and providing greater cargo capacity.

The first new vessel was the *St. Ninian* (I) in 1895. She had spells on most of the main routes, but she was particularly associated with the secondary indirect route for most of her lengthy career. She was effectively an able and sound vessel, bringing the fleet up to 10 ships.On 24th April 1900, on her usual passage from Lerwick to Kirkwall (main indirect service), the *St. Rognvald* (I) ran aground in thick fog on Burgh Head, Stronsay. While all the passengers were safely taken off by the lifeboats, all the livestock was lost. Her deckhouse was subsequently salvaged and now serves as a summer house in a Kirkwall garden.

Unlike their northern routes, where the company had a near monopoly of services, the Norwegian cruising season had attracted quite a few competitors. Both Currie's Castle Line and the Union Steamship Company (prior to

Above: The *St. Nicholas* was built in 1871 for the Caithness service and was the only North Company vessel ever to receive this name. (Bruce Peter collection)

Below: The *St.Rognvald* (II) leaving Leith. (Bruce Peter collection)

their 1899 amalgamation) provided a single cruise in 1887. Wilson's of Hull (from 1886) and Salvesen's of Leith (from 1887) provided regular North Sea crossings/cruises and numerous others were attracted to the scene. Presumably this competition played a part in the North Company's decision to restrict their own Norwegian cruises to a single ship operation following the loss of the *St. Rognvald* (I). After this time the *St. Sunniva*'s programme dropped her longer distance cruises to the North Cape and the Baltic, apart from a Baltic cruise operated in the 1900 season. The programme now consisted of seven fjord cruises followed by the round-Britain cruise lasting about three months at the end of the season. A single fjord cruise in 1902 commenced at Tilbury, apparently the only occasion that this was offered. However, the Norwegian cruising programme was obviously feeling the effects of competition, especially from those companies operating larger ships with better facilities. The Orient Line's *Chinburay* had made a trip from London in 1889 and was joined by the *Garonne* for the July/August season in 1891. In 1907 the North Company only operated six Norwegian cruises while the 1908 season was cut back to two months, although two round-Britain cruises were provided that year, the first cruise sailing anti-clockwise – probably the first time that had ever occurred. Innovation was not entirely lacking though, in 1901 the *St. Sunniva* provided a round-Britain cruise at the end of her Norwegian cruising season proceeding from Leith to Gravesend where the cruise had commenced. This appears to have been repeated every season thereafter. While calls varied from year to year, Torquay, Dartmouth, Plymouth, Isle of Man, Greenock, Oban and Stornoway were usually visited and calls were occasionally made at Dublin, Rothesay and Skye. At least one call was usually made at Stromness, Kirkwall and Lerwick on these cruises, something which rarely occurred on the Norwegian sailings. The year of 1908 saw the end of the Norwegian cruising programme after 23 years. The *St. Sunniva* (I) was converted to a more conventional mail steamer and took over the direct route between Leith/Aberdeen and Lerwick, rarely deviating from this service.

A replacement, the *St. Rognvald* (II), entered service in 1901 and was the second vessel to exceed the 1,000 ton mark. For her first 24 years she was generally operated on the main indirect service. The *St. Giles* (I) was wrecked when she ran aground near Rattray Head lighthouse (between Fraserburgh and Peterhead) in thick fog on 28th September 1902. She was replaced by the *St. Giles* (II) in 1903 which was placed on the direct route. The *St. Magnus* (I) was sold the same year to Gibraltar interests and, whatever perceived failings were attributed to her, she was a most competent vessel during her 36 years with the North Company. Following the disposal of the *Vanguard* in 1868, the *St. Magnus* (I) had been the sole paddler in the fleet. Though little used in the winter periods, she appears to have suffered little from paddle wheel failures and had generally operated a 'long' season, approximately March/April to the end of October. This was curtailed by about a month in the early part of the season from the early 1890s, but from 1896/97 she normally provided the twice-weekly direct service when she was replaced by the new *St. Rognvald* (II). Her final two years were essentially as a 'spare' vessel, being in operation for about nine weeks in 1902

The *St. Nicholas* aground off Wick, c.1902. (Ferry Publications Library)

The *St. Sunniva* (I) was converted to a mail steamer in 1908. (Ferry Publications Library)

This was a small cargo coaster, the first in the fleet, and her intended role is somewhat obscure as she was sold before completion to an Argentinian company.

War and Aftermath (1914–1924)

When the First World War commenced the fleet consisted of eight vessels. The ninth, the *St. Nicholas*, had been lost in June of that year. This was adequate in that five vessels could maintain the main routes with one each allocated to the North Isles and the Pentland Firth, allowing one to be spare. However, during the period 1909 to 1914, two ships had been allocated to the direct route during the summer, reducing the service to one in the winter.

Activities during the war are relatively obscure, although the *St. Ninian* (I) served as a naval ferry for most of the conflict, sailing between Scrabster and Scapa Flow. Three ships, the *Sunniva* (I), the *St. Magnus* (II) and the *St. Margaret* were all chartered out for periods, under the control of G & J Burns Ltd. Perhaps due to this factor, three cargo ships were purchased in 1916, one being the erstwhile *St. Fergus* which, at last, sailed under the company's house flag. The *Temaire* was bought from James McKelvie of Glasgow but only remained with the company for a year before

and only four weeks in 1903. She managed a further 10 years on Mediterranean service, running between Gibraltar and Tangier before going to Dutch breakers.

Another innovation for the company was a Mediterranean cruise departing from London in March 1896, the majority of passengers joining either at Marseilles (on 1st April) or Naples the following day. Lengthy calls were made at Piraeus, Constantinople, Jaffa and Alexandria, returning to Naples on 1st May and Marseilles two days later.

One further vessel remains to be mentioned, the *St. Fergus*, built for the company in 1913.

The distinctive-looking *St. Sunniva* (I). Her cruises ended in 1908 after which she was converted to a mail steamer. This view shows her probably pictured off Aberdeen following her conversion for the Lerwick service in 1908. She was lost in April 1930 after grounding on Mousa. All passengers and crew got ashore safely but bad weather prevented the vessel from being salvaged. (Ferry Publications Library)

being sold again. The third of this trio was the *Cape Wrath* from the Cape Steam Shipping Company of Glasgow.

Three ships were lost during the war, all within a ten-month period. The first was the *Express* which had earlier served on charter on the Pentland Firth for periods between 1890 and 1892. She had been the fourth wartime ship to be purchased in 1917 but was lost in a collision off the French coast in April of that year, achieving the dubious distinction of having the shortest career of any North Company vessel. What she was doing so far from 'home' is unknown, but she could have conceivably been a supply vessel for the British Army in France. On 12th September 1917 the *St. Margaret*, on passage from Lerwick to Iceland, was torpedoed 30 miles east of the Faroes and sank rapidly with the loss of five of her crew. Her master was Captain William Leask who sailed 150 miles to Shetland in a lifeboat with 18 of his crew landing at Hillswick after three days. Captain Leask was later in command of the *St. Clair* (I) when she was attacked by a submarine off Fair Isle on 19th January 1918, when two of the crew were killed. The attackers were driven off and Captain Leask received the DSC for this action. The final loss was the *St. Magnus* (II) due to enemy action off Peterhead on 12th February 1918 while on a passage from Lerwick to Aberdeen. Two passengers and one crew member were lost at that time.

The company made a fifth purchase in 1918 when the *Cape Wrath* was obtained from G & J Burns and renamed the *Ape*, though the change in the name style has never been explained. She was lost post-war after striking rocks in St. Malo Roads on 13th April 1919, suggesting that her role may have been as a replacement for the *Express*.

At the end of the war the fleet stood at nine, one more than in 1914, but there were some major changes. Three of the fleet were now small cargo coasters and there were only four main-line service vessels, the youngest, the *St. Rognvald*, being 17 years old and with the average age of this quartet being 30 years. With the loss of their two newest vessels, the average age of the fleet was 26 years, five years more than when the conflict started.

The conditions in the post-war depression years meant that there was no newbuild programme. The loss of the *Fetlar* (I) was made good by the purchase of the 36-year-old *Cavalier* from MacBraynes in 1919, which was renamed the *Fetlar* (II). She only remained in the fleet for a year and spent part of her service on the North Isles route. A second purchase from MacBrayne's, also in 1919, was their *Chieftain* which was renamed the *St. Margaret* (II) and was employed on the west-side service. Passenger services were curtailed immediately after the war mainly because the *St. Ninian* did not reappear from her post-war reconditioning until the winter of 1919. The 1919 summer programme consisted only of the direct (once-weekly), the main indirect and west-side services. There was no secondary indirect service or Caithness steamer. Services were nearer normality in 1920 but the *St. Sunniva*, although reverting to twice-weekly service between Aberdeen and Lerwick, did not call at Leith. This may have been due to the inflationary cost of coal and numerous strikes at this period, or to the shortage of experienced officers. The Caithness service was not fully restored until the 1921 season.

From 1921 the allocation of main-line service vessels was:

Direct	*St. Sunniva* (I)
Main Indirect Direct	*St. Rognvald* (II)
Secondary Indirect	*St. Ninian* (I)
West-side	*St. Margaret* (II)
Caithness	*St. Clair* (I)

The *St. Ola* and the *Earl of Zetland* operated on the minor routes with the *Cape Wrath* and *St. Fergus* looking after cargo commitments. As the secondary indirect route was a summer-only service, there was always a spare vessel to cover winter overhauls.

Between the Wars (1924–1939)

The economic climate had been improving during the early part of the 1920s and the *St. Magnus* (III) joined the fleet in 1924, the first newbuild ship since the two in 1912/13. She replaced the *St. Margaret* (II) which was sold to Canada in 1925 after only six years in the fleet

The *St. Rognvald* (II) arriving at Leith after the Second World War. She was not broken up until 1951, after 50 years of service. (Ferry Publications Library).

and had a long and honourable career in British Columbia until 1945. The arrival of the *St. Magnus* (III) marked a considerable increase in the size of the main-line vessels. Apart from the two *St. Giles* vessels, virtually all the main-line steamers from 1868 had been between 700 and 1,100 tons gross. The *St. Magnus* (III) was relatively massive at almost 1,600 tons gross and with considerable passenger accommodation, originally 234 berths in the First Class and 84 in the Second Class, a combined total which was not to be exceeded until the introduction of the ro-ro ferries some 50 years later. While many of the cabins were 2/4 or 4-berth, the original configuration included two 16-berth cabins and one 8/18-berth cabin which was in the First Class area! Strangely there were no 2-berth cabins and Second Class passengers were restricted to two 42-berth cabins. The three main public rooms in the First Class section were also

adaptable in that the settee seating around the sides was convertible to an upper and lower bunk configuration and by this means it added 16 berthed passengers in the smoking room, 16 in the winter dining saloon and 24 in the summer dining saloon helping to accommodate the peak of extra summer passengers. The *St. Magnus* (III) also broke new ground in that she had three hatches and corresponding holds, Numbers 1 and 2 forward, and Number 3 aft. Previous vessels had been provided with single holds fore and aft. The impression of size was further enhanced by the three-deck bridge structure, an innovation giving the wheelhouse etc., officers' accommodation and the smoking room (lounge). In all previous vessels the smoking room, where provided, had been sited at the aft deck house. On the introduction of the *St. Magnus* (III) she was placed on the main indirect route, displacing the *St. Rognvald* (II) to the west-side route.

Four years later (1928) the *St. Clement* (I) joined the fleet, replacing the *Cape Wrath* after 11 years of service. The *St. Clement* (I) was another cargo ship but also innovatory in that she had limited passenger accommodation for 12 in the mid-ship accommodation block. Her main duty was as winter Caithness steamer from approximately mid-October to May, although in the late 1930s she was terminating about a month earlier. Her other main duty was to relieve the *Earl of Zetland* (I) for approximately three to four weeks generally during late September–early October, she had only a limited passenger certificate for this duty. During early September she normally spent two to three weeks as a seasonal livestock carrier, shipping sheep and cattle from the islands to Aberdeen. For the remainder of the summer she varied her activities between coping with 'overflows' on the main routes and acting as a general tramping coaster, frequently loading coal cargoes from Granton, Burntisland, Blyth, Seaham, Amble etc. to various destination ports, not necessarily in the northern islands, work which was very much the domain of the *St. Fergus*. Her trading area extended from Stornoway to Hamburg and London.

Loss of the St Sunniva

In 1930 the North Company experienced their final peacetime ship loss when the *St. Sunniva* (I) ran aground on rocks on the island of Mousa on the morning of Thursday 10th April while on passage to Lerwick. All passengers were saved but the ship broke up and sank two weeks later. Her bell was salvaged in recent years and is now displayed in Lerwick Museum. Coming so soon and prior to the beginning of the summer season with only four main-line steamers out of the necessary five, a replacement was needed quickly. This took the form of the *Lairdsbank* (formerly *Laird's Olive* of Burns & Laird). She was renamed *St. Catherine* (I) and commenced her service at the beginning of June on the west-side route for that season. The *St. Magnus* (III) became the direct steamer and the *St. Rognvald* (II) reverted to the main indirect route.

The *St. Catherine* (I) was obviously a stop-gap and a new ship, the *St. Sunniva* (II), entered service at the beginning of June 1931. In many ways the *St. Sunniva* (II) was an anachronism as she perpetuated the clipper bow and figurehead of many of her predecessors and with her white hull, yacht lines and yellow funnel, could easily have been mistaken for a large steam yacht, although the two steam cranes betrayed her true role as a coastal passenger steamer. Although dimensionally slightly larger than the *St. Magnus* (III), her smaller superstructure was largely responsible for her tonnage being about 200 gross tons less than her immediate predecessor. She had 112 First Class berths, less than half the capacity of the *St. Magnus* (III), of which 10 were 2-berth cabins. There were 14 2/4-berth cabins and a ladies cabin sleeping 16. The dining room sat 54 and there was a smoking room in the aft deck house. The Second Class gents cabin was able to sleep 54 in berths, probably the largest number every provided for, and in addition there were settees that could have accommodated a further 16 to 18. The ladies cabin had berths for 18 plus settees for four or five. One peculiarity was that the only access to the ladies cabin was by negotiating the gents cabin!

The *St. Sunniva* (II) was placed on the direct route on which she served for virtually all her peacetime service. The *St. Magnus* (III) and *St. Rognvald* (II) reverted to the main indirect and the west-side routes respectively and while the *St. Catherine* (I) was retained for winter operations, it was the company policy to use the *St. Sunniva* (II) for the summer operations only. From her introduction, the *St. Magnus* (III) was originally a summer-only ship (June to September) but did serve on her own route during the winters of 1935/6 and 1936/7 and on the direct routes during the winters of 1937/8 and 1938/9. The winter service on the direct route became a regular duty for the *St. Catherine* (I) and there was the unusual arrangement whereby the direct route had two vessels allocated to it – a summer boat and a winter boat. The *St. Catherine* (I) made occasional appearances on the west-side route outside her normal winter duty and also relieved the main indirect service at times. In

Showing the style and looks of a private yacht, the *St. Sunniva* (II) was probably one of the most beautiful vessels to serve the Northern Isles. (Bruce Peter collection)

July/August 1933 she had a short charter to the Aberdeen, Newcastle & Hull Steam Company but otherwise the summers were idle at the lay-up buoys in the Victoria Dock, Aberdeen.

The *St. Clair* (I) finished her season on the Caithness route on Friday 30th October 1936 for a winter lay-up and in December was renamed the *St. Colm*, the first and only time this name was used. This was to release the name for the new *St. Clair* (II).

Marginally bigger than the *St. Magnus* (III), the internal layout of the new *St. Clair* (II) had the dining saloon, which always appears to have been described on the deck plans of earlier vessels as 'saloon' or 'dining saloon', now described as the 'restaurant'. The saloon was a deck higher than on earlier ships, on the shelter or upper deck, at the fore end, with numerous windows providing good views of the passing scene. Seating was for 56 in tables for two, four or eight. Above, on the boat deck, was the lounge, which was encircled on three sides by an observation saloon. Aft on the boat deck was a small bar. On earlier vessels the 'bar' had been a small room which was actually a

dispensing compartment. Aft of the saloon, and on the deck below, were the 36 cabins, all 2/4-berth convertibles, making provision for 144 berthed passengers. In Second Class, the smoking room was at the after end of the aft deck house, while the far end had two 4-berth and two 6-berth cabins, somewhat unusually in connected pairs so that a 4-berth had to be negotiated to enter a 6-berth. The entrance lounge with four settees separated cabins from the smoking room. On the main deck below there were four 4-berth and five 6-berth cabins, also a small dining saloon to seat 14, the first time this had been provided in the Second Class area. This was the first ship where 'overflow' bunks were not provided in First Class public rooms, but it was possible to set up a further 10 bunks each in the Second Class smoke room and dining saloon. This gave a total of 86 berths in Second Class.

The *St. Clair* (II) spent her first month in service (May 1937) on the main indirect route, but subsequently transferred to the west-side route which she served for the three summers prior to the outbreak of the Second World War, though winters were spent on the main indirect route.

On the introduction into service of the *St. Clair* (II), the 44-year-old *St. Catherine* (II) was dispatched to the breakers in the middle of May 1937. This was followed by the 69-year-old *St. Colm* at the end of July 1937. Even with the disposal of these two elderly vessels, the remaining nine-strong fleet still included four vessels of between 36 and 60-years-old. It seems possible that with this age profile, the company was considering a rolling programme of replacements, but in the event only one further vessel was ordered and delivered prior to the outbreak of war.

The introduction of the *Earl of Zetland* (II) in August 1939 was as a replacement for her 62-year-old namesake which had been renamed *Earl of Zetland II* – the first occasion this 'II' suffix had been employed by the company. The new *Earl of Zetland* was truly a liner in miniature and was the first diesel-engined vessel in the fleet. All subsequent vessels were similarly engined. On her introduction to service on the North Isles route, her

predecessor was laid up in Aberdeen, her future uncertain.

The Second World War

The 1939 war can be considered to have arrived in 1938 for the North Company. As early as September that year the *St. Clement* (I) was recorded as having made three trips for naval military purposes: (1) Aberdeen to Flotta with a gun pedestal; (2) Leith to Lyness with (telegraph) poles and motor cars; and (3) Rosyth to Lyness with Admiralty mooring gear. Lyness was the main naval shore base on the island of Hoy for Scapa Flow and Flotta which was the largest adjacent island, both being of great importance once the conflict started.

Most succeeding months saw the *St. Clement* (I) and the *St. Fergus* similarly employed, generally to Lyness, although Longhope, a few miles from Lyness, also featured. Where it has been recorded, cargoes were listed as machinery, huts, motors, tipping wagons, rails, railway sleepers, iron, and in one case, a special charter. The *St. Ninian* (I) also got in on the act with five trips divided between

Another distinctive view of the *St. Sunniva* (II) off Aberdeen. This picture was probably taken during builders' trials in 1931. (Ferry Publications Library)

The *St. Rognvald* (II) arriving at Leith. She entered service in 1901 and spent her 24 years generally on the main indirect service. (Bruce Peter collection)

Lyness and Longhope. Two special sailings were made in August 1939 for Scottish Command (the Army), which were probably Territorials' movements. The first was by the *St. Clair* (II), Leith–Lyness–Leith, which she managed to fit into her normal lie-over refit at Leith. A fortnight later the *St. Ninian* (I) operated Leith–Lyness–Scapa (Pier) before reverting to her normal Caithness route. The Lyness traffic had obviously been increasing and in that month the *Naviedale* was chartered to make three Leith–Lyness sailings. In addition, the *St. Rognvald* (II) terminated one of her southbound July sailings in Aberdeen and returned to Kirkwall to bring a contingent of Territorials south for their annual camp, travelling direct to Leith.

Although the war commenced on 3rd September 1939, the company had been monitoring the situation for a few weeks beforehand and there had been an exodus of holidaymakers and visitors from the islands. The first real disruption to normal schedules came

when the *St. Sunniva* (II) terminated her service at Leith on 27th August and returned to Aberdeen two days later when she was handed over to the Admiralty. She was followed by the *St. Magnus* (III) which had arrived in Leith on the 30th, returned to Aberdeen and was handed over to the Admiralty on the following day. In addition, the *St. Clair* (II) had not proceeded beyond Scalloway on her sailing from Leith on the 27th, but otherwise provided her normal weekly schedule for that week. The *Earl of Zetland* (II) was reactivated after only eight days of idleness to make a cargo run from Aberdeen to Scrabster to assist the *St. Ola* (I) on the Pentland Firth route, which was about to begin the busiest ever period in its history. The withdrawal of two of the main-line fleet units necessitated the rescheduling of the remaining vessels and initially the *St. Ninian* (I) took the rescheduled 28th August sailing from Leith in place of the *St. Sunniva* (II) but her next sailing, from Aberdeen on 1st September, was on the main indirect service and this was terminated at

Lerwick. She then proceeded direct to Scrabster, arriving on 4th September and was handed over to the Admiralty to become the naval ferry for the Pentland Firth service. The withdrawn *Earl of Zetland* (II) after only a few days on the Firth, returned to Aberdeen on the same day. By the second day of the war, three of the main-line fleet had been requisitioned, leaving only the *St. Clair* (II) and the *St. Rognvald* (II) to cope. The *Earl of Zetland* (II) was retained until 2nd October taking cargoes from Aberdeen to Wick, Stromness and Kirkwall, but was then laid up until 26th November, her very limited capacity making her unsuitable, even under the circumstances of the time. The *Naviedale*, joined by the *Rimsdale*, were kept on charter throughout September and October 1939 covering the Caithness route at times, and appearing elsewhere as cargo requirements dictated.

As in the First World War, the purchase of second-hand vessels was restarted to make up fleet numbers and the first of these was the *Highlander*, a passenger cargo ship, purchased at the beginning of October 1939 from the Aberdeen, Newcastle and Hull Steam Co., a vessel roughly comparable to the *St. Magnus*

(III) and which had been laid up at the outbreak of war. A further purchase was the cargo ship *Rora Head* from A. F. Henry & McGregor of Leith at the beginning of December 1939 and somewhat similar to the *St. Clement* (I). Early in 1940 a third purchase was the small coasting steamer *Amelia* (built 1894) and at 357 tons gross was even smaller than the *St. Fergus*. This purchase was of a rather different nature in that she had been owned by Cooper and Company of Kirkwall since 1920, operating a direct Kirkwall to Leith service and the purchase was effectively a takeover of Coopers. To the end of her days Coopers retained their own berths, offices and facilities at Leith and Kirkwall, and the *Amelia* remained, with few deviations, on her 'own' route. Some further problems with tonnage resulted in the Caithness route having to be closed; the final sailing was undertaken by the *St. Fergus* from Leith on 5th April 1940. This was followed by the withdrawal of Scalloway calls as from the Leith sailing on 5th May 1940. The west-side service thereafter proceeded no further than Stromness, though it retained the St. Margaret's Hope calls. The *St. Fergus* was also used when the Scalloway calls were terminated.

The *St. Clair* (II) leaving Leith on her maiden voyage on 29th April 1937. (W. Barrie collection)

During 1939 the attempt was made to continue with the long-standing indirect service, but on five different weeks there was no vessel available. The problem was further confounded in that the round trip was taking on average 8/10 days so that it was unusual to find the same vessel making consecutive sailings. Most sailings employed the *St. Rognvald* (II) or the *St. Clair* (II), but the *Highlander* made two trips. The *St. Ninian* (I) and the *St. Clement* (I) also made one sailing each. There were only four sailings in January and February 1940 and one took 16 days for the round journey from Leith. This was followed by a nine-week gap covering March and April. May was unusual in that five sailings were made, thereafter there were only isolated sailings for the rest of the year. As earlier, Leith–Lerwick direct (June to September 1940), Aberdeen–Lerwick (June to September 1940), Aberdeen–Kirkwall (June to November 1940) sailings were provided by the *St. Rognvald* (II), *Highlander* and *St. Clement* (I). Following her de-requisition by the Admiralty, the *St. Magnus* (III) appeared on her old route with a sailing from Leith on 14th August 1940 but this was followed by a ten-week gap. There were only a further few isolated sailings, all provided by *St. Magnus* (III), the last being on 11th January 1941, after which this service did not resume until 1945.

From November 1940 a major change restricted all main services to a link between two ports and from this date there were separate Leith–Kirkwall and Aberdeen–Kirkwall services. The Lerwick direct service was initially continued with the same vessel, generally loading at both Leith and Aberdeen, and while a twice-weekly schedule could not be maintained, the gaps rarely exceeded a week. Initially sailings were divided between the *St. Rognvald* (II) and the *Highlander*, the latter vessel being replaced by the *St. Magnus* (III) from August 1940. Apart from this, the main services were separated into Leith/Aberdeen to Lerwick and Leith/Aberdeen to Kirkwall sailings, the first of these being effectively a continuation of the direct route. Initially an attempt was made to operate the Kirkwall route twice-weekly and until the beginning of

October the *St. Clement* (I) made half the sailings, the rest being shared between the *Earl of Zetland* (II), the *Naviedale*, the *Rimsdale* and the *Highlander*. There was a three-week gap after this, and subsequently sailings were made at about 5/6 six-week intervals on average, but the intervals tended to be erratic in duration. Following the October 'gap' and until mid-August 1940, the bulk of the sailings were operated by the *St. Clair* (II), the *St. Clement* (I) and the *Rora Head*, a few by the *St. Fergus* and only isolated appearances by the *St. Rognvald* (II), the *Highlander*, the *Naviedale*, the *Berriedale* (another charter) and the *St. Magnus* (III). The *Highlander* had been attacked by enemy bombers 10 miles south-east of Aberdeen on 2nd August after leaving Aberdeen while operating the Lerwick to Leith sailings. Managing to shoot down two of them, a part of the wreckage of one was strewn across the afterdeck when it crashed. For this action, Captain William Gifford received an OBE, two crew members received the BEM and three others, including stewardess Miss Cockburn, were commended. After three weeks repairing damage at Leith she resumed service, but it was thought prudent to change her name and she thus became the *St. Catherine* (II). From late August 1940 the Kirkwall service continued as before, the *St. Catherine* (II) taking half the sailings, the others being shared between the *Rora Head*, the *St. Clement* and the *St. Fergus*. It was while thus employed, on 14th November, that the *St. Catherine* (II) (formerly *Highlander*) was attacked once again after leaving Aberdeen for Kirkwall. Fate was against her on this occasion and after a career of just 13 months with the company she sunk rapidly with the loss of Captain J.G. Norquoy, 13 crew (including seven from the engine room) and one passenger.

Initially, during 1939, the Lerwick service was attempted as a twice-weekly sailing but this was difficult to maintain, October having a particularly poor service with no sailings after the 2nd until the 31st. Most sailings were provided by the *St. Rognvald* (II), the *St. Clair* (II) and the *Highlander*, with the *St. Ninian* (I), the *St. Clement* (I) and the *St. Fergus* all making appearances. From January 1940 the service tended to be approximately weekly with the *St. Rognvald* (II) and the *Highlander* generally alternating until July, the latter vessel being replaced by the *St. Magnus* (III) thereafter. Two 'strangers' appeared, the *Kildrummy* (possibly a charter) for one trip in August and, from May 1941, the *Blyth* (allotted by Ministry of War Transport) which joined the *St. Rognvald* (II) and the *St. Magnus* (III) until August 1941 when the joint Leith/Aberdeen sailings terminated.

The *Earl of Zetland II* was reactivated on 2nd October 1939 and returned as second vessel for the Pentland Firth route, this occupying her until 22nd January 1940. She then returned to her old haunts, the North Isles of Shetland, for the duration of the war and was normally relieved by the *Earl Sigurd* from Orkney. The new *Earl of Zetland* was requisitioned by Scottish Command and used initially for troop movements from Scrabster and within Scapa Flow. Military control was exercised from Stromness and for the first two months she was a regular visitor to Scapa (Pier), Lyness and less frequently to Longhope and Flotta. Overnight lie-overs were shared between Scrabster and Stromness but occasionally Scapa and St. Margaret's Hope were used. From April 1941 she fell into a fairly regular pattern of leaving Scrabster around 12 noon, crossing over to Stromness, often with a call at one of the Scapa Flow ports, and then returning similarly to Scrabster, arriving about 5pm/6pm. From about September the Scrabster departure was brought forward to 9am/10am, returning around 3pm/4pm. Scrabster was very much her home port during the war but the Saturday sailing was generally northbound only, providing the weekends at Stromness and resuming service from there on Mondays. The naval ferry the *St. Ninian* (I) was based at HMS *Dunluce Castle*, moored at Scapa Flow, making a return crossing daily from there to Scrabster. She was joined by the *Morialta*, a new ship from the Caledon yard for Australian owners, but requisitioned by the Admiralty and apparently managed by the North Company from October 1940.

For the rest of the war four ships were required to operate the Pentland Firth routes while the *St. Ola* (I) on the commercial service

The *St. Clair* (II) arriving at Aberdeen in a storm on 20th November 1950. (Ferry Publications Library)

was normally relieved by the *Earl of Zetland*, which, operating as a military ferry, was relieved by the *St. Ninian* (I). The naval ferry continued as a two-ship operation until June 1945 and when the *Morialta* terminated her service at the end of August 1943 she was replaced by the Faroese steamer the *Tjaldur*, which had entered the service from June 1943 and was also managed by the North Company. In all, some 21 vessels made appearances on the Pentland Firth routes, some for only very short periods. Both the 'Earls' and the Great Western Railway's Plymouth tender, the *Sir Richard Grenville*, had the distinction of serving on commercial, naval and military services. Other vessels which had significant spells on the Pentland Firth were the *Calshot* (Southampton tender) and the escaped Norwegian coastal steamer *Galtesund*, while another Plymouth tender, the *Sir John Hawkins*, appeared on the military service at times.

To return to September 1939 where the *St. Sunniva* (II) and *St. Magnus* (III) lay at Aberdeen under Admiralty requisition, both later sailed from the port on 8th October, the *St. Sunniva* (II) as an accommodation ship in Scapa Flow and the *St. Magnus* (III) to Kirkwall Bay where she became a guard ship for contraband control. Both were briefly diverted in April 1940 for a troopship voyage from Aberdeen to Norway, the third ship in the convoy being Bank Line's *Cedarbank* which was torpedoed and sunk off the Norwegian coast. The *St. Magnus* (III) had a number of other diversions

The *St. Clair* (II) at Leith during her early career. (Bruce Peter collection)

from her static role in Kirkwall Bay and on some of these her place on duty was taken by the *St. Sunniva* (II). On 15th May 1940 the *St. Magnus* (III) made a voyage from Kirkwall Bay to Lerwick with a contingent of Royal Air Force units, returning on the following day. She departed again on 1st June 1940 and the evidence suggests that she went to Scapa Flow, berthing alongside at Lyness, where embarkation (presumably naval personnel) took place that afternoon. She sailed on 3rd June arriving at Rosyth the following afternoon where her 'passengers' disembarked. She left Rosyth on 8th June, probably for Scapa/Kirkwall where 43 officers and 305 other ranks of army personnel had embarked. The *St. Magnus* (III) sailed around 1pm on 16th June, arriving at Aberdeen at 5am the following morning where the troops disembarked.

War losses were the *St. Fergus*, following a collision, and the *St. Catherine* (II) by bombing, both in 1940. The *St. Clement* (I) was lost by bombing in 1941. The *St. Sunniva* (II) foundered without trace off Newfoundland in January 1943 with the loss of 64 crew.

Services following the Second World War

At the end of the war in Europe on 7th May and Japan on 14th August 1945, the North Company services were still essentially on a wartime footing, although the *St. Clair* (II) had been handed back to the company at Aberdeen on 19th June for refitting. There were still four allocated ships in the fleet (the *Blyth* and three General Steam Navigation Co. vessels) serving traditional ports. In addition a further two vessels had been allocated on 16th December 1944 as military transport. These were the *Nova* (Bergen Steamship Company) normally operating Aberdeen–Faroe (until September 1945) and the *Lochnagar* (Aberdeen Steam Navigation Company Ltd.) normally operating Aberdeen–Lerwick (until February 1946). Owned vessels on their regular services were the *St. Magnus* (III), St. *Rognvald* (II), *Rora Head*, *Dunleary*, *St. Ola* (I) and the *Earl of Zetland* (II).

The *St. Ninian* (I) and the *Earl of Zetland* remained as naval and military ferries on the Pentland Firth.

There was a general derequisition of all

allocated vessels as from 2nd March 1946 once voyages were completed and the last of the 'outside' fleet departed on 26th March. However, with a severely depleted working fleet, the *Edina* was taken on commercial charter (March to June 1946), as was the *Naviedale* (April to June 1946). On the release of the *Earl of Zetland* from military duties, she returned to the North Isles route (December 1945 to March 1946), but was then transferred initially to the Aberdeen–Kirkwall service, which had reverted to a twice-weekly passenger service before finally returning to her 'own' route. Her predecessor, the old '*Earl*', was reallocated to the Pentland Firth for general assisting duties from December 1945 to early March 1946, followed by a final stint on the North Isles service until June 1946 when she returned to Aberdeen to lay up. The *Earl of Zetland* (II) was sold in November of that year and left Aberdeen on 5th December 1946 for a new life in the Mediterranean.

For the period June 1945 to June 1946 there was an interim phase during which the Aberdeen–Kirkwall and Aberdeen–Lerwick services were provided on a twice-weekly basis. The Kirkwall route was provided by the *St. Rognvald* (II) or the *Earl of Zetland* (March to May) leaving Aberdeen on Tuesdays and Fridays and Kirkwall on Mondays and Wednesdays, while Lerwick was served by the *St. Magnus* (III) or *St. Rognvald* (II) (April to May), leaving Aberdeen on Mondays and Thursdays, and Lerwick on Tuesdays and Saturdays. After a full year refitting and converting for her peacetime role, which included conversion to oil burning, the *St. Clair* (II) took up the twice-weekly Lerwick service on 17th June 1946 and thereafter the 'direct' route but did not include a Leith call.

The indirect service resumed in July 1945 though there was one major difference: the main sailing was now one at the beginning of the week, normally Monday from Leith, while the secondary sailing left Leith on the Thursday. Initially the main sailing was operated by the *Blyth* or the *Aire* (September to November) but calls were not made at Aberdeen in either direction. This service terminated again in mid-December but resumed with the *St. Magnus* (III)

in June 1946 on the traditional pattern of calling at Aberdeen both northbound and southbound. The most pressing problem for the company was the purchase of new vessels and on 26th September 1946 the new *St. Clement* (II) made her maiden voyage from Aberdeen to Kirkwall. She replaced the *Dunleary* which had been sold the previous month to Greek buyers. Like her earlier namesake she was a cargo ship but included some features not provided for on earlier vessels. While her predecessor had been provided with a saloon for the statutory 12 passengers, the new ship was fitted with 2-berth cabins for this number and the master had the novelty of both a day room and a bedroom. One of the main duties envisaged for the *St. Clement* (II) was the carriage of livestock and she incorporated a ramped walkway from the upper (shelter) deck, accessible from the starboard side down to the main deck, so that livestock did not require to be lifted by crane off and on. There was also a portable walkway from the main deck down to the lower hold and during the major livestock movements this was regularly left in place. The *St. Clement* (II) fell into a fairly regular pattern during her early years of livestock sailings (September–November), secondary indirect service (November–May) and North Isles (March–April). At other times she effectively acted to clear backlogs or was used for supplementary sailings. The secondary indirect service had recommenced in September 1945 and notionally was operated fortnightly by the chartered *Edina*, but the service lapsed during March–May 1946. Like the main service, no Aberdeen calls were made in either direction. It reverted to something approaching its pre-war appearance from June 1946 when the *St. Rognvald* was allocated to the Thursday sailing from Leith. The main difference now was that the service terminated at Kirkwall all year round.

New Tonnage

The west-side service, effectively the Stromness boat with fortnightly calls at St. Margaret's Hope, was covered by the *Rora Head* although the *St. Clement* (II) was employed for periods during late summer and autumn; the *Naviedale,* on charter, was also used. The *St. Ninian* (I) was finally derequisitioned at Aberdeen in December 1946 and lay there unused for about two years before going to the breakers in 1948 at 53 years of age. Perhaps the most unusual feature of these immediate post-war years was that the *St. Rognvald* was used to relieve the Pentland Firth and the North Isles services during April/May 1947. Perhaps surprisingly it was not until 1950 before a main-line vessel was built, though obviously the years of austerity and inflation in the immediate post-war period may have been the reason. The new vessel was the *St. Ninian* (II) and was innovatory in that she was the first twin-screw vessel in the fleet, indeed the only one until the car ferries appeared 26 years later. She also introduced a rather different profile with only one hold forward and two aft. First Class cabins, mainly 2-berth with some 4-berth, were spread over four decks and, for the first time, the decks were identified A (prom deck), B (shelter deck), C (main or upper deck) and D (lower deck). Second Class cabins (4-berth and 6-berth) were situated on C and D decks. The Second

Class dining room and the lounge/bar were located at the fore end of the accommodation block on B deck and the First Class dining saloon, seating 60, was located directly above. This was rather a high location for such a public room and during mealtimes caused continual difficulties in service in adverse weather conditions. As in the earlier *St. Clair* (II), there was an enclosed observation shelter surrounding the saloon on three sides and in the first year it had to serve as an overflow dining saloon during the peak season. It could seat a further 40 (later increased to 50) and meal service was only possible in that there were two communicating doors between the dining saloon and the observation area. There were very few cabins on A deck and the after end of this section was divided to form separate lounge and bar areas. The crew were located aft, the first time this had been done, although stewards were mainly on C deck (port side).

On the introduction into service of the *St. Ninian* (II) in June 1950 she was allocated to the main indirect route, displacing the *St. Magnus* (III) to the secondary sailings, which now, as in pre-

The *St. Ninian* (II) entered commercial service in 1950. Some 21 years later she was sold for further service. (Late Alastair Robb Collection)

war years, were extended to Lerwick during the June–September period. The *St. Rognvald* operated the Stromness service that summer. The year of 1950 was the only post-war year that the company operated four main-line vessels, still one less than in 1939. The *St. Rognvald* finished service in October 1950 and after being laid up for a few months was sold to breakers. The *St. Ninian* (II) was thus effectively a replacement ship for the *St. Rognvald*.

The other improvement to services that summer was the re-establishment of the Caithness route and the *Rora Head*, being effectively surplus, was available to cover this route. One change was that Wick was the only Caithness route call until the end of October when Kirkwall was also included. From November the Caithness and Stromness services were generally operated jointly, apart from the summer period.

In 1951 the final ship in the post-war reconstruction programme was built. This was the *St. Ola* (II), built to replace her elderly 59-year-old namesake. She commenced service at the end of May 1951, her predecessor going to the breakers. In appearance she was an enlarged *Earl of Zetland* but had no well deck forward. With twin lifeboats on each side she was easily distinguishable from the '*Earl*'. Internally the shelter deck had a large, rather spartan deck shelter on the fore end, while the after end was given over to a large well-furnished lounge/bar. The dining saloon was below this on the main deck and six 2-berth passenger cabins were located on the starboard side. There were also two rest rooms on the lower deck, male and female, furnished with settees and a comfortable area where passengers could lie down on a bad day on the Firth. The *St. Ola* (II) was also the first Single Class ship (cargo vessels excluded) in the fleet.

At the end of the war in 1945 the fleet consisted of ten vessels, including the two time-expired veterans (the *Earl of Zetland* (II) and *St. Ninian* (I)) with an average age of 37 years, four of the fleet being in excess of 50! At the end of this reconstruction programme six years later, the eight-strong fleet now averaged 15 years, although this still included the 57-year-old veteran *Amelia*.

The Traditional Period 1951–1974

This quarter century can perhaps be defined as a period of stability with no major changes, although the 'Steam Navigation' became the North of Scotland, Orkney & Shetland Shipping Co. Ltd. in 1953. Only three ships joined the fleet, one being second-hand, but four departed. It can be divided into two separate periods. From 1951 to 1966 services still largely followed the traditional pattern and with considerable resources devoted to expanding the all-inclusive cruise and hotel holiday concept. The period from 1967 to 1974 was one of contraction, other than on the freight side, when the main-line fleet diminished to only one vessel and all services from Leith ceased.

In 1900 the company had built the St. Magnus Hotel in Hillswick, Shetland, a four-month seasonal establishment, which until 1939 had formed an essential seven-day stop-over link in the 12-day holiday packages from Leith/Aberdeen employing the services of the west-side steamer. The 1939 cost was £12 (Leith) and £11.50 (Aberdeen). This particular 12-day holiday resumed in 1946 but as there was no longer a Hillswick vessel the 'cruise' part was in the care of the *St. Magnus* (III) or *St. Ninian* (II) from 1950 and passengers were taken by coach from Lerwick to Hillswick. In 1947 the Standing Stones Hotel at Stenness, Orkney was purchased, which was open all the year round and tourists could now select either hotel or have a week at both.

As the post-war austerity conditions diminished the company commenced 'signing up' various other local hotels to act as booking agents on their behalf. Three hotels in Shetland joined the scheme in 1955 and were all serviced by the *St. Magnus* (III) with her considerable passenger capacity. One hotel was on the island of Unst and this required 'cruisers' to transfer to the *Earl of Zetland* (II). In 1956 the *St. Clair* (II) was brought into the range of holidays offered and five hotels participated that year. In 1957 an additional hotel was offered and numbers remained at five or six until 1965, although there were seven in 1959. In addition the two principal North Company hotels at Hillswick and Stenness continued to be served by the *St. Ninian* (II). Apart from all these inclusive cruise/hotel holidays, it was always possible to undertake the round trip on some of the ships as a pure cruise. These were certainly available from 1902 on selected vessels, from 1950 were available on any of the passenger vessels, and from 1955 included the cargo vessels (12 passengers) as well. One trip which was very popular was the mini-cruise, though this descriptive title was not used until 1972. Their origin can be traced back as far as 1898, although at that time they could only be arranged on a stage-by-stage basis and involving a main-line vessel to Lerwick before transferring to the *Earl of Zetland* and returning similarly. From 1946 the mini-cruise was offered as an all-inclusive *St. Clair/Earl of Zetland* package and the basic concept exists to this day, albeit without the North Isles extension, employing the ro-ro ferries.

The company had been considering a new ship for some time, one that can perhaps be considered an 'intermediate' vessel, as her design was for only 50 passengers. She was envisaged as the Caithness steamer with her other main role being to relieve the main-line vessels when they were off on annual refit. Perhaps the additional trade anticipated during the construction of the various nuclear installations at Dounreay, only a few miles west of Scrabster, had influenced this decision. Whatever the reason, the design was significantly altered after the order was placed. What appeared in 1955 was a large cargo vessel with cabins for 12 passengers, eight of which were single-berth, an innovation in the fleet. This was the *St. Rognvald* (III) and she introduced a completely new profile to the fleet. There was a large deckhouse amidships extending from side to side and this incorporated store rooms, the cargo refrigerating machines and, most importantly, the access for the cattle ramp which linked the shelter deck with the 'tween deck. Unlike the *St. Clement* (II), this cattle ramp could be rigged at either side of the ship to suit loading requirements, though it was almost permanently rigged on the starboard side.

Both holds were fitted for livestock carriage

and there was a portable ramp installed to load livestock into Number 2 hold, something which previously had only been fitted to the *St. Ninian* (II). The *St. Rognvald* (III) largely took over the duties of the *St. Clement* (II) and normally spent September/October on livestock traffic, which saw her visiting Baltasound and occasionally Fetlar, as well as the main ports. During the winter she operated what was effectively the secondary indirect service vessel, while the *St. Magnus* (III) was relieving on other routes. In the spring and summer she normally operated a freight service to Kirkwall, St. Margaret's Hope (fortnightly) and Stromness.

On the introduction of the St. *Rognvald* (III), the *Amelia* was withdrawn and scrapped and the *Rora Head* generally covered Cooper's freight service, sometimes loading in Leith at both Cooper's and the North Company berth. In 1956 the Caithness service was withdrawn due to high operating expenses and the *Rora Head* was sold to Lerwick owners. The *St. Clement* (II) had also taken over some of the Cooper's sailings and it was around this time that Cooper's shed and office at Leith was relinquished and all the traffic concentrated at the Victoria Dock complex. It was also around 1954 that the company started the practice of calling at non-standard Orkney ports during March/April. About four or five sailings would be made calling at Stronsay, Sanday and Westray, and occasionally Longhope, normally combined with Caithness and Stromness sailings. The *Amelia* was employed in 1954, the *Rora Head* in 1956 and the *St. Clement* thereafter for about a decade. Cargoes were invariably manufactured manures and feeding stuffs for livestock. By 1956, with the introduction of the *St. Rognvald* (III), the sale of the 61-year-old *Amelia* and the 35-year-old *Rora Head*, the fleet was reduced to seven ships, with the average age being 13 years. This included the elderly *St. Magnus* (III) which had been built in 1924. However, when the *St. Rognvald* (III) joined the fleet the opportunity was taken to modernise the *St. Magnus* (III) and she was withdrawn from service for three months (February–May 1956) to be converted into an oil-burning vessel. The Second Class and crew's accommodation was remodelled

The *St. Ola* (II) at Stromness. She maintained the Pentland Firth crossing between 1951 and 1974. (Late Alastair Robb Colection)

from dormitory style to cabins. The First Class accommodation was less affected but the 18-berth ladies' cabin was converted to two 4-berth and one 6-berth cabins, and additional showers and toilet facilities were also installed. Like many of the earlier ships, some of the deck areas were convertible, i.e. First Class cabins in summer, livestock accommodation in winter! On the *St. Magnus* (III) this latterly consisted of a block of 12 2-berth cabins (converted from dormitory style earlier) and these were altered to provide four 4-berth and eight 2-berth cabins. (These cabins were forever known to the crew as the 'cattle stalls' with the resultant entertainment of the occupants when they found out.) A further two 2-berth cabins were built on the shelter deck amidships. These alterations still provided berths for 224 First Class passengers, only 10 less than the originally built arrangement.

Enter the Third St Clair

Another main-line vessel joined the fleet in 1960 in the form of the *St. Clair* (III), significantly larger than the *St. Ninian* (II). She had a more 'built-up' profile than anything previously, and

reverted to the two holds forward and one aft. The four deck infrastructure allowed cabins to be located higher with all First Class completely above the waterline. The dining saloon was located aft of the engine casing, reverting to the shelter deck, thus at the same level as her namesake. First Class cabins were distributed over four decks and consisted of four 4-berth and 82 2-berth. As with the *St. Ninian* (II), the Second Class was located in the forward section of the midships superstructure. Her namesake had been renamed the *St. Clair II* some time earlier and the introduction of the new *St. Clair* (III) resulted in the *St. Magnus* (III) being sold for scrap. The *St. Clair II* was then renamed *St. Magnus* (IV). The new *St. Clair* (III) took up the direct Aberdeen–Lerwick route, while the *St. Magnus* (IV) transferred to the secondary indirect route.

In 1961 the fortnightly call to St. Margaret's Hope had been reduced to a call every third week and 3rd May 1966 marked the withdrawal of calling there. The entire fleet was affected by the lengthy seamen's strike between mid-May and the beginning of July although the *St. Rognvald* (III) had been allowed to make a few

The *St. Clair* (III) dressed overall arriving at Lerwick on her maiden voyage. (P&O Library)

trips with emergency supplies. The first ship to resume sailing was the *Earl of Zetland* (II) (Lerwick–Kirkwall–Aberdeen), bringing down the 'North' company seafarers to crew the fleet which was laid up in Aberdeen and Leith.

Towards the end of 1966 it was announced that the *St. Magnus* (IV) was to be withdrawn and would be replaced by a cargo/livestock vessel. The *St. Magnus* (IV) was renamed the *St. Magnus II* in October and she is unusual in having operated under six different names under the one ownership: *St. Clair*, HMS *Baldur*, *St. Clair, St. Clair II, St. Magnus* and *St. Magnus II.* Her replacement was the *City of Dublin* which was overhauled and converted for North Company service at Ardrossan over six months and entered service on 30th March 1967, from Leith on the secondary indirect service. She had been renamed the *St. Magnus* (V) a fortnight earlier and at a distance was almost indistinguishable from the *St. Rognvald* (III). The main-line fleet was now down to only two vessels. This also resulted in the contraction of the cruise/hotel programme, only three hotels being signed up for the 1967 and 1968 seasons, although the *St. Ninian* (II) continued

additionally to serve Hillswick and Stenness hotels.

An unusual situation occurred in February 1970 when the *St. Clair* (III) was chartered to relieve the Liverpool–Belfast service for about two weeks while the *Ulster Queen* and the *Ulster Prince* were on survey. This arrangement was repeated in 1971 but covered four weeks and was facilitated by the fact that both companies were part of the Coast Lines Group which had taken over the North Company in 1961.

Early in September 1970 the company had discussed their plans with the local island authorities for the restructuring of the fleet and services. This envisaged three ro-ro vessels, one each for the Pentland Firth, Lerwick and Kirkwall routes, the last one being a 12-passenger vessel, but none would be in service before 1975. In addition Leith would be closed down and the *St. Ninian* (II) would be withdrawn. Stromness (apart from the Pentland Firth sailings) would also fall victim, all of these changes targeted for early 1971.

The final scheduled Stromness call was made on 24th February 1971 by the *St. Clement*

(II), but it was stated that calls would be made if inducements were favourable. There were a few infrequent isolated calls thereafter. The *St. Magnus* (V) made the final sailing from Leith on 9th March 1971. The *St. Ninian* (II) which was relieving the *St. Clair* (III) made her last sailing when she arrived in Aberdeen on 28th February and was subsequently sold to Canadian interests, leaving Aberdeen on 26th April 1971 with basically a North Company crew on the delivery voyage. The Lerwick service continued to operate from Matthew's Quay, but Orkney freight services were transferred to Jamieson's Quay, which was the Coast Lines complex and the basic pattern became: the *St. Rognvald* ex Aberdeen (Mondays), Kirkwall (Tuesdays), Lerwick (Wednesdays), Aberdeen (arr. Thursdays). The *St. Clement* ex Aberdeen (Tuesdays), Kirkwall (Wednesdays/Thursdays), Aberdeen (arr. Fridays). The *St. Magnus* ex Aberdeen (Tuesdays), Kirkwall (weekend), Aberdeen (arr. Tuesdays).

While this appeared to be poor utilisation of vessels, it eliminated expensive weekend discharging of cargo and the three vessels were basically required, in that the *St. Clement* (II)

normally spent 10 weeks in the summer assisting with car traffic on the Pentland Firth and many additional sailings would be required during the autumn livestock season, while allowances had to be made for the annual refits of all six vessels. During 1971 only the *St. Clair* (III) was advertised in the summer season brochure, but 1972 saw a reversion to the indirect service being promoted (either the *St. Rognvald* (III) or the *St. Clement* (II), depending on whether early or late summer) and from May 1972 this sailing included a Kirkwall call southbound, arriving Aberdeen on Friday. A further contraction in the operations was the sale of the St. Magnus Hotel, Hillswick around May 1972, the Stenness Hotel having been sold as far back as 1953 although still included in the holiday packages up to 1970.

In October 1972 yards in both the UK and Europe had been requested to tender for a new ferry for the Aberdeen–Lerwick service. Meanwhile, the contract was given to Hall Russell, Aberdeen for a new Pentland Firth ferry on 12th December for delivery during spring 1974.

In perhaps the worst mishap since the war,

The *St. Clair* (III) leaving Lerwick for Aberdeen in the evening sun. (Lawrence Macduff)

The *St.Ola* (II) berthed at Stromness following her morning arrival from mainland Scotland. (Bruce Peter collection)

the *St. Rognvald* (III) ran aground on Thieves Holm (Kirkwall Bay) on 4th May 1973 and was re-floated two weeks later. As the *St. Ola* (II) was off on refit at the time, the *Clarity* was chartered for about two weeks until her return. The *St. Rognvald* (III) returned to service on 25th June.

P&O Takeover Services

The Aberdeen–Lerwick ro-ro ferry order was eventually given to Hall Russell's at Aberdeen in July 1973 for delivery in May 1975; but the shipyard subsequently withdrew from the contract citing pressure of other work and it was back to square one. Coast Lines who had been taken over by the P&O Group in February 1971 looked at other vessels in their fleet that might fit the role instead of a newbuild. Two vessels were considered in late 1974, the *Lion* and the *Norwave*.

The new Pentland Firth vessel, the first ro-ro ferry in the fleet, the *St. Ola* (III), was launched at Aberdeen on 24th January 1974 with delivery planned for mid-June. It emerged that the first choice of name had been the *St. Olaf*, perpetuating the name of the first North

Company vessel to operate on the route, but that name was unavailable. In preparation for the arrival of the new ferry the existing vessel on the route had been renamed the *St. Ola II*. The new *St. Ola* was delayed and made her visit to the Firth of Forth in mid-September for dry docking and speed trials, and then carried out final trials in Aberdeen Bay on 29th October 1974, later sailing overnight to Stromness. By arrangement, she met up with the *St. Ola II* off Houton (near Stromness) at 9am the next morning. An official reception was held on board for local dignitaries on the arrival day and the *St. Ola* (III) was open to the public on 31st October. On 1st November local schoolchildren were granted a special holiday and 420 visited the new ship. However, the delays at the shipyard paled into insignificance compared with the delays at Scrabster where the terminal was nowhere near ready. The *St. Ola* (III) lay unused for three months at Stromness before entering service.

Another part of the operations that had been seeing significant changes was on the North Isles of Shetland. In the summer of 1970 Zetland County Council received approval for

Above: The *St. Clement* (II) is seen here at Lerwick during her layover at the port on 8th October 1972. (Lawrence Macduff)

Below: The *St. Ola* (II) arriving at Scrabster on 5th August 1974. The St. Clement (II) is at berth while assisting the St.Ola on the route with car traffic during the summer peak period. (Lawrence Macduff)

Above: The *St. Ninian* (II) leaves Leith for Aberdeen on one of her final sailings. (Lawrence Macduff)

Below: The *St. Magnus* (V) at Aberdeen on 31st May 1976 with a pale blue funnel. (Lawrence Macduff).

their inter-island car ferry service which would attract a 75 per cent Government Grant. At that stage this required four vessels and 10 purpose-built terminals, although a fifth vessel (spare) was later added to the initial concept. The *Earl of Zetland* (II) was 31 years old and replacement by another conventional vessel was not a realistic option. The first of Zetland County Council's ferries, the *Fivla*, entered service on 21st May 1973 between Toft (mainland) and Ulsta (Yell), and after a transitional period the *Earl of Zetland* (II) progressively dropped her various calling ports in the North Isles as each new ferry was introduced. Calls at Mid Yell (Normally Thursdays) and Cullivoe, Yell (Fridays only) were discontinued after 1st August 1973, while final calls at Uyeasound, Unst (Mondays/Tuesdays overnight and Wednesdays, Fridays/Saturdays) and Baltasound, Unst (Fridays/Saturdays overnight) were made on 14th and 15th December respectively. The latter two ports were actually 'closed' by the *St. Ola II* which was on relief duties at the time. The overnight stopovers, which had been part of the North Isles' history since 1877, terminated after 97 years, not quite making their century. From 17th December 1973 a new pattern of services commenced:

Mondays only Lerwick 8am – Whalsay, Skerries, Fetlar, Whalsay, Lerwick (arr. c. 5pm).

Wednesdays only Lerwick 9am – Whalsay– Lerwick (arr. c. 12 noon).

Fridays only Lerwick 10am – Whalsay, Fetlar, Whalsay, Lerwick (arr. c. 5pm).

Meanwhile on 22nd November the final Fetlar call was made.

In June 1974 the *Ortolan* of GSN (General Steam Navigation another division of Coast Lines/P&O) appeared on an inter-group charter and assisted the *St. Clair* (III) with freight trips. However, the first practical signs of the North Company's involvement with North Sea oil was imminent when she made a number of trips to Flotta (which eventually became the Occidental Oil Company oil terminal) and also called at Lyness. The *Ortolan* appears to have been employed intermittently until mid-December.

The *Earl of Zetland* (II) laying off Houbie, Isle of Fetlar during livestock movements on 15th October 1973. The 'flitboat' is astern of her. (Lawrence Macduff)

The New Generation of Ferries

On 26th January 1975 the new *St. Ola* (III) made a circumnavigation of Hoy for crew familiarisation purposes to test all machinery systems. On the 28th she made a VIP crossing to Scrabster and on the following day she made her maiden voyage from Stromness to Scrabster. At long last ro-ro had come to fruition, some 11 years after its introduction in MacBrayne territory in the Western Isles. With her better speed, some schedule adjustments were made. Internally the passenger accommodation was confined to the shelter (or upper deck) with a large observation saloon at the fore and a cafeteria/bar at the after end which was divided down the centre line on an open-plan layout. An entrance foyer and

The newly built St. Ola (III) fitting out at Hull Russells Shipyard, Aberdeen in 1974 prior to entry into service. (Lawrence Macduff)

The *St. Clair* (IV) leaves Aberdeen for Shetland in April 1979, with her black livery and blue funnel prior to receiving the new P&O livery. (Lawrence Macduff)

purser's office was amidships. Vehicles had the use of the entire main deck with two wing decks above accessed by lifts and frequently used for livestock.

The *St. Ola II* departed for Aberdeen on 29th January 1975 and after a few days was sold for use as a seismic survey vessel. Less than a month later the *Earl of Zetland* made her final voyage on 21st February. As a mark of the close relationship between the ship and the community, the crew on the *Earl of Zetland* held a private dinner party on board that evening and a few days later were the guests of the Provost at a reception in Lerwick Town Hall. A week later she left Lerwick for Aberdeen, played out by the town band, and was sold for further work as a seismic research vessel. Latterly she had been serving Whalsay and Skerries only and Zetland County Council took over the Skerries route from the end of February 1975. While all five of the Zetland County Council ferries had now been delivered, there were no terminals ready at Symbister (Whalsay) or Laxo (mainland) to allow the Whalsay service to operate. Instead, the *Grima* from the quintet was chartered by the North Company and provided a Symbister–Lerwick service until January 1976 when the Zetland

County Council ferry service commenced. She was island-based and the schedule was to leave Symbister 9am Tuesdays only and 7.30am/1pm Fridays only and Lerwick 2pm Tuesdays only and 10am/4.30pm Fridays only.

Meanwhile during March 1975 the *Lion* was put out to tender for conversion to become the Lerwick ferry, but mounting losses on P&O's long routes (Lisbon, Tangier and San Sebastian) forced a rethink and in October it was announced that the former *SF Panther* would be employed instead. She had operated on the Southampton–San Sebastian route until its closure in 1973, and then had been chartered out to Da-No Linje for service in Norway and renamed the *Terje Vigen*. With what was effectively a five-ship fleet, which only included one ro-ro vessel, a relief vessel had to be chartered from outside. The *Clansman* relieved the *St. Ola* during the first half of November that year and in fact fulfilled this role every year until 1982/83.

While the *St. Clair* and the three cargo ships continued as before, the most significant change during that first year of ro-ro was that the Pentland Firth sailings were increased during the summer. The old *St. Ola* had operated extra summer crossings for many years, but these were invariably only as required and traffic patterns generally confined these to the Friday to Monday period while Sunday sailings had become part of the advertised schedule from 1959 (July/August only) onwards. From the beginning of June the *St. Ola* (III) made an extra 3pm Wednesdays only crossing from Stromness, while on Thursdays five single crossings, commencing at 8.45am from Scrabster, were provided until the end of August. This was mainly to provide a day excursion on Thursdays from the Caithness side but on a number of occasions the Wednesday evening service was employed for charter cruises along the coast or through Scapa Flow and this arrangement continued for a number of years.

At the beginning of October 1975 the North Company title disappeared, the company initially trading as P&O Ferries (Orkney & Shetland Services) and the *St. Ola* (III) reappeared from refit in November with P&O pale blue funnels, the first of the visual alterations.

During 1974 preliminary site work had commenced at the Aberdeen and Lerwick terminals, though the construction phase did not commence until 1976 at Aberdeen and effectively became an extension of the then current Kirkwall freight berths. In the same month all vessels commenced using the new Lerwick facilities at Holmsgarth except for the *St. Clair* (III) which continued to use the 'mail' berth at Victoria Pier. The Matthew's Quay complex at Aberdeen was finally vacated at the end of October with the *St. Clair* transferring to a temporary berth at Regent's Quay.

In 1975 indications that North Sea oil was to be a major force, particularly in the northern North Sea, resulted in the freight-only ro-ro vessel the *Helga* being purchased by P&O for management by the North Company. She was renamed the *Rof Beaver* (Rof signifying 'roll-on freighter'), the 'Beaver' being in accord with P&O's then stated policy of using the Burns' fleet animal names for all their ferries. She was Leith-based and with no North Company presence there by then, agents were appointed to look after her. She carried no passengers. She was overhauled in Marseilles and made her

delivery voyage to Immingham in May, loading for Sullom Voe. During that first year she visited Peterhead, Belfast, Stromness, Sandwick (Shetland) and Lerwick, as well as her more frequent visits to Flotta and Sullom Voe. She even got as far as Rotterdam on one occasion!

The *Ortolan* was again also frequently employed on charter, obviously on oil-related work, and she visited Leith, Inverkeithing, Dundee, Peterhead, Flotta, Kirkwall, Sandwick and Sullom Voe. Sister vessel the *Orlole* also made a few appearances apparently on traditional North Company routes from Aberdeen to Kirkwall and Lerwick.

In the islands there was continuous criticism of the 'blue' funnels which became more vociferous at the thought that their cherished 'Saint' names could disappear to be replaced with 'animal' names, but this criticism was allayed when an announcement was made that the *SF Panther* would be renamed the *St. Clair* (IV). The blue funnels remained but the 'Beaver' was to be the only 'animal' to enter the fleet list.

The *Rof Beaver*'s stern ramp allowed her to discharge on to a quayside, which she invariably did at Leith, and she was the first vessel to use the Lerwick linkspan in June 1976. She largely confined herself to Lerwick and Sullom Voe sailings, but did make single calls at Lyness and Middlesborough. There were many more inter-group charters that year, principally the *Ortolan*, visiting London on one occasion with the *Petrel* and the *Dorset Coast* also making appearances. One non-P&O vessel to be chartered was the *Rosemarkie,* which briefly appeared, apparently on traditional freight work. At the beginning of December 1967, the *St. Clement,* the smallest of the freight ships, was sold to the Greeks and renamed the *Aghios Georgios.*

With the entry into service of the *St. Clair* (IV) on 4th April 1977, Shetland now had full ro-ro services to the outside world. A new lower fares structure from the islands (southbound) was introduced at this time. The *St. Clair* (III) was re-registered as the *St Clair II* to release the name for the new *St Clair* (IV), she then continued to make some freight sailings, including two indirect route sailings, relieving the *St. Rognvald* (III) and making rare calls at Kirkwall. She finished early in June, being sold on as the *Al Khairat* to the Meat Foodstuff Company of Kuwait.

The *St. Ola* (III) had a breakdown at the start of 1977, running on reduced power at first and missing some sailings if the weather was poor. The *St. Magnus* (V) was called in to take some cars south from Kirkwall to Aberdeen (New Year holiday traffic) while the *St. Rognvald* (III) helped out with an extra crossing of the Pentland Firth. In May 1977 the *St. Magnus* (V) was sold on to Sun Star Lines of Limassol, Cyprus as the *Mitera Eirina*. The *Ortolan* and the *Petrel* had again helped out on the freight side in September 1976, with the *Petrel* again in June 1977. The *Lairdsfox* and the *Dorset Coast* also appeared in June 1977 and from July to September 1978. In September 1977 the *Ortolan* finished with the P&O Group.

Livestock sailings by chartered vessels on an annual seasonal basis commenced with the *Angus Express* on 17th September 1977. This situation was as a result of the introduction of ro-ro operations and the demise of the *St. Magnus* (V) and the *St. Clement* (II). This arrangement continued until 2007 for periods of one to three months annually. These livestock sailings gradually ceased making local calls with both island groups, concentrating on Lerwick (Shetland) and Kirkwall (Orkney). Aberdeen was the principal mainland port, but Invergordon and Peterhead had been used occasionally.

The *Bussard*, a Danish ship, was chartered for three to four weeks for services from Aberdeen to Kirkwall, sometimes extending the service to Lerwick. The ro-ro freighter *Dorset* (built as the *Donautal* in 1970) appeared on charter in February 1978 to relieve on the freight side on the Pentland Firth, after which P&O (Orkney & Shetland Services) decided to purchase her and to send her to Belfast for refit. She took up services in the North with the name *St. Magnus* (VI) on the indirect service, substituting Stromness for Kirkwall, immediately causing consternation with the authorities in Kirkwall who saw a need for a linkspan to retain links with Aberdeen and the South!

The *St. Magnus* (VI) started a Scandinavian service to Hanstholm in Denmark and Kristiansand in Norway, and a regular pattern emerged, which fitted in with her other duties, while the *St. Rognvald* (III) was sold to Naviera Winton S/A Panama as the *Winston*.

A chartered Norwegian vessel, the *Nornan Fjord*, brought in animal foodstuffs to the islands over a ten-day period while the following year she reappeared as the *Sea Fisher* to relieve the *St. Magnus* (VI). The *Condor* also appeared for a month to help out.

Fares were increased in March 1980 and brought a change to the rebate system, an increase on the passage subsidy and also a subsidy for accompanied cars from the islands.

A second linkspan, the Eurolink, in Aberdeen Harbour was used by one of the charter ships and was to be used by company ships on occasions over the years.

The Highlands and Islands Development Board (HIDB) was set up to promote development in the Highland area and produced a report suggesting that Scrabster should be the port for Shetland. However, this was not acceptable to the Shetlanders who campaigned to keep the Aberdeen connection.

When the *St. Magnus* (VI) was overhauled in 1982 some Orkney-bound freight was sent by road to Scrabster from Aberdeen. This set a trend for the future and road improvements north of Inverness reduced the overall journey times to the Caithness port.

The *Smyril*, a car and passenger ro-ro ferry of Strandfaraskip Landsin (Faroese Government Shipping Department), was used to relieve the *St. Magnus* (VI), which in turn relieved the *St. Clair* (IV) and also the *St. Ola* (III). The *St. Magnus* (VI) made a trip for the *Rof Beaver* on 1st March 1982 incorporating a return visit to Leith.

In May 1982 the *St. Clair* (IV) was used for a fundraising event for the Lerwick Lifeboat and this became an annual event, as did the cruise around Bressay and the bird sanctuary at Noss. The *Earl of Zetland* had previously made this cruise on similar charters during the fifties!

In autumn 1982 the *Smyril* relieved the *St. Clair* (IV), followed by the *St. Ola* (III). However, the *Smyril* had to return to the Faroes before the *St. Ola*'s (III) refit was complete, so the *St. Magnus* took over for the short time until the

The *St. Clair* (IV) leaving Aberdeen on 12th April 1982 with the P&O house flag on her funnel. (Ferry Publications Library)

St. Ola (III) was able to return to her route. A fire aboard the *St. Ola* (III) delayed her return and the *St. Magnus* (VI) was then assisted by the *Rof Beaver* and the *Orcadia* when she was available. In late November the *Clansman* of Caledonian MacBrayne was called in to cover the route, but in January the *Clansman* had to return to service on the west coast and the interim arrangements were resumed, with the *St. Magnus*, the *Rof Beaver* and the *Orcadia* working the route between them until the *St. Ola* (III) resumed service on 7th February 1983. During this time, when she was on the Pentland Firth, the *Orcadia* sailed from Kirkwall to Scrabster but on at least two occasions she called at Wick. Meanwhile, Brittany Ferries' *Penn-ar-Bed* relieved the *St. Clair* (IV) for two weeks in February 1983.

On 9th May there was an unusual sailing to Gothenburg by the *St. Clair* (IV) for the final of the European Cup Winners Football Cup (Aberdeen versus Real Madrid), which Aberdeen won. A mini-cruise to Bergen took place in September 1983.

The *St. Ola's* (III) next relief was carried out in 1984. Because of her fire, the previous certificate had been issued in the spring of 1983, and from then on her overhaul was in the January–February period. The *St. Magnus* (VI) was given a passenger certificate for 50 passengers on the Pentland Firth crossing so she was used now regularly to relieve the *St. Ola* (III).

The *Smyril* was used again for two weeks, for relief duties, in 1984 at which time the *St. Clair* (IV) was refitted with extra cabins. During May the ship offered a mini-cruise to Harlingen in Holland.

The *Norröna,* owned by Smyril Lines, had replaced the *Smyril* on the link between Faroe, Shetland and Norway in June 1983 and in 1985 they advertised through links to Britain using P&O (Orkney and Shetland Services) as their UK agents.

Around this time the Highlands and Islands Development Board, and Orkney Council, assisted some local shareholders in setting up a new company, Viking Island Ferries, to operate a service linking Orkney with Shetland. They chose Kirkwall, Westray and Scalloway as their ports and the *Devonian (ex Scillonian II)* was the ship chosen. She arrived at Westray from Torquay on 17th November 1985, visiting Kirkwall the following day, and was renamed the *Syllingar*. The ship made her maiden voyage on 15th December but the service suffered

Above: The *St. Sunniva* (III) at Stromness in the morning sunshine during her first season with P&O Scottish Ferries, prior to her departure for Shetland in the early afternoon. (Lawrence Macduff)

Below: The *St. Magnus* (VI) at Lerwick on her early evening arrival at the port in May 1988. (Lawrence Macduff)

from breakdowns and weather problems and by May 1986 the company was in receivership.

Daily Sailings to Shetland

P&O announced at this time that they would acquire a second passenger ship/ferry to operate the Aberdeen, Stromness, Lerwick route and additional direct sailings between Aberdeen and Lerwick.

The *nf Panther*, formerly of P&O Normandy Ferries' Dover–Boulogne route, was purchased by the company. Built as the *Djursland* for Jydsk Faergesfart of Denmark in 1972, the contract to refit her was awarded to Hall Russell's Aberdeen shipyard. The ship was refitted as an overnight ferry with cabins forward on main and upper passenger decks with restaurant, shop, TV room and bar on the main deck. A self-service restaurant-cum-cinema doubled up with reclining seats as the overnight lounge on the upper deck, with more cabins on the port side aft.

The proposed pattern of services was: Mondays to Friday evening departures northbound and southbound on Sundays to Thursdays with an additional Saturday midday sailing northbound via Orkney. The Friday sailing southbound was to leave Lerwick at midday via Orkney. The *St. Clair* (IV) would take the Monday, Wednesday and Friday northbound sailings while the second ship would take the Tuesday, Thursday and Saturday northbound sailings. Sailings on a daily basis to Shetland for passengers had returned.

In 1986 the *Orcadia* was chartered to P&O to operate a weekly inter-island service from Kirkwall to Scalloway and on occasions diverted to Lerwick.

The *St. Magnus* (VI) continued on the *Rof Beaver*'s roster until the *nf Panther* was ready for service. Plans were made to have more mini-cruises for the spring and autumn when the new ship took up the routes but the *St. Clair* (IV) eventually undertook most of them. Mrs Olivia Ford renamed the *nf Panther* the *St. Sunniva* (III) on 27th March 1987, however the bridge windows were damaged on the maiden voyage and electrical problems resulted in the ship having to return to Aberdeen. The special party of invited guests were given a later

The *Rof Beaver* arriving at Leith in May 1985. (Lawrence Macduff)

opportunity to sail on the *St. Sunniva* (III) and a decision to use stronger glass in all forward windows was made after this voyage!

In 1987 the company brochure had a two-page feature on the 150th anniversary of P&O with various events taking place, for example, the opening of the Bod of Gremista (birthplace of Arthur Anderson, founder of P&O Company), two visits to Leith on consecutive weekends, and an Orkney week promotion was held in Aberdeen.

The *St. Magnus* (VI) now regularly used the Eurolink. She was chartered to the Ministry of Defence in November 1987 when she sailed to Loch Ryan in south-west Scotland. The *St. Sunniva* (III) became the relief vessel for the fleet from 1988 onwards.

Plans to visit the Glasgow Garden Festival in summer 1988 were announced in the autumn of 1987. The *St. Sunniva*'s (III) Glasgow visit was incorporated with a southbound direct sailing to Aberdeen from Lerwick, returning to Stromness with passengers who boarded at Aberdeen, before cruising through the Western Isles to Glasgow. Sadly due to industrial action the passengers had to be flown north after an extended visit to the Glasgow Garden Festival, where the ship was used as a floating exhibition centre for isles businesses.

In January 1989 the company changed the title of their North services once again when P&O Scottish Ferries was adopted, and the company took over their own dock labour staff on the demise of the National Dock Labour Scheme.

The *St. Ola* (III) pictured at Govan, Glasgow following her overhaul and repainting with the P&O Ferries livery. (Lawrence Macduff)

Also during 1989 the *St. Magnus*'s (VI) freight sailings to and from Leith were altered to Grangemouth for six/eight weeks while the dock gates in Leith were being repaired.

The *St. Clair* (IV) made a mini-cruise to Maloy in Norway in the spring of 1989. At this time she was involved with further safety exercises involving Lifeboat, Coastguard and Military personnel as guinea pigs to test evacuation procedures. The *St. Clair* (IV), and later the *St. Ola*, came under close scrutiny as the costs of new safety measures, said to be in the order of £335,000 for the passenger fleet, were implemented following the *Herald of Free Enterprise* ferry disaster. It was suggested by company officials that the *Norröna* should be bought to replace the *St. Clair* (IV).

The *St. Sunniva* (III) added mid-week northbound calls each Tuesday at Stromness during the peak season, leaving Aberdeen at midday and Lerwick at midday on Wednesdays. This was linked with a call of about an hour and a half in each direction at Stromness from 1989.

A freight service to Hanstholm (Denmark) had again been suggested in 1988 and an additional freight ship was required for this service, so a charter of the *Marino Torre* from Italian owners took place in 1989. She had 50 per cent more freight capacity than the *St. Magnus* (VI) so she was eventually bought in as her successor on the indirect service. She was renamed the *St. Rognvald* (IV).

The *St. Magnus* (VI) was relieved by the

Juniper of Limassol in July 1989 before leaving for a charter on the Southampton to Cherbourg service and being offered for sale. The *Smyril* was chartered briefly to operate the new Scandinavian link and also operated on the Stromness to Lerwick service while the *St. Magnus* was away. A second-hand replacement for the *St. Clair* was now planned and £15 million set aside for this purpose.

The *St. Clair* (IV) took part in the Forth Bridge Centenary celebrations opened officially by HRH Prince Edward who switched on the floodlighting.

During the overhaul period in 1992 the *St. Rognvald* was damaged in heavy weather, requiring her to be towed to Aberdeen when the *Smyril* was chartered for a week to cover. During this time she combined the rosters of both the *St. Sunniva* (III) and the *St. Rognvald* (IV). At this time it was announced that the *Smyril* would operate the route to Aberdeen on its Faroese service in lieu of Scrabster.

In 1991 the link had been maintained by the *Teistin*, another Faroese Government ship.

The Second Generation of Ferries

The *Tregastel* of Brittany Ferries was bought in 1991 and was due to commence service in 1992 after some conversion work was done. The *St. Ola* (III) was to be replaced by the *Eckero* of Eckero Lines of Finland.

The Stromness berth was proving too short for both the *St. Sunniva* (III) and the *St. Rognvald* (IV) and so work was put in hand to extend it. While this was being done the *St. Sunniva* (III) served Kirkwall in lieu of Stromness on some sailings and the *St. Rognvald* made additional calls there in addition to her Monday calls. The *St. Ola* (III) spent more time at Scrabster, sometimes on 'light' sailings as well as others already timetabled.

In the summer of 1991 the Tall Ships Race was staged at Aberdeen and the *St. Sunniva* was used by VIPs reviewing the fleet cruise.

In 1992 the *Tregastel* joined the fleet as *St. Clair* (V). Built as the *Travemunde* in 1971 for Moltzau Line, she had four passenger decks and two car/vehicle decks and was the largest ship in the fleet. The passenger cabins were mainly on C and D decks; the bar, lounges,

Above: The *St. Ola* (III) passes the Old Man of Hoy inbound to Stromness on 17th May 1991. (Lawrence Macduff)

Below: The *St. Sunniva* (III) makes a fine sight as she passes Erskine in the River Clyde on 14th May 1988, following her appearance at the Garden Festival at Glasgow. (Colin J. Smith)

Above: The *St. Clair* (IV) arrives at Aberdeen from Lerwick. (Lawrence Macduff)

Below: The *St. Ola* (IV) leaves Stromness for Scrabster in August 1993. (Lawrence Macduff)

Above: The *St. Sunniva* (III) swings off the berth at Stromness to allow the St. Ola (IV) to use the berth. (Miles Cowsill)

Below: The *St. Clair* (V) makes an impressive view off the coast of Shetland outward-bound from Lerwick. (Miles Cowsill)

Above: A wintry scene with the *St. Ola* (IV) at Scrabster with the impressive Ward Hill behind her. (Willie Mackay)

Below: The *St. Clair* (V) prepares to sail from Lerwick during her last season in service with P&O Scottish Ferries. (Miles Cowsill)

restaurant, children's play area, and ship's office on B deck, and the reclining seat lounge on A deck.

In preparation for her own replacement on the Pentland Firth service, the *St. Ola* (III) was given the suffix 'II' before retiring to Leith on the sale list. The *St. Clair* (IV) was also given the suffix 'II' but on 26th February 1992 was sold to Malaysian interests. Before entering service the *St. Ola* (IV) visited Kirkwall on a 'show the flag' cruise. As visits had been made to Scapa Pier by previous incumbents of the name this was an unusual occurrence. Stromness and Scrabster visits and berthing trials then followed and the *St. Ola* (IV) entered service on Wednesday, 25th March 1992. The main deck had a television lounge forward, ship's office in the foyer, restaurant and shop, while the bar was on the upper deck. She was built by Jos L. Meyer at Papenburg in 1971 as the *Svea Scarlett*. She was able to carry 500 passengers and up to 110 cars and/or 20 commercial vehicles. As the *Cecilia*, the old *St. Ola* (III) was chartered to Svenska Rederi A.B. for a Denmark to Sweden crossing but was eventually sold to Greek owners.

The *St. Ola* (IV) made her first visit to Lerwick

The *St. Rognvald* (IV) at her berth at Lerwick pending her evening departure to Aberdeen. (Miles Cowsill)

after the *St. Sunniva* (III) had an engine failure and was grounded at Stromness. She made her crossing on Saturday evening, arriving on Sunday morning and leaving an hour or so later, reaching Stromness in the late afternoon and taking up her Scrabster sailings in the evening. Her return sailing was cancelled on the occasions this happened.

When it was announced at the end of August 1992 that the *Norröna*'s calls at Lerwick

The St. Clair (IV) leaving Aberdeen on 12th April 1982 with the P&O house flag on her funnel. (Ferry Publications Library)

The *St.Ola* (IV) at Scrabster in her last months of operation. The building works for the new linkspan for NorthLink operations can be seen behind her. (Willie Mackay)

were to cease, pressure from the Local Authority, Tourist Board and others led to a decision to send the *St. Clair* (V) to Bergen in the high season of 1993. This used the Friday departure from Aberdeen at 6pm to Lerwick, departing from Lerwick during late Saturday mornings for Bergen and arriving at 10pm local time, with the return sailing to Lerwick and Aberdeen two hours later. This renewed a link with the past, to when the North Company had offered Norwegian sailings for 23 years until 1908. This service continued in June, July and August for the next three years with slight timetable adjustments.

The *St. Rognvald* (IV) was the relief vessel in most winters, releasing the *St. Sunniva* (III) in the January to March period to relieve the *St. Ola* (IV) and the *St. Clair* (V) to have their own overhauls. The *St. Rognvald* (IV) was usually overhauled first for a week or so and the *St. Sunniva* (III) made her own regular sailings to clear backlogs in traffic which occur each year.

The *St. Rognvald* (IV) was chartered during summer weekends to Ferrymasters for their Middlesborough to Gothenburg service during 1993 and in 1994 she was chartered to Color Line for their Tyne to Bergen route. She

continued with her own single weekly round trip to the Northern Isles during these years.

A report at this time suggested that a complete fleet replacement would cost around £100 million. Napier University suggested that by using aluminium-constructed catamarans, each costing £40 million, up to 800 passengers and 100 cars could be carried, thereby saving up to two-thirds of the journey time to Shetland.

In 1993 investigative reports for H.I.E. and Shetland Islands Council into more economic ways of providing ferry services to and from Aberdeen suggested that the Government provided and owned the ships, with P&O Scottish Ferries or others managing them.

Chapter two

Tendering the Routes

By 2002 the Northern Isles stood at the edge of the most significant changes to their shipping services since the arrival of P&O Scottish Ferries.

The introduction of new freight services to Orkney and Shetland by Orcargo, which ceased to trade in 1999, and Streamline Shipping, led to overcapacity thus reducing the viability of the existing lifeline services provided by P&O Scottish Ferries. As a result the existing Tariff Rebate Subsidy (TRS) scheme was replaced with a block grant system from 1st May 1995,

with the new system benefiting a single carrier on a competitive tender basis for car and passenger traffic only. TRS had been divided amongst all of the available operators. Only livestock sailings would continue to receive subsidy on the TRS basis until 2006, when it was deemed to be unlawful under EU State Aid Rules. In the summer of 1995, the Scottish Office invited companies to tender for the new contract to serve the Northern Isles but the west coast operator Caledonian MacBrayne was excluded from the tendering process. The

P&O Scottish Ferries *St. Clair* (V) makes a majestic departure from Aberdeen on 26th June 2002. (Colin J. Smith)

The *St. Sunniva* (III) leaves Aberdeen on her midday departure outward bound for Stromness and Lerwick. (Colin J. Smith)

General Election and change of Government in May 1997 led to delays in completing the tender process and on 24th July 1997 the new Secretary of State for Scotland, Donald Dewar MP, confirmed that P&O Scottish Ferries had won the contract for a further five years in the face of competition from Sea Containers and Orkney Ferries. However, with the P&O vessels ageing, new Safety of Life at Sea (SoLAS) regulations being introduced (with which the ships might not comply) and Scottish devolution on the horizon, a new tendering process for the operation of the services beyond 2002 began almost immediately. This time around, Caledonian MacBrayne could participate and expressions of interest were invited in summer 1998.

Meanwhile, on Saturday 28th November 1998, the *St. Ola* (IV) departed from Stromness on her morning crossing of the Pentland Firth. As she headed east through Scapa Flow on account of a heavy westerly swell, an unfamiliar ship with a much more modern profile emerged from the mist off Cava and slipped into the vacated pier at Stromness. The mystery

visitor was the three-year-old Caledonian MacBrayne ferry *Isle of Lewis*, making a courtesy call to Orkney on her return from her annual overhaul on the Tyne. During her four-hour visit she was opened to the public and the modern facilities of the *Isle of Lewis* impressed Orcadian residents, councillors and business people alike. Caledonian MacBrayne had made their intentions clear – they intended to compete strongly for the privilege of serving the communities of Orkney and Shetland.

'Cal Mac and Friends'

On 17th December 1999 the Scottish Executive, answerable to the Scottish Parliament on transport matters, announced that four companies – P&O Scottish Ferries, Serco/Denholm, Sea Containers and Caledonian MacBrayne and its partners – would be invited to submit tenders by March 2000 to operate the new contract. As part of their respective tenders the participating companies were obliged to make public their plans for the future services. The P&O tender was initially based on acquisition of second-hand vessels for the Aberdeen routes and engine upgrading/replacement on the *St. Ola* (IV). The deadline was extended to the end of May 2000 during which time P&O revised their proposals to include new ships at a cost of around £100 million, with the proposed vessels very similar to those which subsequently appeared with NorthLink. The company appeared confident of continuing their association with the Northern Isles. The Serco/Denholm bid was based on a single passenger vessel operating on a 24-hour basis. Such a service – daytime one way and overnight the other – would have been unlikely to meet the main customer requirement for an end of day departure and overnight crossing. Additionally, the timetable was tight and allowed no flexibility for bad weather or other delays. Meanwhile Sea Containers withdrew from the bid process.

Caledonian MacBrayne anticipated growth on the routes, estimating around £8 million greater passenger revenue than P&O. They led a consortium which included the Royal Bank of Scotland, funders and owners of the new ships, the Isle of Wight ferry operator WightLink, National Express and the shipbuilders Ferguson of Port Glasgow and Devon-based Appledore Shipyard. In the event the final consortium was an equal partnership between CalMac and Royal Bank of Scotland with WightLink and other partners having ended their interest prior to submission.

During a courtesy visit to Stromness by *Clansman* on 31st January 2000, Caledonian MacBrayne gave details of the three new vessels they would provide if successful. Two large ferries with capacity for 600 passengers would be built for the two Shetland routes with a 600-passenger, 110-car ferry for the Pentland Firth crossing. The initial Expression of Interest was submitted on behalf of 'CalMac and Friends' then changed to 'CalMac NorthLink' and finally to 'NorthLink'. Further work was required on trading names for the new company, with Norlantic being one option. However, the name 'NorthLink' was subsequently adopted and continues to the present day.

The role of Caledonian MacBrayne in Northern Isles ferry services stems from 5th October 2000, when Transport Minister Sarah Boyack MSP announced to the Scottish Parliament that the Caledonian MacBrayne partnership with Royal Bank of Scotland was the successful tender bid and that the new operation would begin in late 2002. For P&O Scottish Ferries it was the end of a long history serving Orkney and Shetland, but for Caledonian MacBrayne, it was a significant, if somewhat logical extension of their operations. NorthLink Orkney & Shetland Ferries was quickly established and, with headquarters in Stromness, they set about ordering the

The *Isle of Lewis* made a courtesy call to Stromness on 28th November 1998. (CalMac)

Above: Old and new at Aberdeen as NorthLink's *Hjaltland* waits at Regent's Quay pending berthing trials, whilst the P&O ferry *St. Clair* (V) prepares to depart on 18th September 2002. (Colin J. Smith)

Right: This view shows *St Sunniva* (III) leaving Stromness for the last time on 14th April 2002. (Andrew MacLeod)

Below right: The *Faye*, formerly the *St. Sunniva* (III) is framed by the bow of the new *Hamnavoe* at Leith on 5th November 2002. (Colin J. Smith)

Below left: A courtesy visit to Stromness by the *Clansman* on 31st January 2000. (Willie Mackay)

promised car and passenger ferries for introduction in October 2002. Although CalMac was a joint venture partner providing technical and ship management services, NorthLink was to be an otherwise autonomous business with its own staff, management and way of delivering services.

Farewell to P&O

The last days of the P&O vessels were not trouble free. The *St. Clair* (V) made her final sailing on 30th September 2002, operating the final northbound P&O Scottish Ferries sailing from Aberdeen to Lerwick. She sailed to Leith the next day and was subsequently sold to Saudi Arabian owners to be based in Jeddah for Pilgrim traffic on the Red Sea, under the name of the *Barakat*. Her new sphere of operation was thus a far cry from the wild seas of Shetland. On 26th October, en route to the Netherlands for overhaul she ran short of fuel off Hook of Holland and was towed into port by two tugs. She was still registered under the Saudi Arabian flag in 2016 as *Noor*, operating in the Red Sea from Jeddah.

The final few months of the *St. Sunniva* (III) were full of minor incidents – a food poisoning scare, engine failure, repeated turbo charger problems and a cracked sewage pipe – all of which led to delayed or cancelled sailings and

dry docking for repairs. With the imminent arrival of NorthLink in October 2002 and the need for the pier at Stromness to be upgraded in advance of the new services, the *St. Sunniva* made her last call on 14th April 2002. Using Kirkwall for the remainder of her season, she paid off on 30th September 2002, operating the final 6pm departure from Lerwick to be replaced next day by the new arrivals. She sailed to Leith for lay-up and was sold to Al Thurya of Dubai for further trading as the *Faye*. She departed from Leith on 15th November 2002 entering service between Dubai and the Iraqi port of Um Qasr in January 2003. Two months later, the US-led invasion of Iraq consumed the country and the *Faye* was subsequently scrapped at Alang, India in early 2005.

The future for the *St. Ola* (IV) was more auspicious. On 30th September 2002, under the command of Captain Willie Mackay, and with 147 passengers on board, she made her final sailing from Stromness to Scrabster, prior to sailing to Leith and onwards to Estonian ferry operators Saaremaa Shipping Company. Her departure from Orkney brought to an end 110 years of continuous service of the four ships to bear the name *St. Ola*. Departing from Leith on Wednesday 9th October 2002, she passed her successor *Hamnavoe* off the south coast of

The *Barakat* (ex *St. Clair* (V)) laid up at Rotterdam following her sale to Saudi Arabian interests for Pilgrim traffic operations on the Red Sea. (Ferry Publications Library)

Above: The *Hrossey* fitting out on 24th April 2002, with Hjaltland in the background. (Andrew MacLeod)

Right: The *Hjaltland* at the fitting out berth, after float out from the building dock. The funnel of Tallink's Romantika is in the background. (Andrew MacLeod)

Below left: The *Hjaltland* nearest with Hrossey double berthed alongside the fitting out quay on 24th April 2002. (Andrew MacLeod)

Below right: The *Hjaltland* in her final stages of construction. (Andrew MacLeod)

Above: The *Hamnavoe* pictured in the building dock on 28th May 2002. (Andrew MacLeod)

Left: An aerial view of all three Northlink vessels in their final stages of construction. (STX Europe)

Hrossey & Hjaltland

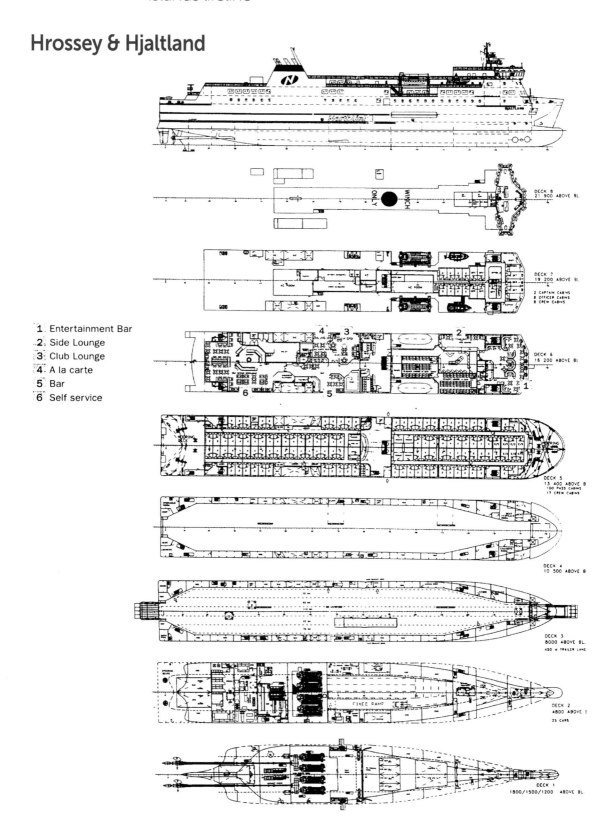

1. Entertainment Bar
2. Side Lounge
3. Club Lounge
4. A la carte
5. Bar
6. Self service

The *Hjaltland* undergoing painting works in the dry dock at Aker Finnyards, Rouma. (STX Europe)

Sweden and joined her near sister *Regula*, on the Kuivastu–Virtsu route. She occasionally reappeared in Northern Isles waters when en route to the Faroe Islands to undertake relief sailings for the ferry *Smyril*.

The final sailing of the *St. Rognvald* (IV) for P&O Scottish Ferries took place on 28th September 2002, following which she was sold to Gulf Offshore of Aberdeen and chartered by the newly established Norse Island Ferries, continuing to serve Shetland for a time. By this fortuitous set of circumstances, one of the old P&O order had slipped through the net, albeit temporarily.

The New Fleet Arrives

The new NorthLink vessels for the services from Aberdeen were impressive. Both were built by Aker Finnyards of Rouma, Finland at a contract price of around £32 million each and were designed specifically to serve the direct and indirect routes from Aberdeen to Lerwick (Holmsgarth) via Kirkwall, where they would use a new terminal at Hatston, rather than Stromness. In effect, the Kirkwall call revived in its entirety the former 'North Company' indirect route. Timetables for the new, faster vessels would be markedly different from their predecessors, with later departure times from Aberdeen and earlier island arrivals. NorthLink

would operate seven days per week and offered 12–14 hour crossings even travelling via Orkney, which now received calls on four days a week northbound and three days a week southbound, thus opening up major new inter-island opportunities as well as giving Orkney residents a new Kirkwall–Aberdeen service which has been heavily used from the outset.

There were to be no more 'saints'. The names chosen for all three new ships and the fourth vessel – a somewhat elderly but reliable freight vessel – were chosen in a competition by island residents and reflected the desire of NorthLink to be very much at the heart of the islands, rather than being perceived as a company based in distant Aberdeen. Reflecting the Norse heritage of the Northern Isles, the two larger ships were named *Hjaltland* and *Hrossey*, these being the Old Norse names for Shetland and Orkney respectively. To cement their roots in the island communities the company transferred as many P&O staff as possible into their fleet on similar employment terms. On 1st October 2002, the brand new *Hjaltland* set out from Aberdeen, bound for Kirkwall and Lerwick, whilst the *Hrossey*, departed from Lerwick southbound heralding the dawn of a new era of ferry links between the islands and mainland Scotland.

Hjaltland

Work started on the first vessel at Aker on 20th August 2001 when the project consultant John Horton symbolically stamped his initials onto a metal plate to be used in the steelwork of *Hjaltland*. Following Finnish tradition, the keel of *Hjaltland* was laid over 15th century 'good luck' *rheingulden* coins on 4th October 2001, she was floated out of her construction dock on 25th March 2002 and was delivered to her new owners on 12th August 2002. With the handover of the first ship, the new NorthLink Chief Executive, Bill Davidson, took up the post, having been involved in the project since its very earliest days. The *Hjaltland* sailed to Leith on 16th August 2002 under the command of Captain David Wheeler who described her as 'beyond expectations'. Following further fitting out the *Hjaltland* was welcomed to the new Holmsgarth terminal at Lerwick for the first time on 12th September where she towered above the *St. Clair* and displayed the new NorthLink house flag, almost identical to that of the old 'North Company', except for a lighter shade of blue, thereby acknowledging the heritage of a bygone era. On 14th September she was named by Narene Fullarton who had suggested the ship's name, and was opened to the public at Victoria Pier where she met with favourable comment and was inspected by a significant proportion of the Shetland population. She departed for Aberdeen via Kirkwall where berthing trials took place at the existing P&O terminal at the Town Pier. The *Hjaltland* took up service on 1st October 2002, departing from Aberdeen on the first northbound sailing, complete with the 'Lerwick Up Helly Aa Jarl Squad' aboard to add to the celebrations.

Hrossey

On 4th October 2001 Orkney Islands Council convener Councillor Hugh Halcro-Johnston stamped his initials into steel destined for sister ship the *Hrossey*. The keel was laid on 1st December and the ship was floated out on 20th April 2002 then handed over to NorthLink on 7th September. The *Hrossey* left Rauma on 12th September and sailed to Leith for a week of further fitting out with her master Captain Clive Austin describing her as 'a wonderful, wonderful ship'. She arrived in Kirkwall on the 24th September and, prior to opening to the public, was named by Kirsten Kelday, daughter of Alan Kelday who had suggested her name. On 1st October 2002, *Hrossey* undertook the first sailing southbound from Lerwick with thick fog delaying her arrival at Aberdeen for three hours.

The *Hjaltland* on sea trials off the coast of Finland. (STX Europe)

Above: The *Hjaltland* and *Hrossey* together at Leith for a VIP/Press reception on 23rd September 2002. (Andrew MacLeod)

Below: Another view of the *Hjaltland* and *Hrossey* together at Leith. (Andrew MacLeod)

Chapter three

The Era of NorthLink

Raising the Standards

Both the *Hjaltland* and *Hrossey* were drive-through ferries, 125 metres in length with gross tonnage of 12,000 and capacity for 600 passengers, including 300 overnight berths. Both ships were designed by the Finnish marine design consultants Deltamarin, whose design stable includes an impressive pedigree of excellent ferries and cruise ships including *Disney Magic, Disney Wonder, Voyager of the Seas, Europa, Armorique, Ulysses, Viking XPRS* and vessels of the Superfast fleet from *Superfast I* to *Superfast XII*. Deltamarin also designed *Blue Star Ithaki* built in Korea in 2000 for Strintzis Lines whose parent company, Attica were sufficiently impressed with the NorthLink ships to make an

unsuccessful offer to buy them in 2003.

Central to the NorthLink concept was the intention to offer passengers an altogether higher standard of service, with modern cruise-ferry style cabin accommodation, a choice of dining options, entertainment facilities, cinema, children's play area, shopping and other on-board services including four disabled cabins. Interior design was undertaken by the Essex-based Lindy Austin Partnership and the new vessels' interior design reflected the close links between the ships and the two island communities which they would serve. Hence the *Hrossey* has an Orcadian theme and displays Kirkwall as her port of registry whilst the *Hjaltland* offers a Shetland theme and her port of registry is Lerwick.

The main reception foyer was located on Deck 5, from where 2- and 4-berth en suite cabins were located fore and aft on both sides of the vessel with the outside cabins boasting large windows. The reception area was floored with chequered polished granite incorporating a compass motif and was fitted with a large gently curved stone-topped reception desk behind which a model of the vessel was displayed. A central stairwell lead up to Deck 6 where all other passenger facilities were located. The use of wood panelling effect, mirrors and stainless steel fittings gave both vessels a cruise-ferry ambience with leather seating and carpets all of high quality. Each vessel had two bars, the Midships Bar and Filska Bar aboard *Hjaltland*, Midships Bar and Skyran Bar on *Hrossey* and in September 2004, well ahead of Scottish legislation, a no smoking policy was introduced, meaning that both

On board the *Hrossey* at Kirkwall on 23rd September 2002 at the naming ceremony. From left to right: Rosie Wallace, Rebecca Parkin, Jim Wallace (Deputy First Minister), Hannah Barbour, Kirsten Kelday, Bill Davidson and NorthLink's Non Executive Director Lex Gold. (NorthLink)

Above: The *Hjaltland* leads her sister *Hrossey* as they pass beneath the Forth Bridge on 23rd September 2002. (Colin J. Smith)

Below: The *Hjaltland* makes a fine sight in the evening sunshine as she passes the Forth Bridge on 23rd September 2002 carrying invited tourism industry guests on their familiarisation cruise (Colin J. Smith)

The *Hjaltland* departing from Aberdeen on 18th March 2003. (Colin J. Smith)

vessels were now entirely smoke-free throughout their enclosed spaces. Both the *Hrossey* and *Hjaltland* offered a cinema lounge incorporating recliner seats and airline style suspended LCD screens with headphones showing up to three films per evening. The Orcadian theme aboard the *Hrossey* was continued with the positioning of a contemporary 'leaping salmon' sculpture in the reception area adjacent to the central stairway, whilst aboard the *Hjaltland* the position was occupied by a sculpture in stainless steel of a (left handed!) Viking warrior.

Both vessels boasted impressive à la carte restaurants serving local products and cuisine from Orkney and Shetland, together with excellent self-service restaurants. In March 2009, in response to demand, the number of covers in each of the à la carte restaurants was increased from 30 to 37.

The *Hrossey* and *Hjaltland* also offered shops that stocked the best of Shetland and Orkney crafts and produce, with a wide selection of jewellery, knitwear, wines and spirits, including Orcadian single malt whisky and Shetland gin, on offer.

External areas included a small gallery deck astern of the self-service restaurant with stairways leading up to outside areas on the upper level above the crew accommodation block at bridge level. Crew accommodation,

two rescue boats, a pair of lifeboats, fully enclosed bridge and officers' mess were situated on Deck 7 with a helipad located on the uppermost level, Deck 8. Navigational radar was carried on both ships' forward masts and both also possessed stern radar for berthing.

Both ships were capable of a cruising speed of 24 knots, compared to the 16 knots of their predecessors, reducing the journey time on the direct route to Lerwick to 12 hours instead 14 hours by P&O. The *Hjaltland* and *Hrossey* could make the crossing in 8.5 hours if required as both vessel's four engines allowed permutations ranging from very economical through to flat out.

To comply with SoLAS regulations, Deck 3, the vehicle deck, was over one metre above the waterline and offered 450 metres of 'truck-width' lane space, whilst a lower garage on Deck 2 could hold 25 cars and was accessed via a fixed ramp. There were no cabins below the waterline. For the first time on Scottish-owned vessels the bow doors were of the clamshell type, replacing the bow visor common on Caledonian MacBrayne vessels. Both vessels had a crew complement of 37.

Prior to commencing service NorthLink organised a special event in Leith for the many people and firms who had been heavily involved in the creation of the company, the design of the ships, the preparation of the

Above: In her original condition the *Hrossey* makes a departure from Aberdeen for Kirkwall on 22nd April 2004. (Colin J. Smith).

Right: The Filska Bar on the *Hjaltland*. (STX Europe)

Below left: The Midships Bar on board the *Hjaltland*. (STX Europe))

Below right: Wide staircases on both the *Hjaltland* and her sister Hrossey give ease of access all deck for passengers. (STX Europe)

Hamnavoe

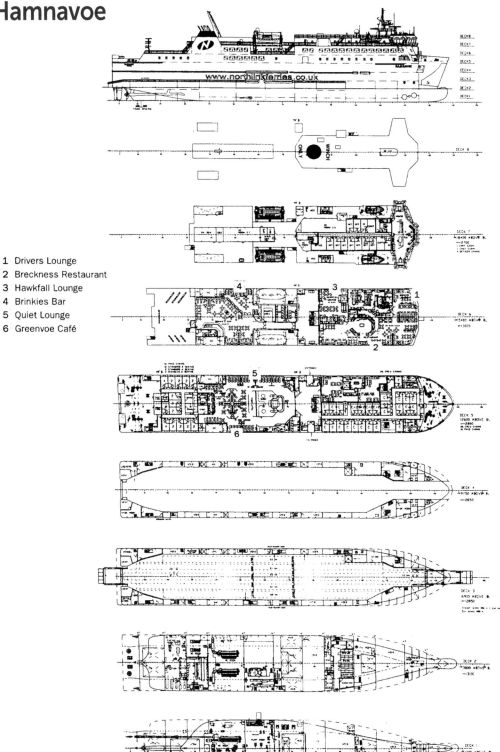

1 Drivers Lounge
2 Breckness Restaurant
3 Hawkfall Lounge
4 Brinkies Bar
5 Quiet Lounge
6 Greenvoe Café

winning bid to operate the lifeline services and the financing of the new ships. This 'corporate day' was then followed by a three-night trip to Orkney and Shetland for over 100 invited tourism industry guests from home and overseas. The trip, undertaken by the *Hjaltland*, launched NorthLink's drive to grow tourism to the Northern Isles through their 'NorthLink Cruise Tours' brand. On 23rd September, prior to departure from the Forth, the *Hjaltland* departed from Leith, having embarked her invited guests, and led the *Hrossey* on a cruise upriver beneath the Forth Bridges to Rosyth, which had been adopted as NorthLink's bad weather diversionary port.

The introduction of the new ships was accompanied by some of the worst weather ever experienced in the Northern Isles and North-East Scotland, but the vessels acquitted themselves well. Gale force winds on 21st October 2002 led to the closure of Aberdeen and the first diversion by the *Hrossey* to Rosyth. So severe was the weather that all NorthLink sailings were cancelled, resuming on 24th October 2002. On 3rd November 2002, the *Hrossey* encountered easterly Force 11 winds and seas so mountainous that she sought shelter to the west of Shetland, returning to Lerwick almost 24 hours after her departure

The Shoormal self-service restaurant on the *Hjaltland*. (STX Europe)

with minor damage to her foredeck fittings. Meanwhile, on one crossing, the *Hjaltland* arrived in Lerwick after 40 hours at sea, having been forced to omit her Kirkwall call. However, there were to be only three diversions in the next seven years. It was an unlucky start for the new service.

Initially, the two larger vessels experienced difficulties at Aberdeen on account of silting in the harbour channel, which was rectified by dredging in late 2002. Both the *Hjaltland* and *Hrossey* regularly undertook RNLI charters

The *Hjaltland* departs from Aberdeen whilst the paddle steamer *Waverley* rests at Atlantic Wharf during a break in her long trip from Great Yarmouth to the Firth of Clyde on 10th June 2003. (Colin J. Smith)

An impressive view of the *Hamnavoe* approaching Rora Head, north bound from Scrabster. (NorthLink)

organised in Shetland and Aberdeen with the ships being made available at no cost, whilst sponsors and suppliers donated services free of charge to ensure that 100 per cent of ticket sales and bar and shop profits went to the RNLI, with all the fuel costs being donated. In February 2009 both *Hrossey* and *Hjaltland* visited Fredericia in Denmark for overhauls, which saw application of an antifouling paint coating, together with the construction of a forecastle deckhouse to prevent recurrence of previous wave damage to the fo'c'sle doorway leading to the crew accommodation area.

In general, problems were few and the ships became accepted and admired by their many passengers over the years, whilst being immaculately maintained by their crews and officers who served aboard with great pride.

Hamnavoe

The £28 million *Hamnavoe* was a smaller version of the new twins, with capacity for 110 cars and 600 passengers, including 37 overnight berths in 16 cabins. A letter of intent to build the ship had been placed with Ferguson Shipbuilders of Port Glasgow in October 2000 but on 11th December of that year Ferguson's notified NorthLink that they could not formalise the contract due to the

tight 22-months deadline for completion. Within 18 hours a further letter of intent was placed with Aker Finnyards Shipyard in Rauma, with the contract signed for the third ship on 19th January 2001, the Aker yard being able to complete the smaller *Hamnavoe* thanks to a gap in their order book caused by lapsing of an option for SeaFrance. The keel of *Hamnavoe* was laid on 4th March 2002 and she was floated out on 5th June 2002, with confident predictions that, in spite of minor delays in construction, she would be ready for the 1st October commencement of the Pentland Firth service. In the event, although the *Hamnavoe* herself was ready, the new pier at Scrabster was incomplete. Aker had constructed the new vessel, from keel laying to handover, in less than seven months.

The *Hamnavoe* arrived at Leith on 9th October 2002 and had been given the Old Norse name for Stromness meaning 'Safe Haven'. En route she passed her predecessor *St. Ola* (IV) off the Swedish coast. She then visited Stromness where she was named on 19th October by her sponsor Linda Harcus, and was opened to the public for two days. Following this, she returned to Leith, sharing the Ocean terminal for a time with the former Royal Yacht *Britannia* and her predecessors

The *Hrossey* leaves Lerwick on her evening sailing to Orkney and Aberdeen. (Miles Cowsill)

Barakat (ex *St. Clair*) and *Faye* (ex *St. Sunniva*). She was laid up for seven months pending the completion of the new pier at Scrabster whilst the CalMac ferry *Hebridean Isles* provided the Pentland Firth service and experienced cancellations during the worst of the winter weather.

With more delays occurring on the completion of the new pier at Scrabster an interface platform was built for the forthcoming season, during the calmer weather, to allow *Hamnavoe* to load from the old pier, which was not to be completed until September 2003 – a year late. It was not until 7th April 2003 that the *Hamnavoe* finally left Leith, undertaking berthing trials at Aberdeen, Lerwick, Hatston and Scrabster over the next few days. Following modifications to the old Scrabster pier to allow her to berth, she was open to the public at the Caithness port on 13th April 2003 and she undertook two Charity Cruises for the RNLI on Saturday 19th and Sunday 20th for the Stromness and Thurso branches respectively. She then spent two days 'shadowing' the *Hebridean Isles* on the Pentland Firth prior to taking up service on the 9am crossing on Monday 21st April 2003, but operated on a modified schedule until the new pier at Scrabster was completed.

Like her larger consorts *Hamnavoe* was fitted out to a cruise ship standard, the interiors having been designed by Lindy Austin Partnership who subsequently undertook the interior design for CalMac's Polish-built Islay ferry *Finlaggan*. On-board facilities included the Breckness self-service restaurant, the Greenvoe Café, the Hawkfall Lounge, Brinkie's Bar, which opened onto a large open deck area overlooking the stern, games room and a children's play area. *Hamnavoe* had 13x 2- and 1 x 3- and 2 x 4-berth cabins for use mainly by passengers overnight and then on the first departure of the day from Stromness. Being permanently associated with the shorter Pentland Firth crossing to Orkney, the *Hamnavoe* was registered in Kirkwall. The centrepiece in her reception area was a sculpture called 'The Mither o' the Sea', representing the benign force of the summer sea, one of the oldest elements of Orcadian folklore, whilst the writings of the celebrated Orcadian writer and lifelong Stromness resident, George Mackay Brown, author of the poem 'Hamnavoe' were etched on glass throughout the ship.

On 16th May 2004 *Hamnavoe* sailed to Bremerhaven, returning to service on 25th May where remedial work on fissures in the A-frame

The *Hjaltland* arrives at Lerwick at 06.30 on her overnight sailing from Aberdeen. This view shows the additional accommodation which was added to the upper deck at the stern to provide further cabins. (Miles Cowsill)

structures supporting the propeller shafts was carried out prior to the start of the main tourist season. Her replacement for a one-week period was the freighter *Hascosay* which carried all cars, freight and up to 12 passengers, with support from the John o' Groats ferry *Pentland Venture* to transport all other passengers. On 16th May 2006 the *Hamnavoe* struck the Outer Holm at the mouth of Stromness Harbour due to an electrical failure but was not damaged and in April 2008, during overhaul at Fredericia, she was modified to burn low-sulphur fuel – a cheaper intermediate fuel oil instead of expensive gas oil.

To allow her to relieve the *Hamnavoe*, the *Hjaltland* undertook berthing trials at Scrabster and Stromness on 14th April 2007 whilst en route to Birkenhead for overhaul and the addition of a new cabin block. Her first spell of service on the Pentland Firth took place between 13th and 29th April 2008, making her the largest vessel ever to serve on the Pentland Firth crossing, a task she has repeated in subsequent years.

The NorthLink Freighter

In addition to the three newbuilds, the company undertook to operate a fourth vessel for livestock and commercial vehicles only, acquiring the 6,136 ton vessel *Sea Clipper* and renaming her *Hascosay* after an uninhabited Shetland island lying between Yell and Fetlar.

The *Hascosay* was built in 1971 at Kristiansand, Norway as the *Juno,* and was sold in 1979 to Finnfranline of France, being renamed the *Normandia* and was chartered to Finncarriers for service between Finland and France. In 1982 she was chartered to Sucargo for service between France, Algeria and the Middle East, then in 1986 she was sold to Mikkola of Finland, renamed the *Misidia* and chartered to Transfennica for services between Finland and Northern Europe. In 1990 she was sold to Kristiania Ejendom of Norway and was renamed the *Euro Nor,* then another name change was to come in 1991 when she was chartered to Commodore Ferries becoming the *Commodore Clipper* serving the Channel Islands, and in 1996 she was replaced by the

Commodore Goodwill and sold to Goliat Shipping and was renamed the *Sea Clipper*.

In 1998, the vessel was chartered to the Estonian Shipping Company (Esco) for service between Germany and Estonia as the *Transbaltica*. She was renamed the *Sea Clipper* in 2001 and chartered to Fjord Line, prior to joining NorthLink early 2002. The *Hascosay* was an ice-class vessel, able to carry over 36 trailers or, in livestock container mode, accommodate 5,500 lambs or 1,000 cattle on a daily basis, as well as about 20 trailers at a maximum speed of over 17 knots. In preparation for her new role she underwent a major refit at the Remontowa Shipyard, Gdansk, Poland and entered service on 8th May 2002, not on Northern Isles services but on charter to Caledonian MacBrayne for freight runs between Ullapool and Stornoway. The *Hascosay* was the first vessel to don the new livery of NorthLink Ferries and on 1st October 2002 she transferred to Aberdeen to take up the route for which she was intended, namely Northern Isles freight sailings.

During a period relieving for the *Hamnavoe* in May 2004 the *Hascosay* carried 12 passengers between the mainland and Burwick, but by this time, her smart livery had given way to a more sombre dark blue hull, having failed to stand up to the rigours of winter on such an old ship.

Harbour Investments

To handle the new ferries, major upgrading of terminal and berthing facilities at Aberdeen, Scrabster, Stromness, Kirkwall and Holmsgarth (Lerwick) was undertaken.

At Kirkwall, the construction of a completely new 161-metre ro-ro terminal at Hatston one mile north of Kirkwall facilitated the reintroduction of the seven times weekly indirect route, with vessels calling in each direction at Kirkwall on passage between Shetland and Aberdeen. In addition to the ferry terminal, Hatston offered a 225-metre deepwater berth for large cruise ships, rapidly becoming a central feature in the tourism industry in Orkney. The Hatston terminal opened on 21st October 2002. At Lerwick, the new Holmsgarth terminal, designed by the

Aberdeen-based architects Arch Henderson, was opened on 1st April 2002. The terminal was also capable of accommodating the new Smyril Line vessel *Norröna*, introduced in 2003 to link Shetland with Iceland, Denmark and the Faroe Islands. Aberdeen also witnessed major reconstruction of the terminal areas in 2002/2003, with much of the life-expired P&O infrastructure at Aberdeen razed to make way for new marshalling areas and a new livestock shed. Aberdeen Harbour Board also provided a new award-winning two-storey passenger terminal designed by Arch Henderson, with covered boarding walkways and new check-in and luggage storage facilities.

At Stromness, the pier was strengthened and modified through addition of an upper level walkway and covered boarding bridge and replacement linkspan. In Caithness, construction of the new pier at Scrabster, named Queen Elizabeth Pier, was delayed by around a year, being officially opened by HRH Prince Charles, the Duke of Rothesay on 6th August 2003 and the new passenger terminal at the pier became operational on 10th August 2004, almost two years after the start of NorthLink services.

Freight and Livestock

The movement of livestock and freight all year round is central to the economies of Orkney and Shetland. Prior to handover to NorthLink, the handling of livestock needed to be modified to comply with the new livestock welfare regulations of the EU; NorthLink proposed carrying livestock using specially designed livestock 'cassettes'. Today the company utilises a fleet of 12-metre and 6-metre trucks, 48 of these units were built by Stewart Trailers of Inverurie and in support of these trailers, new lairage facilities were provided at Lerwick, Hatston and Aberdeen.

As the peak livestock season straddled the change of operator from P&O to NorthLink, it was agreed that P&O would start and finish the 2002 livestock season, using the chartered *Buffalo Express* alongside the *St. Rognvald* during October 2002, even though their passenger services ended at the end of September.

Above: The chartered Norwegian freighter *Clare* departs from Aberdeen in the company of the harbour pilot launch on 21st April 2004. (Colin J. Smith).

Right: In her original NorthLink livery the freighter *Hascosay* is seen departing from Aberdeen on a sunny day on March 18th 2003 (Colin J. Smith).

Below left: The MN *Toucan* was chartered for freight work during an extended absence of the Hascosay for rudder repairs in early 2007. (Willie Mackay)

Below right: The *Hascosay* arrives at Lerwick inward-bound from Aberdeen. (Willie Mackay)

Above: The *Hascosay* swinging off the berth at Lerwick inward-bound Kirkwall. (Willie Mackay)

Left: The *Hamnavoe* loading cars at Stromness. (NorthLink)

Freight Competition

In July 2002, the three main haulage companies in the Northern Isles – Northwards, JBT and Shetland Transport – came together with Cenargo and Gulf Offshore North Sea to launch a new freight company, Norse Island Ferries (NIF). On 24th July 2002 this company announced it would link Aberdeen and Shetland from the end of August that year using the former Norse Merchant Ferries vessel *Merchant Venture*, then laid up at Birkenhead, offering a service from Aberdeen and Lerwick six days a week, with the *St Rognvald* following as their second ship in October 2002. For NorthLink, this represented the loss of about 90 per cent of the freight on the existing route and as such was a major blow. Competition ensued, with the reliability of the new NorthLink ships proving increasingly popular for freight operators. The *Merchant Venture* proved troublesome, with NIF having to charter the *European Mariner* to cover for her extended absence due to mechanical problems. These problems led to the *Merchant Venture* being permanently withdrawn in February 2003. Meanwhile financial difficulties at Cenargo gradually impacted upon Norse Island Ferries and, as a result, the company graciously bowed to the inevitable on 7th June 2003. For NorthLink, the demise of NIF saw freight

demand increase sharply requiring additional capacity through the immediate charter of the erstwhile *St. Rognvald* to meet the additional demand. As a result NorthLink's costs rose dramatically in the wake of a period when freight traffic revenue had been significantly undercut, threatening the very survival of the company.

In November 2003 the *St. Rognvald* was sold to Middle Eastern interests and on to India for scrap in January 2004. She was replaced by the Danish vessel *Clare* on 5th December 2003. Built at Bremerhaven in 1972 as the *Wesertal*, she was renamed *Meyer Express* upon delivery, reverting to *Wesertal* in 1973. She subsequently carried the names *Vinzia E*, and *Dana Baltica*, when operating between Denmark and Lithuania for DFDS Baltic Line, and was subsequently operated by Smyril Line between Torshavn, Lerwick and Hanstholm between 2001 and late 2003, when she was chartered to NorthLink. On 30th July 2004, the *Clare* suffered an engine explosion, which necessitated her withdrawal for repairs, returning to service on 25th August during which time she was replaced by the *MN Colibri*, a ship employed in carrying components of the ESA Ariane rocket vehicle. A similar vessel, the *MN Toucan* was chartered for freight work during an extended absence of the *Hascosay*

The *Clare* prepares for her morning sailing to Kirkwall. (Miles Cowsill)

for rudder repairs in early 2007.

In support of the autumn livestock sailings NorthLink continued to charter the livestock carrier *Buffalo Express,* or her near sister *Zebu Express*, for sailings from Aberdeen. These arrangements continued only until 2007 since when livestock sailings have been handled by NorthLink vessels using the new livestock containers which started to become available during 2008.

Orkney Competitor

In 2001 a new company began sailings on the route between St. Margaret's Hope in Orkney and Gills Bay in Caithness, formerly the location of the terminal for the ill-fated Orkney Ferries short sea crossing venture in the 1980s. Pentland Ferries was the brainchild of Andrew Banks whose family had been involved in operating work boats at the Flotta oil terminal and who acquired the former Caledonian MacBrayne ferry *Iona* dating from 1970, and subsequently the 1979-built side-loader *Claymore*, renaming the former the *Pentalina B*. The initial impact of Pentland Ferries was to attract around an estimated 30 per cent of the 180,000 passengers conveyed by P&O on the

Scrabster–Stromness route. However levels recovered with NorthLink's passenger numbers on the Stromness crossing steadily increasing by 55,000 between 2002 and 2005. Pentland Ferries now operate the *Pentalina*, an 18-knot RoPax catamaran with capacity for 30 cars and 250 passengers which was built in the Philippines in 2008.

Thanks to the new NorthLink vessels, the arrival of Pentland Ferries on the Pentland Firth and new competitors in the shape of Norse Island Ferries, a total of eight large ferries were available to serve the Northern Isles from mainland Scotland for a time in 2002–2003. Islanders had never had it so good. But the good times could not, and did not, continue indefinitely.

'It Wasn't Broke. But it is now. And How.'

So ran the editorial in the *Shetland Times* of 9th April 2004. On the previous day, the Transport Minister, Nicol Stephen MSP, unexpectedly announced that as a result of huge trading losses at NorthLink, the tendering process would be repeated with a new contract to serve the Northern Isles coming into force in 2005, two years earlier than the planned date

Above: The small town of Stromness plays host to the cruise ship *Hanseatic*, while the *Hamnavoe* leaves for Scrabster. (Willie Mackay).

Right: The *Hjaltland*, *Clare* and *Hascosay* at Lerwick during a weekend lay-over. (Willie Mackay)

Below left: The weather conditions on the Pentland Firth can at times be very rough. This view shows the *Hamnavoe* outward-bound for Scrabster with the island of Hoy behind her in the setting sun. (Willie Mackay)

Below right: An interesting collection of vessels at St Margaret's Hope. From left to right, the *Claymore*, *Pentalina B* and the new *Pentalina*. (Willie Mackay)

Above: The *Hildasay* alongside at Lerwick prior to taking up service. (NorthLink)

Right: NorthLink's Commercial Director Cynthia Spencer with Sophie Wishart and CEO Bill Davidson at the renaming of the *Hildasay*. (NorthLink)

Below: A full turnout for the renaming of the *Hildasay* at Lerwick, including Jarl Squad. (NorthLink)

The *Hascosay* and *Helliar* offer regular freight only services from Aberdeen to both Orkney and Shetland (Colin J. Smith)

of September 2007. An additional £13.4 million had been made available to NorthLink between October 2002 and April 2004 to offset losses incurred as a result of unforeseen circumstances, including the need to charter the *St. Rognvald* and subsequently the *Clare*, which had adverse impacts on the NorthLink business plan.

The successful NorthLink bid had been prepared on the basis of historic traffic and market conditions data provided by P&O Scottish Ferries but, even before the arrival of NorthLink in October 2002, fundamental changes and unforeseen events had adversely affected the financial model on which the bid had been prepared and accepted by the Scottish Executive. These included delays due to Scrabster Harbour Trust being a year late in completion of facilities for the Pentland Firth service, the consequent tie up of the £28m *Hamnavoe* at Leith for six months, with the resultant revenue loss on the route, together with the need to charter the *Hebridean Isles* and the start-up of rival Pentland Ferries. The arrival and subsequent demise of Norse Island Ferries had an adverse effect on NorthLink's fragile freight revenue, putting the company

onto the financial back foot even before services began. Audit Scotland concluded that 'NorthLink got into financial difficulties because competition reduced its income and some of its costs were higher than expected'. The business NorthLink had planned to run was not the one they were actually running and by summer 2002 it was clear that refinancing was required.

The situation had been under discussion with the Scottish Executive since the summer of 2002 pending the outcome of a funding agreement that was acceptable to the European Union. NorthLink continued to operate the services until a revised tender could be undertaken. Expressions of interest were invited in late April 2004 and the detailed tender was published on 27th May 2004. P&O announced withdrawal from the process on 30th June 2004 and on 19th July 2005 Transport Minister Tavish Scott MSP announced the tender shortlist and specifications, which included a reduced tariff for freight on the Aberdeen routes, improvements to the timetable and new provision for the carriage of livestock.

Chapter four

NorthLink 2

The NorthLink brand name, logo, and identity were offered for sale to bidders if they wished to use it. Three companies, V Ships UK Ltd, Irish Continental Ferries plc and Caledonian MacBrayne Ltd were invited to tender for the services, with operation and leasing of the NorthLink vessels transferring to the successful bidder. Although they had no involvement in the tendering process, the Royal Bank of Scotland would continue to own the three new ships, with a charter arrangement set up between the bank and the successful operator. In a memo to all staff on 19th July 2005, NorthLink CEO Bill Davidson made it clear that whilst his own companies' interest in the tender was at an end, a successful bid by Caledonian MacBrayne would effectively mean that NorthLink Ferries would continue as a wholly owned subsidiary of the west coast operator, in the guise of what he termed 'NorthLink 2'. It was intended that services would transfer to the new operator on 1st April 2005 but the start date was revised to July 2006.

Only two companies submitted tenders, the Irish operator withdrawing from the process, and on 9th March 2006 the Transport Minister announced that Caledonian MacBrayne had been successful. Under the six-year contract, Orkney saw a 19 per cent reduction in freight tariffs, while Shetland's reduced by 25 per cent.

On 6th July 2006, control passed to the new operator, NorthLink Ferries Limited. This company was a wholly owned subsidiary of none other than the dormant David MacBrayne Ltd, (DML) which was reactivated to become the parent company of the operator of the Northern Isles contract. David MacBrayne Limited now owned NorthLink Ferries Limited and remained in the ownership of Scottish Ministers, as did Caledonian MacBrayne Limited, which remained

a separate operating company. The ships themselves remained the property of the Royal Bank of Scotland. To the travelling public everything remained pretty much the same as before. Somewhere in heaven, old Mr. MacBrayne, master at last of all he surveyed, poured himself a celebratory dram.

The subsequent re-tendering of services and the takeover by parent company DML did not halt the growth in traffic generated by NorthLink. By 2007 it was necessary to increase cabin capacity on the larger ships by 20 per cent, from 280 to 356 berths out of their total passenger complement of 600. To provide the additional berths on both vessels a new crew accommodation module was constructed on the deck above the cafeteria whilst existing crew cabins on the passenger cabin deck Deck 5 were refurbished for passenger use. The work was undertaken by Northwestern Shiprepairers at Birkenhead during annual survey and overhaul on *Hjaltland* during April and May 2007 and on *Hrossey* over a three-week period from 26th February 2007.

In summer 2009 NorthLink began consulting on possible changes to their schedules which would see the introduction of additional daytime sailings between Orkney and Shetland to free up overnight accommodation for passengers on the Aberdeen–Lerwick sailings, and with a reduction in wintertime passenger capacity on the direct service. Responses to the proposals were mixed with the tourism industry welcoming the proposed increases in summer passenger capacity whilst other sectors, mainly the aquaculture industry, were concerned about the effect on delivery times and winter capacity to Aberdeen and as a result the proposals were shelved.

The charter of the *Clare* ended in December

Above: The *Hamnavoe* at Scrabster in the morning sun on 11th April 2010. (Colin J. Smith)

Below: The *Hjaltland* leaving Aberdeen on evening sailing to Shetland 8th July 2014. (Colin J. Smith)

2010 and she was replaced by another vessel of the *Hildasay* type, the 122 metre Seatruck Ferries ro-ro vessel *Clipper Racer* built in 1997 by Astilleros de Huelva SA, Huelva, Spain as the Lehola for the Estonian Shipping Company of Tallinn. For Northern Isles service, the vessel was renamed *Helliar,* after Helliar Holm, an island near Shapinsay.

The economic recession which began in late 2008 had an unexpectedly positive impact as NorthLink's passenger and freight carryings continued to increase throughout 2009. However with limitations on the capacity of the *Hascosay* NorthLink turned to the Irish Sea for a replacement. This was the 121 metre, 7,606 ton *Shield*, built in 1999 at Huelva in Spain for Esco. Following a refit at Birkenhead, which included modifications to her stern ramp, the *Shield* was renamed *Hildasay* on 10th February by Shetland schoolgirl Sophie Wishart and took up service for NorthLink on 18th February 2010. The previous day the *Hascosay* made her last sailing from Lerwick to Aberdeen, having covered 432,000 miles for the company. On 13th March 2010 *Hascosay* departed from Kirkwall for the last time, her destination Beirut, where she would be refitted for another chapter in her long career as a livestock carrier sailing to Jordan from Brazil, Georgia and Romania.

Re-tendering of Routes to the Northern Isles Services

Services to Orkney and Shetland were re-tendered during 2011/12 by Transport Scotland as NorthLink Ferries Ltd's contract came to an end. Initially, the contract's two services (Aberdeen–Lerwick and Scrabster–Stromness), which were to be de-bundled, became available. Eligible bids for the services were received from Pentland Ferries (which expressed interest in the Scrabster–Stromness service only), Sea-Cargo A/S (which expressed interest in the Aberdeen–Lerwick service only), P&O Ferries, Shetland Line (1984) Ltd (part of local haulage and freight company Streamline Shipping Group), Serco, and the incumbent NorthLink Ferries Ltd. The Scottish Government subsequently re-bundled the routes when insufficient interest was shown in the separate routes.

On 4th May 2012, Transport Scotland announced that Serco was the preferred bidder. This decision was legally challenged in the Court of Session by rival bidder Shetland Line (1984) Limited, on the basis that the Scottish Government had allegedly not taken into account that their proposed service scored higher in a quality test than Serco Ltd – suspending the securement of the contract. However, on 29th May 2012, the court overturned the suspension and Serco Ltd was confirmed as the new operator, ending Caledonian MacBrayne's 10 years of involvement with Northern Isles ferry services.

The contract was for a six year period until 2018 and worth £243m. Serco Group, using the same vessels and branding as its predecessor, began operation of the Northern Isles ferry services at 3pm on 5th July 2012. The new contract between both parties stated that Serco, in addition to running the operations to the Northern Isles, would undertake that there would be no repetition of the dry dock problems of the previous contract, that they would streamline services for freight operators from the islands and also build on improvement to the passenger experience.

Commenting on the appointment Transport Minister Keith Brown said:

The Scottish Government is absolutely committed to providing the very best ferry services to Orkney and Shetland to meet the needs of residents, business and visitors alike.

Building on the work by NorthLink over the last six years, today we are taking the Northern Isles ferry services forward. Following a full public consultation exercise and a period of open and transparent competition, Serco Ltd have won the contract to deliver ferry services to the Northern Isles from summer this year until 2018.

The new contract rectifies many of the difficulties of the one we inherited, in particular the recent difficulties with the extended dry dock period.

The new arrangements ensure we will avoid the situation where vessels have been laid up for long periods of time. The *Hjaltland*

A very rare view of the two sister ships, the *Hjaltland* and *Hrossey* together off Aberdeen, taken on Sunday 16th March 2014. Hrossey had just arrived ex Birkenhead refit in her new livery as Hjaltland departed for Orkney and Shetland on the scheduled evening sailing having dry docked herself in February of that year. (NorthLink)

and *Hrossay* will not be used to relieve the Scrabster–Stromness route as has happened in the past. A different replacement vessel will be used to cover *Hamnavoe*'s dry-dock periods.

The needs of vital time-sensitive freight exports like fish and seasonal livestock and vital imports like supermarket goods will be met, and the services available for passengers will be improved. Passengers will see improvements to the journey experience with improved ticketing arrangements, premium reclining seats added on board overnight services, and improved catering, hospitality and customer care facilities.

Crucially, clear commitments that crossing times, including the 90-minute crossing between Scrabster and Stromness, will also be retained. Given cuts by Westminster to the Scottish Government's budget, it is also essential that we make the very most of every penny spent in Scotland, so we will also see the new contract deliver value for money for Scotland's taxpayers.

Serco Ltd has prepared a thorough start-up plan setting out what is required to be done to ensure a seamless and managed handover from the current operator, including transfer arrangements for staff under TUPE regulations, in time for the start of the new service. Beyond this new contract, there is more we want to do for communities in the Northern Isles. We made clear in our Draft Ferries Plans that we see RET as the basis for setting fares in Scotland and have stated our clear aim to implement RET-based fares across every route in Scotland, including the Northern Isles. We will set out, next year, our proposals on how and when that will take place. I look forward to the beginning of the new contract this summer which will ensure that people travelling to and from Orkney and Shetland will continue to have access to safe, reliable and affordable ferry services in the future.

Angus Cockburn, Serco's Chief Financial Officer said:

Since commencing the operation of the Northern Isles ferry service in 2012, Serco has introduced the Caledonian Sleeper service to our Scottish portfolio, building on our increasingly strong presence in the country.

Serco's successful customer-led approach to managing two such iconic Scottish services on behalf of Transport Scotland has allowed us to demonstrate our expertise in the transport and maritime industries as well our dedication to providing good value for the tax payer, something we are proud to deliver across our eleven operations in Scotland.

As part of our approach, we are committed to supporting local business and local communities by employing nearly 3,000 people in health, transport, justice, immigration, defence and housing. We focus employment on areas close to our operations and have a policy to 'buy local'

Above: An impressive view of the *Hamnavoe* outward bound Scrabster on her morning sailing to Orkney. (NorthLink)

Below: The *Hjaltland* captured with vista of Lerwick, following her morning arrival from Aberdeen. (NorthLink)

wherever possible, proudly working with over 270 Scottish suppliers, of which 75 per cent are SMEs.

This contract allowed Serco to build on their experience of managing and transforming critical local transport services such as Northern Rail, Scatsta Airport on the Shetland Islands and London's Woolwich Ferry.

Serco Take Control

Modifications to accommodation and on-board catering services on the *Hrossey* and *Hjaltland* were undertaken during the first winter from Thurso was quickly recognised. Outer island customers were also offered the bed and breakfast service on the *Hamnavoe* over the winter period, which became seven days per week as a further improvement in operations, to tie in with evening arrivals of many of Orkney Ferries' services.

Following internal modifications to the *Hjaltland* and *Hrossey*, Serco NorthLink Ferries rolled out their revised on-board services in February 2014 along with a new 'Magnus' logo and livery emphasising the islands' Viking/Norse heritage. The former à la carte restaurants and attached lounge were rebranded as the exclusive

Above: The new exclusive sleeping pods offer an alternative to a cabin on the *Hjaltland* and *Hrossey* for overnight sailings. (NorthLink)

Right: The Magnus Lounge offer peace and quiet to work or unwind on the longer routes from Aberdeen. (NorthLink)

under the management of Serco. This included the provision of much-improved sleeper seats designed by the Norwegian company Georg Eknes in the Forward starboard reclining seat lounge, maintaining the current cinema/reclining seat area and the fitting of further reclining seats in the area adjacent to the shop.

Reductions to two sailings per day commencing on 3rd January 2013 on the Scrabster–Stromness route were also announced. These would be at 6.30am/8.45am and 4.45pm/7.00pm Monday–Friday with Saturday and Sunday remaining at 9.00am/12 noon and 4.45pm/7.00pm There was some debate about the new scheduled timings but the benefits of an early morning departure from Orkney to connect with ongoing public transport

Magnus' Lounge on both vessels. A charge was introduced for the use of the new exclusive area, which included an extensive range of complimentary offers and access to a range of newspapers and magazines. Premium and Executive Cabin users were now also able to use Magnus' Lounge as part of the upgraded service for these cabin types.

The original reclining-seat area on the starboard side forward was removed and replaced by more comfortable 'Premium Sleeper-seats' later to be branded as 'Sleeping Pods'. The special seating, the first of their kind on any ferry, came with a large table, adjustable lighting and a USB socket. The individual seats reclined back to allow passengers to relax and sleep without intruding on the space of the person behind. The price included a token for a free shower. The new seating proved very popular and was very much modelled on airline 'Club' seating.

As an improvement request from the pre-contract community engagement programme, showers were also introduced on-board for those passengers travelling without cabin accommodation. One of the showers was specifically designed with low level wheelchair access for passengers with reduced mobility.

The restaurants on all three vessels were renamed 'Feast' for 2013, still providing the main dining area, but with hot snacks also available in the bars for longer hours. A premium 'cooked to order' menu, largely based on local quality produce, was now offered with personal service in part of Magnus' Lounges, in a slightly simplified version of the previous operator's à la carte menu on the Aberdeen service. In addition to the refurbishment, which was completed on the run, on timescale and within budget, the annual surveys for this year were carried out while the ships were in service during February and March.

The Aberdeen terminal reception was modified in 2015 to have a lower reception desk to allow for easier check-in for those in wheelchairs. All lifts were altered to have improved signage, and larger and more visible button controls in addition to audio announcements. On-board the passenger directional signage was also improved to offer black on chrome contrast, tactile and braille to make the passage easier for those with impaired visibility. This included all cabin door numbering.

Just hours after NorthLink held public presentations on the islands, showcasing their recent refurbishment programme, the *Hamnavoe* suffered an engine shutdown on her evening crossing from Scrabster on 25th April 2013. Following her arrival at Stromness the following morning's sailings were cancelled while ongoing mechanical investigations revealed serious crankshaft damage on the starboard engine, which was obviously going to mean a considerable time out of service for the ship. While arrangements for replacement parts, and locating a shipyard with available facilities, were being put in place, NorthLink Terminal staff arranged alternative arrangements via the Aberdeen–Kirkwall route and Pentland Ferries.

Attempts were made to source a replacement vessel while the ship's staff, assisted by service engineers, continued to dismantle the engine. After six days the *Hamnavoe* sailed to Rosyth. She was repaired afloat in the non-tidal wet basin, which allowed stern-ramp vehicle access, while temporary access hatches for large engine parts were made in the vehicle deck. As no suitable replacement passenger ferry could be sourced, the freight vessel the *Helliar* was mobilised from Lerwick to provide a twice-daily cargo and 12-passenger service, which continued until the *Hamnavoe* returned on 23rd May.

Sadly this whole scenario led to much ill-feeling in Orkney, particularly against the Scottish Government and the operator, as the 2012 state-run ferry contract allowed for no utilisation of one of the Aberdeen–Kirkwall–Shetland vessels on the Pentland Firth route. NorthLink rivals Pentland Ferries obviously benefited greatly from the problems with the *Hamnavoe* and added some extra weekend sailings to cope with demand. The Aberdeen–Orkney–Shetland indirect service also saw increased traffic as a result of the *Hamnavoe* being off-service.

Cargo traffic from Shetland was sufficient that the two-ship summer freight service by the *Hildasay* and *Helliar* was resumed early in 2013 at the beginning of June, two weeks earlier than planned. This gave two southbound trips from Kirkwall to Aberdeen with the particularly important Monday service catering for the main cattle sale at the beginning of each week, and the latter part of the week then concentrating on aquaculture and white fish volumes from Shetland. The northbound Aberdeen–Orkney–Shetland service also saw increased traffic due to a considerable upturn in oil and gas sector work in Shetland.

NorthLink Ferries Today

Today NorthLink Ferries lies at the epicentre of island life. A trade route for agriculture, fisheries and businesses, and a transport link for residents, it is also a bringer of the essential tourism business which underpins so much of the island economies. The initial assentation that

Above: The *Hamnavoe* swings off the berth at Stromness on her morning sailing to mainland Scotland. (Miles Cowsill)

Below: The *Hjaltland* makes a fine sight in the evening sunshine during June 2016 as she sails outward bound for Aberdeen. (Miles Cowsill)

An outstanding view of Stromness with the Island of Hoy in background. The *Hamnavoe* can be seen at berth in the heart of harbour. (NorthLink)

The Reception Area on the *Hjaltland*. (NorthLink)

there was scope to generate growth in traffic to the Northern Isles continues to be borne out with just under 300,000 passengers carried per year between the Islands and mainland Scotland, a 6.3% increase in passengers since Serco Limited commenced Contract management in July 2012 and with a 2% increase in freight traffic on 2012 volumes compared to those recorded in 2015.

NorthLink is a significant generator of employment in the islands and a strong supporter of community activities. The company employs 81 shore-based staff over its five operating sites, the majority in the islands, with the call centre, marketing, social media and freight activity all being centred in Stromness. 260 crew are employed directly on its three vessels; *Hamnavoe*, *Hjaltland* and *Hrossey*, with a similar number of contractors providing stevedoring, security and shore facility services across the route network.

Since 2012 a specific focus on local recruitment has led to increasing numbers of employees drawn from the islands, from the North East of Scotland. As ever employees are also drawn from further afield in the UK and Europe.

To offer travellers a taste of the islands, NorthLink buys local goods and services as far as possible by applying its' Buy Local Produce' policy, currently it procures 85% of its food and beverage from businesses based within a 50 mile radius of the company's operating ports. Since 2012 Serco NorthLink had a comprehensive sponsorship programme providing a broad range

of support to individual sportsmen and sportswomen, teams, societies and many groups representing the social whirl of the Islands and North East communities they serve. From Food & Drink festivals to RNLI fundraising days, Island Games travel, Shetland Folk Festival, fiddlers to the Edinburgh Tattoo, sports teams, swimmers, track athletes, horse jumpers and more. Support to Kirkwall's St. Magnus Festival, the Shetland Classic Motor Show, Stromness Shopping Week and the RSPB Orkney Nature Festival are all essential aspects of recognising and working with their local communities. In 2016 in particular two new initiatives recognised NorthLink Ferries embracing both traditional craft building and key agricultural stakeholders with their sponsorship of both the Portsoy Traditional Boat Festival and the ANM Christmas Classic Livestock Sales at the Inverurie Mart.

All part of a programme of support allowing real community spirit and pride to be shown throughout the route network and demonstrating the close working relationship developed with key stakeholders.

The ships themselves, flagships of the overall £100 million investment package, remain as superb as the day they first sailed, reflecting the great pride taken in them by their crews. They are still owned by the Royal Bank of Scotland on the basis of a 15-year ownership agreement over three tender periods meaning that any future operator would be able to use them, unless they opted to provide alternative vessels of their own.

At the outset of the service there was some nervousness about the new era and indeed some of the islanders suggested that the ships were too opulent for the Northern Isles, whilst other commentators did not regard them as particularly beautiful. Inevitably there were yearnings for the old days of P&O and their predecessors. Over the years, however, the ships of NorthLink Ferries have won over the hearts and minds of islanders and visitors alike, firmly securing their place as worthy successors to their predecessors and proud ambassadors for the people of Orkney and Shetland. Indeed in 2016 the readers of the Guardian and Observer newspapers rated the NorthLink vessels as number one in their 'Best Ferry' award.

Chapter five

Keeping the Freight Moving

The lifeline service that NorthLink provides to the islands cannot be underestimated. Three passenger ferries, the *Hrossey*, *Hjaltland* and *Hamnavoe*, and two freight vessels, the *Hildasay* and *Helliar* transported a staggering 478,000 lane metres of freight (the equivalent of 35,000 articulated trailers) in the contract year July 2015 through to June 2016.

Kris Bevan, NorthLink's Freight Manager, has good reason to be proud of the service that continues to offer reliable, regular and convenient sailings from Orkney and Shetland to the mainland, and which has a strong focus on local communities. The ferries are an integral part of the supply chain, with daily connections between Orkney and Shetland allowing for next-day deliveries between the islands and the mainland. Local businesses, supermarket chains, the construction industry, oil and gas renewables, and seafood suppliers all benefit from the lifeline service along with the islands' livestock producers. Anything and everything that needs to get to Orkney and Shetland can take advantage of the services provided by NorthLink. The fleet's dedicated freight vessels, which cater for outsize and abnormal loads, can accommodate dangerous goods (e.g. bottled gas for islanders or chemicals for the oil and gas industry) as well as livestock, temperature controlled goods and building materials. With strong industry and stakeholder cooperation NorthLink is there for the businesses that need it.

Over 2,100 sailings a year are utilised, depending on timetable requirements and the weather are used to service this lifeline obligation contract. Satisfied clients are fundamental to the business — the customer service centre in Stromness is in operation from 8am–8pm seven days a week and along with a regularly refreshed website allowing online booking, NorthLink has embraced social media, with its Facebook and Twitter accounts being especially active and showing the best of the Islands, the North East and Caithness. Being at the mercy of the weather (the Aberdeen - Orkney–Shetland route takes about twelve hours) communication with customers is seen as an essential part of the remit. Despite there being very few cancellations, if there is a chance of bad weather, passengers and businesses are kept up to date, with daily updates issued to hauliers and stakeholders detailing when vessels are due to depart and arrive.

A key contract commitment is the shipment of livestock, with NorthLink providing a dedicated service from Orkney and Shetland. With peaks in September and October on average 137,000 sheep (predominantly from Shetland) and 25,000 cattle (23,000 from Orkney) are transported each year. The bespoke livestock containers, which have garnered interest from around the world, are double-decker platforms for sheep and cattle, allowing for safe, high-volume transportation of animals in line with strict animal welfare regulations. Smaller volumes are moved inter-island and between Orkney and Caithness, mainly for breeding purposes. The shipment of livestock by NorthLink is vital in ensuring the continued economic sustainability not only the agriculture sector, but the island economies in general.

Loading supermarket essentials aboard the *Helliar* at Aberdeen. (Colin J. Smith)

Shetland's largest commodity sector is the fishing and aquaculture industry, worth around £300 million each year to the island's economy, and reliable, efficient transport links are vital to all involved. Around 300,000 boxes of fish are landed annually, with around 40,000 tonnes of farmed salmon also being produced. The rapidly growing mussel farming industry is especially strong, a popular commodity – the product has placed Shetland on the map for producing some of the highest quality mussels available in Europe and over 5,500 tonnes are exported annually. Most have to be carried off-island and delivered quickly to buyers in the UK and throughout Europe. To meet export connections, the seafood industry requires the current sailings of seven days per week. Arrival time in Aberdeen by 8am ensures that shipments can be unloaded for departure to the transport hub at Bellshill in Glasgow to meet onward connections to markets across the UK, Europe, and the rest of the world. It is vital for the industry – and its reputation – that this highly perishable product reaches its destination on time.

Recent innovations have ensured the fishing and aquaculture industry can better understand their impact on the services NorthLink provide, improve quality and encourage growth. These innovations include the commodity capture database, which currently shows that a third of all volume exported from the Northern Isles is fishing and aquaculture sector related (mainly from Shetland as Lerwick is still one of the major fish landing ports in Scotland) and shipment of bulk bags on deck, which utilises spare deck space to transport salmon feed or building materials. Although revenues from freight and passengers are roughly equal, the majority of freight business comes from four main customers; Northwards, JBT, Streamline and Shetland Transport. They specialise in island transport and logistics and utilise the drop trailer service (where trailers are shipped without driver and handled by NorthLink at the port) to provide efficient transport solutions.

Supermarket traffic is also now vital to the islands. Supermarkets provide a massive variety of produce at low cost, which is of huge benefit to locals, and is something which is seen as the

A Shetland Transport lorry loading at Lerwick harbour for the evening sailing to Aberdeen. (Colin J. Smith)

Above: The *Hildasay* makes an early morning arrival at Aberdeen. (Colin J. Smith)

Below: The *Helliar* leaves Lerwick on her evening freight sailing to Aberdeen. Both freight ships have proved good tonnage on the Northern Isles services since their introduction. (Miles Cowsill)

norm for modern living. For better or for worse Islanders no longer have to rely on locally-grown produce or expensive imports. However supermarkets tend to operate a JIT (Just in Time) delivery system, which means that little to no stock, is warehoused on the island, meaning fresh and time-sensitive produce is very susceptible to periods of adverse weather. This JIT delivery system is well-suited to mainland operations but perhaps less so for island communities. As a consequence, however, during times of unavoidable, but rare, disruption it is often the local retailer who is most resilient, given that they tend to keep small stock of essential items and are also supplied by the larger wholesalers who have large warehouses of stock on-island. Nevertheless, for both types of retailer, the daily service NorthLink provides to the mainland is vital for importing a wide range of produce.

But it's not all easy sailing for NorthLink – fares are set within the contract (including freight fares), which can make maintaining market share difficult, particularly where other operators are present and dependency on the weather, in a sometimes harsh operating environment means that accurate forecasting is vital and helps managers to keep on track. Changes in volumes can affect services, meaning freight and passenger levels are monitored closely and predicting levels helps stakeholders understand how markets develop, for example the Shetland boom in oil and gas traffic and construction sector traffic to Orkney due to the Schools for the Future and Three Port Strategy projects all had to be factored in to ensure the services provided are fit for purpose.

The provision of the service is a combined effort; NorthLink employs 260 employees on ship and 81 on shore, many of whom are local, ensuring NorthLink themselves provide high quality employment opportunities to the communities they serve. Where possible goods and services are also procured locally and over £5 million is spent annually on goods and service procured within 50 miles of each port, these range from food and drink for on-board services to repair and maintenance of ship and shore machinery.

Being a socially responsible company, with their customers' needs at the forefront of operations, NorthLink is a true lifeline to the islands.

Northwards

Formed in 2002 after a management buyout from P&O Scottish Ferries Ltd, Northwards Ltd uses NorthLink's services to stay on track with their freight, haulage and maintenance operations in and between Aberdeen, Orkney and Shetland. Operating out of depots in Shetland, Orkney, Aberdeen, Inverness, Scrabster and Glasgow, the company can accommodate any type and size of cargo and operates next day deliveries to and from both Shetland and Orkney, something which is vital to many businesses on the islands.

With rapid, but focussed, cargo volume growth and continued geographical expansion the company have gone from strength to strength, and with Sea-Cargo Aberdeen Ltd becoming majority shareholders in 2011, links to Scandinavia have grown stronger along with the already implemented global transport links throughout the rest of the UK, Europe and beyond. Customers are now connected with efficient and reliable transport services that were cost-inhibitive or even unavailable in the past.

Freight is shipped seven days a week to Orkney and Shetland, with groupage freight (consolidating goods with other consignments) allowing customers a more cost-effective daily shipment throughout Scotland. Goods of any size can be accommodated, from a single box to an abnormal load, and from temperature controlled and chilled goods with remote-controlled tracking to hazardous cargoes. Northwards are also specialists in the transport of dangerous goods, with freight staff trained to OPITO standards.

Along with utilising NorthLink's freight vessels, Northwards provide their customers with warehousing, storage and skip hire, along with a wide variety of trailers and modern vehicles. As members of the United Pallet Network (UPN) the company can quickly distribute deliveries and collections throughout the whole of England, Scotland, Ireland and Wales

Both NorthLink and Northwards are community focussed, and on many occasions have transported goods for worthy causes, having the island communities' interests at heart. While providing a lifeline support to the islands, they have also transported some weird and wonderful cargoes over the years, a giant stuffed turtle to name but one.

On working with NorthLink, Murray Prentice, Managing Director of Northwards, said 'Today we see the Serco set up carrying on the lifeline service better than it has ever been. The management have a strong understanding of the commercial aspects of the business and this continues to improve.'

Shetland Transport

Established in 1982, by Hamish Balfour, Shetland Transport is a Shetland-based, family-run freight haulage company with depots in Shetland, Aberdeen and Coatbridge, Glasgow. They utilise NorthLink's freight vessels to provide a top-quality customer experience offering reliable and efficient daily freight and shipping services to satisfy their clients' diverse needs.

With a transport fleet consisting of 35 trucks and 96 trailers, the company have expanded greatly from their initial Shetlands-only service in the early days. They pride themselves on their range of highly versatile modern vehicles and keep up-to-date by replacing a number of the fleet every three years, fitting their vehicles with all the latest technology to adhere to the latest diesel engine emission legislations. Offering a reliable and efficient freight service to all customers, whether sending a single package or a large consignment, are supported along the way as the fleet work through the UK and onward into Mainland Europe.

Goods are carried to and from Orkney and Shetland via NorthLink's overnight ferries, both on trucks from the fleet and on tailor-made trailers – whatever the load the company can carry it. But Shetland Transport don't stop at day to day business traffic. As designated freight agents for Swedish furniture store IKEA, no Shetland resident has to be without the latest in affordable furniture. Every two weeks goods are collected from IKEA's Edinburgh store and

transported to Shetland, either for pick-up at the Lerwick depot or delivered to the customer's address on the next delivery to their area.

Household removals is also an important part of the business. For those moving into and out of Shetland, Shetland Transport will try to make the move as easy for their customers as possible. All the work and planning is carried out by the company, keeping the customer informed throughout while providing a quick and accurate service. They understand how stressful it can be to relocate, and with a community spirit will help make any move as smooth as possible.

Shetland Seafood Auctions

The fishing and seafood industry is of vital importance to Shetland, meaning that a reliable, frequent transport service is a must. Placed at the heart of Northern European fishing grounds, Shetland has a rich fishing tradition, and today the seafood industry is worth £300 million to the local economy, with £67 million coming from the fishing fleet alone. Around 60 per cent of the fish, weighing roughly 60,000 tonnes, brought into the island annually consists of herring and mackerel and is worth an average of £43 million, while the remainder consists of haddock, cod and monkfish along with the more valuable species.

Today's modern technology ensures that quality catches are made widely available, and to trade quickly and effectively Seafood Auctions has two unique systems in place – an online 'landings page' and an electronic Dutch auction for purchasing consignments.

Every day boats detail their catch to Lerwick-based fishing agents LHD Ltd, then all white fish are recorded on Shetland Auction's landings page 18 hours before an electronic auction is due to start. Boats lay out boxes according to a market plan from early afternoon until around midnight, when auction staff grade and weigh the high value species and ensure accurate box weights. Six per cent of the boxes are also sample weighed as further quality assurance. Work is finished by 6am before the auctioneers catalogue the landings and produce the auction catalogue, which is then transferred to

All the NorthLink terminals offer modern and comfortable areas for the travelling public. (NorthLink)

the database. The landings page allows buyers to see which species have been landed by each vessel at both Scalloway and Lerwick, along with the grades and size of the fish, and the overall total landed. This gives purchasers the luxury of planning their auction strategy well in advance.

Registered local buyers are allowed to see the catch from 6am and, once the catalogue is ready at 7am, over 200 companies in the UK, France and Spain are contacted and begin planning their purchases. Remote companies gain access to the catalogue via the landings page from 7am giving them the ability to bid on consignments from their own offices, with transport arranged by the auction company. Approximately 50 tonnes of white fish are sold every day through the auction.

When auction time comes seating is provided for 23 local buyers in the auction room above Lerwick fish market, and a viewing gallery allows a glimpse of the action. Larger boxes are available to view, while all landed fish, both from Lerwick and Scalloway, are sold at the one sitting. At 8am every weekday the auction begins: the lots are described on screen with an opening price set at a higher amount than expected and a countdown drops by one penny per kilo until a bidder stops the auction for that lot. This type of auction allows purchasers around the world to set the price based on the quality of the fish and the price

they are willing to pay. Since the electronic auction was introduced in August 2003 white fish landings have increased by 84 per cent and the value of fish at Shetland's markets has also increased in recent years. A new technological enhancement, funded via the European Fisheries Fund 2007-13 Axis 4 programme and Shetland Islands Council, has been the introduction of an electronic recording and printing system, further enhancing the traceability of each catch for discerning buyers.

Shetland Auction also provides seafood sellers with a flexible process to take advanced orders via their online seafood sales system, thus giving them complete control of their businesses. By allowing producers to input quantities, sizes and grades of seafood available each day and setting the prices they are willing to accept, deliver the goods to a chosen distribution depot when they are available and invoicing the buyer direct, Shetland Auction will then add products to the system, pass on details of the successful buyers and invoice their commission on a monthly basis. In this way buyers can source whole, gutted or filleted salmon, along with mussels and white fish, in any quantity of their chosen grade and from fully traceable suppliers, with the minimum of fuss, and with next day delivery to the UK, guaranteeing the freshness of this delicate commodity.

The success of Shetland Auction is proving not only what a vital business sector the fishing industry in Shetland is, but that proximity to the fishing grounds and the high quality of the product has produced a trade that is recognised worldwide for its quality and fast delivery.

Seafood Shetland

The seafood industry is vital to the Shetland economy, it has supported generation after generation of Shetlander, protecting rural communities and remaining an integral part of our lives. It is currently worth in excess of £300 million a year to the islands and surpasses the value of the oil, gas, agriculture, tourism, and creative industries combined.

Seafood Shetland is the industry body that represents the interests of companies involved in all aspects of fish processing and shellfish growing. All year round, members export premium quality farmed and wild fish and shellfish products all over the world. Fundamental to the success of the industry – and protecting the quality of the product and retaining loyal customers – is excellent transport links.

To give context to the volume of seafood exports, in 2015, 7,450 lane metres of seafood was exported from Shetland via Serco NorthLink, this comprised 67% salmon, 22% wild fish and 8% mussels. The busiest day of the year was 14th December when 25 trailers of seafood left the islands – bound for festive feasts across the globe!

Commenting on the level of service provided by Serco NorthLink, chief executive of Seafood Shetland, Ruth Henderson, said: 'The climate and weather conditions that prevail in Shetland is what makes our seafood special and, conversely, those are the very conditions that can, on occasion, present our greatest challenge when it comes to transportation to the UK mainland and beyond.

'When our members have harvested and processed a highly perishable product ready for transportation to an expectant customer, to then discover that a sailing has had to be postponed or cancelled due to the weather, it is not only costly and wasteful, it can affect customer confidence and longer term business prospects. Unfortunately, there is nothing that can be done about the weather, but what Serco NorthLink has been extremely good at is keeping the industry informed of potential disruptions well in advance, giving producers the time to make alternative arrangements. This, coupled with the company's clear commitment to its freight customers and regular dialogue through the industry transport group, has led to the seafood industry as a whole being very satisfied with the Serco NorthLink service since its inception.

'From an island location, reliable transport is indeed a lifeline: vital to the economy and its ultimate survival. For Seafood Shetland, NorthLink Serco plays that crucial role particularly well.'

The *Hamnavoe* leaves Stromness with another full loading of passengers from Orkney. (Miles Cowsill)

Chapter six

Looking after the Fleet

Having spent all of his career in marine services Chris Adams is passionate about his work and the people around him, and being Technical Manager for NorthLink means that he is in constant demand. Chris and his team keep the fleet in the water, maintaining the vessels and allowing services to run smoothly throughout the year – no mean feat on such an important route.

Since taking over the service in 2012 the five-strong fleet has been improved and made more efficient, something Chris is proud of, but which most customers may not even notice – smooth, uneventful sailing is the order of the day. The blue Magnus logo, boldly pointing journeyward on the side of the ferries, is something that passengers do notice with its striking design making the NorthLink vessels immediately recognisable while at sea and in port. However, the casual observer may not realise that the logo is not painted but is a huge vinyl decal sourced from a company in Germany. Tough and durable, the vinyl has worked well and does not peel or require heavy duty maintenance.

Efficiency savings have steadily rolled through the fleet under Chris's management. The funnels on the Hrossey, Hjaltland and Hamnavoe are now stainless steel, making them lighter and more efficient than the previous mild steel funnels, which were prone to rust. This change has lead to fuel savings - a small amount but still useful in times of high fuel prices. Ventilated covers on the side of the ships are now also stainless steel, again a small

but useful addition, and with hulls of self-polishing paint, meaning when washed they shine up themselves and feel like silicone to the touch, maintenance is now easier.

Annual inspections have also been improved on over the years. Rather than rely on dry-docking, which takes each vessel out of commission, each hull is now inspected annually by divers while the ship is still in service. This is a useful saving in both manpower and lost trippage. When dry-docking is needed the ships have recently docked in either Birkenhead or Rosyth. Use of a Scottish yard allowed a quicker turnaround of the *Hamnavoe* in 2016; the journey to and from the dock being a short day sail each way. Dry docking in March helps to avoid condensation and allows the hull to be painted quickly, but of the 14 days in dock, up to nine of these can be used to simply paint the ship. Whether the ships are dry-docked or not they are checked once a year and are then checked three months later to make sure all is as intended. Of course each vessel is checked regularly by its captain, mate and chief engineers.

A high volume of sailings across some of the world's most demanding seas brings its challenges. A crankshaft split on the *Hamnavoe's* Scrabster to Stromness evening sailing of 25th April 2013 meant a journey on one engine to reach its destination port. The ship was immediately taken out of service due to serious mechanical failure and five days later sailed to Rosyth for repairs. The damage was not due to lack of maintenance or external

Above:This is the bow section of the *Hrossey*, taken in 2013 during in dry-dock. (NorthLink)

Below: The *Hrossey* having her 'Anchor housing' painted. (NorthLink)

Above and below: These show the arrival of *Hjaltland* into dry-dock with her 'Old Livery' which is being replaced.

Above left: This shows the forward under water area before; and after being water washed. The hull has no further painting except for minor repairs.

Above right: Scaling and painting of the car deck and repairs to the lower car deck ramp..

Left: The *Hjaltland* stern door opened for maintenance..

Right: Painting out of the 'Old Logo'

Below left: Bow thrusters from the Hjaltland.

(All photos NorthLink)

LT BY *Aker Finnyards*

Above: The new logo on the *Hjaltland*. (NorthLink)

Right and below: Flooding up of the dry-dock. (NorthLink).

The *Hjaltland* sailing from dry-dock at Birkenhead. (NorthLink)

forces, but as the crankshaft was irreparable it required a complete stripdown of the engine. NorthLink's freight vessel *Helliar* began a cover service, at close to the normal timetable, on the Stromness to Scrabster route, but was limited to 12 passengers although cars and commercial vehicles were accommodated. This eased the pressure on the other ferry operators, especially Pentland Ferries who had arranged extra sailings to cope with additional passenger levels, but was far from ideal. The subsequent repair timetable was efficient and effective – despite having to replace a damper once the vessel returned to Stromness, the *Hamnavoe* was returned to normal service in less than a month.

Internally the ships are now better than their predecessors, however Chris likes to inspect areas himself whenever possible. The bilges are inspected often, for example, spotting any potential leaks allows the technical team to flag any concerns before they become problematic. The stabilizers for each ship are also closely monitored, with divers being able to adjust where necessary to avoid lengthy dry dock visits for repairs.

Maintenance and repair of NorthLink's three ferries and two freight vessels is not an easy

task, but with a good team the service has gone from strength to strength.

Anchor chain waiting to be ranged. (NorthLink)

Chapter seven

The Passage North

Good afternoon Ladies and Gentlemen, welcome on board *Hjaltland* for this evening's trip to Kirkwall and onwards overnight to Lerwick. Shell doors have been closed and the vessel will shortly leave the berth. Sea conditions are expected to be reasonably good with light to moderate westerly winds expected, though there may be a bit of westerly swell between North Ronaldsay and Sumburgh Head in the early hours of the morning, therefore I suggest people take care when moving around the ship, particularly when going through doorways and onto the external decks.

The ship departs Jamieson's Quay at the west end of Aberdeen's Victoria Dock, where the Northern Isles passenger vessels have been berthed since the introduction of Ro/Ro sailings from Aberdeen in 1977. The NorthLink terminal building is in almost the same location as the previous P&O Scottish Ferries building, which was replaced in 2003 shortly after NorthLink took over the services. The most significant difference being the introduction of airline-style baggage trolleys, a covered walkway and lift facilities for passengers.

We then head seawards past Blaikie's Quay, which is normally used by offshore supply vessels and also by Streamline Shipping's container service to Kirkwall and Lerwick. We

Above and right: The *Hrossey* at the port of Aberdeen. (NorthLink)

The *Hrossey* loading cars and passengers at Aberdeen. (NorthLink)

then head through the 'Cut', which was formerly fitted with two sets of lock gates and St Clements Bridge until the Dock was significantly dredged to facilitate 24-hour access by oil and gas related vessels in the mid-1970s. As we move clear of this we pass Aberdeen's 2nd Linkspan, regularly used by the chartered NorthLink freighters *Hildasay* and *Helliar*. This facility, opened in 2001, is also used by the weekly container and Ro/Ro freight service from Stavanger operated by Sea-Cargo. Interestingly this site was the base of the North of Scotland, Orkney and Shetland Shipping Company (taken over by Coast Lines and subsequently P&O Group) until 1977, but today it maintains a link to Orkney and Shetland being the Aberdeen base for Northwards Transport (formerly P&O Scottish Ferries Haulage division).

Crossing the turning basin we then pass the oil installation at Point Law to starboard as we turn to port approaching the 'Pilot Jetty'. This is obviously a bit 'tricky' due to the limited width of the dredged channel, particularly at low water with a 125-metre-long vessel normally sailing close to the 5.4 metre maximum draft,

this is the reason sailings are sometimes delayed if there is any significant swell from the east. As we head parallel with the North Pier we pass one of Aberdeen's Municipal Golf courses and the remains of the 'Torry Battery' which was built to defend the approach to the harbour in earlier times. Today there is a car park situated there, which is a good vantage point for watching the ships coming and going and the fairly common dolphin/porpoise activity around the end of the North Pier. This sea life can sometimes be viewed from the outside decks of the ship particularly just as we begin to increase speed passing clear of the dredged channel. The vessel will frequently pass fairly close to other shipping waiting to enter and there are regularly a number of vessels anchored just north of the Aberdeen Fairway buoy.

Once clear of waiting vessels we then set a course more or less parallel with the coast, passing the mouth of the River Don and the fine sandy beaches at Balmedie towards the Ythan river mouth at Newburgh. The next significant point north of that is Cruden Bay, home of a well-known golf course and just

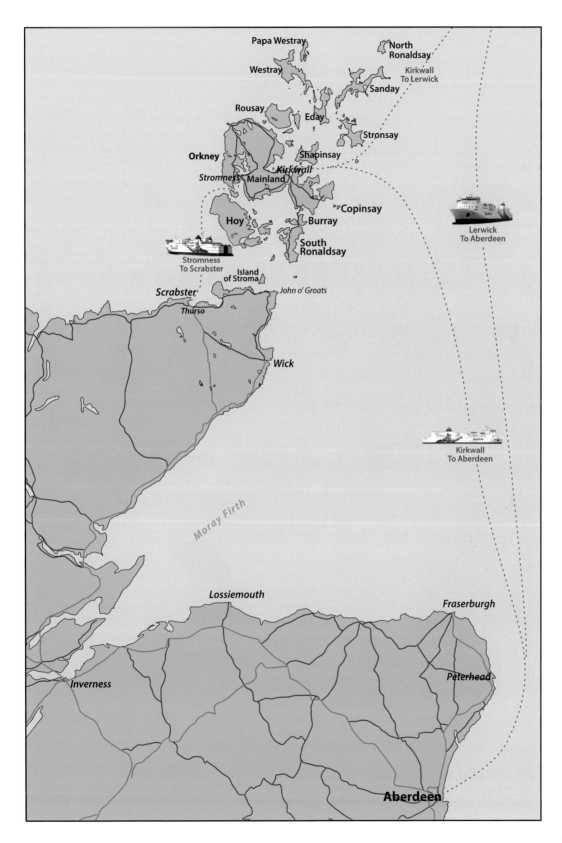

Papa Westray

North
Ronaldsay

Westray

Kirkwall
To Lerwick

Sanday

Rousay

Eday

Stronsay

Orkney

Shapinsay

Stromness Mainland

Kirkwall

Copinsay

Lerwick
To Aberdeen

Hoy

Burray

South
Ronaldsay

Stromness
To Scrabster

Island
of Stroma

Scrabster

John o' Groats

Thurso

Kirkwall
To Aberdeen

Wick

Moray Firth

Lossiemouth

Fraserburgh

Inverness

Peterhead

Aberdeen

The *Hrossey* at the entrance to Aberdeen harbour. (Stuart MacKillop)

north of this the ruins of Slains Castle, which was built around 1600 by the Earl of Erroll. It was later famous because Bram Stoker allegedly used the ruin as a setting for Dracula's Castle at the end of the 19th century. Slightly further north we can see Buchan Ness lighthouse and the tall chimney of Peterhead Power Station.

At this point we turn north towards Rattray Head lighthouse; passing the busy fishing and oil related port of Peterhead and the massive St Fergus Gas Terminal before passing Rattray Light Tower which stands on its own seaward of the sand dunes. We then alter course further to the north-west, leaving the other large fishing port Fraserburgh off to port.

We now have nearly three hours of open water till we approach Orkney's eastern extremity, the island of Copinsay, which is now a RSPB reserve purchased in memory of naturalist James Fisher in the early 70s. Copinsay lighthouse was completed in 1915 and the keepers' families lived on the island till 1958, the light was automated in 1981. North of this we soon pass the Horse of Copinsay then abeam of the Mull Head on Dearness we turn towards the Helliar Holm lighthouse on the north side of the channel known as 'The String' between Shapinsay and the Orkney Mainland. On the south side we pass Kirkwall Airport at the head of Inganess Bay, then on towards the Head of Work which is opposite the lighthouse. Just west of Helliar Holm is Balfour village where the ferry *Shapinsay* is based. Further west we pass Balfour Castle, a small Baronial style castle completed for the laird David Balfour in 1850. On the port side we are now approaching the low-lying island of Thieves Holm where we head south into Kirkwall Bay. As we slow down approaching the Hatston Terminal on the west side of the bay, the old town provides a pleasant backdrop with the skyline dominated by the spire of St Magnus Cathedral which was built in the 12th century by Earl Rognvald in memory of his uncle who was an early Christian martyr, having been slain on the nearby island of Egilsay.

Departing from Hatston we come astern off the berth, just over a ship's length and bearing in mind the relatively shallow water just north

of the Orkney Cheese Factory, promptly swing to starboard and head north through Kirkwall Bay to pass just west of Thieves Holm, where we turn to head towards the south of Helliar Holm.

Once past the lighthouse we then head due east to pass Auskerry Light, which is on a small island south-east of Stronsay. This is the point where we head in a more north-easterly direction passing approximately 7–10 miles to the east of Sanday and North Ronaldsay, both fairly low-lying and marked by significant lighthouse towers at Start Point and Dennis Head. North Ronaldsay, with a population of approximately 50, is Orkney's most remote inhabited island. It is home to a unique breed of native sheep who are kept on the seashore outside a stone dyke and survive on a diet that mainly consists of seaweed. This gives the meat a unique flavour and in recent years it has been exported to some of Britain's top restaurants. The fleeces are used to produce fine knitwear on the island.

Normally the route between Kirkwall and Lerwick takes us reasonably close to the west side of Fair Isle. Despite its relative remoteness it still has a population of approximately 70 who are mainly engaged in sheep-rearing with some inshore shell-fishing carried out in summer months. Due to its remote location Fair Isle is often visited by many fairly rare migrating birds and there is an observatory with modern residential accommodation on the island. The island is also famous for its uniquely-patterned knitwear with some designs believed to originate from survivors of a Spanish Galleon wrecked on the island in 1588. The island is served by the 18-metre passenger (12)/cargo ferry *Good Shepherd* which is based on the island but is hauled clear of the water in winter to avoid risk of damage. Sometimes she can be storm-bound for as long as 3–4 weeks in winter but fortunately there has been a regular eight-seat air service from Shetland for over 40 years which maintains essential supplies and communication.

The passage between North Ronaldsay and Sumburgh Head is generally reckoned to be the most exposed part of the trip. While it can be a very pleasant seeing the spectacular cliff

Above: Slains Castle. (Visit Scotland)

Below left: Rattray Head. (Visit Scotland)

Below right: Copinsay Lighthouse (www.orkney.com)

Bottom view: Copinsay from the sea.
  (www.orkney.com)

Top left: Balfour Castle. (www.balfourcastle.co.uk)

Top right: The *Shapinsay* leaving Kirkwall. (Miles Cowsill).

Above: The *Earl Siguard* laid up at Kirkwall in the evening sun after an intensive operating day. (Miles Cowsill)

Left: The 'Weeping Window' at St Magnus Cathedral, Kirkwall in 2016. (Miles Cowsill)

Above: St Magnus Cathedral, Kirkwall in the setting sun. (www.orkney.com)

Left: Auskerry Lighthouse. (www.orkney.com)

Top left: Sanday.
(www.orkney.com)

Top right: North Ronaldsay.
(www.orkney.com)

Above: Fair Isle. (Tommy H.
Hyndman/fair-
isle.blogspot.com)

Below: The lighthouse on
Fair Isle. (www.shetland.org)

The harbour at Fair Isle. (www.shetland.org)

scenery (best seen southbound on a long summer evening) it can be very different in winter and the experienced NorthLink masters often have to vary the passage considerably to provide as safe and comfortable a trip as they can.

Sumburgh Head is the most southerly point of the Shetland mainland and has had a lighthouse since 1821. Obviously the light has been modernised several times since then and following automation the buildings, apart from the Light Tower, were taken over by the Shetland Amenity Trust. Part of the complex housed a bird observatory unit for several years but then a major upgrade costing £5m saw the complex open in 2014. It is a spectacular visitor centre covering aspects as diverse as lighthouse history, wartime radar station use, and local marine-life and wildlife with a new observation lounge providing weatherproof views covering the neighbouring coastline, the historic Jarlshof, and Shetland's main airport which, as well as providing daily links to the Scottish mainland and helicopters serving oil platforms, is base for a Coastguard Rescue

helicopter.

We then proceed north along the east coast of Shetland and pass just east of the island of Mousa, which is home to one of the best preserved Pictish brochs in Scotland and a

The *Good Shepherd IV* outward bound from Sumburgh. (Miles Cowsill)

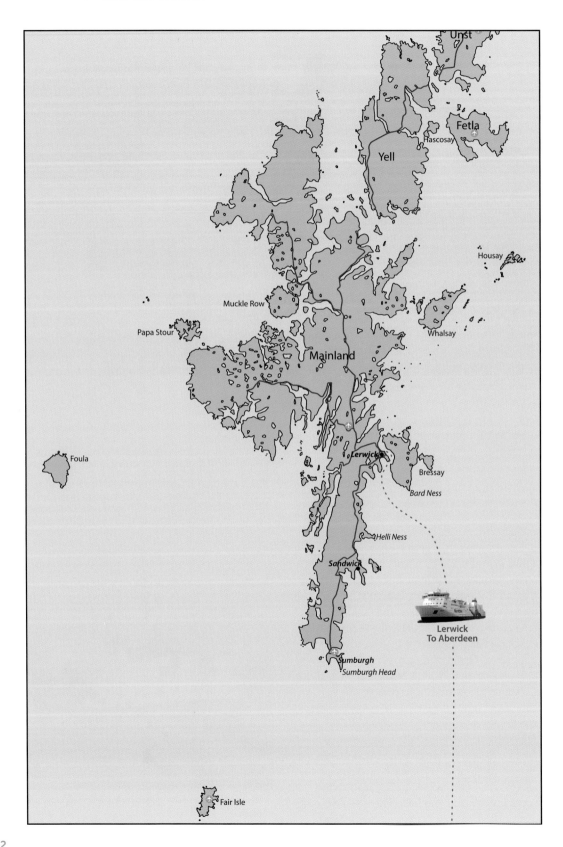

Sumburgh Head. (www.shetland.org)

colony of Stormy Petrels. Day trips to uninhabited Mousa are made by a small ferry *Solan III* from Sandsayre on the Shetland mainland in summer.

As we approach the south entrance to Lerwick Harbour we become sheltered from the east by the islands of Bressay and Noss. Bressay is home to approximately 350 people with a frequent 10 minute Ro/Ro ferry service to the centre of Lerwick where many are employed, but it also has some of the best farms in Shetland on its relatively sheltered west side. Noss by contrast is a national nature reserve and only inhabited by a couple of wardens in the summer months but, along with cliffs on the south of Bressay, Noss is home to spectacular numbers of seabirds particularly Gannets.

We pass the harbour limits for Lerwick port abeam of Kirkabister lighthouse where there is nowadays a less powerful light and radar station operated by Lerwick Port Authority, while the former lightkeepers' houses are let as

self-catering holiday homes. To the west of this, roughly from an area stretching from Gulberwick to Breiwick Bay on the Shetland Mainland, is used as an anchorage, mainly by waiting shuttle tankers and other offshore related units. From the 70s till the late 90s this

Very much at home are the puffins at Sumburgh Head. (Miles Cowsill)

Above: Bard Ness, Bressay. (Miles Cowsill)

Right: The lighthouse on Sumburgh Head. (Miles Cowsill)

Below: Lerwick harbour and town from the ferry (Miles Cowsill)

Above: Lerwick with Swan Hellenic cruiseship the *Minerva* and the Bressey ferry. (Miles Cowsill)

Left: The Bressey ferry *Leirna* leaves Lerwick on her 10 minute crossing. (Miles Cowsill)

area was commonly used by mainly East European 'Klondykers' or fish factory ships engaged in transhipping herring and mackerel from the Shetland and Scottish fleets.

As we approach the narrower confines of the harbour we pass the headland known as the Knab and the Lerwick cemetery to port, then as we are gradually reducing speed we pass the Widows homes built by Shetlander Arthur Anderson, then chairman of P&O in 1865. We are soon passing Victoria Pier, which was the Aberdeen and Orkney Shipping terminal till the introduction of Ro/Ro ferries in 1977, and now there are pontoons for visiting yachts and tenders from liners too large to berth alongside in the summer months. We get a good view of the older part of the town as we sail slowly north passing the harbour offices, Bressay Ferry Terminal, Malakoff ship repair yard and the fish market before turning to a more north-westerly course through the buoyed channel at North Ness. Here we pass the modern 'Mareel' music and film centre and the Shetland Museum buildings which are well worth a visit, especially the restaurant with its excellent range of food and panoramic view over the North Harbour. We are now heading for the tall exhaust of the diesel fired power station, which is gradually taking less load as the number of renewable energy projects in the islands steadily increases. That heading brings us up to the Holmsgarth terminal where the passenger ship berths on the north side bow-in and most days the freighter *Hildasay* or *Helliar* will arrive a little later to berth on the south side at Holmsgarth No 3. The Lerwick passenger terminal was built just before NorthLink took over from P&O in 2002 and with reasonable space on two floors it is well able to cope with a significant load of passengers travelling without vehicles.

Captain Willie MacKay